THE POLITICS OF AUSTRALIAN CHILD CARE

THE POLITICS OF AUSTRALIAN CHILD CARE

From Philanthropy to Feminism

DEBORAH BRENNAN
Department of Government
University of Sydney

CAMBRIDGE UNIVERSITY PRESS

Published by the Press Syndicate of the University of Cambridge
The Pitt Building, Trumpington Street, Cambridge CB2 IRP, UK
40 West 20th Street, New York, NY 10011-4211, USA
10 Stamford Road, Oakleigh, Melbourne 3166, Australia

© Cambridge University Press 1994

First published 1994

Printed in Australia by McPherson's Printing Group

National Library of Australia cataloguing in publication data
Brennan, Deborah.
The politics of Australian child care.
Bibliography.
Includes index.
1. Child care services – Australia. 2. Child care – Government policy – Australia. 3. Day care centers – Australia. 4. Child care services – Government policy – Australia. I. Title.
362.7120994

Library of Congress cataloguing in publication data
Brennan, Deborah.
The politics of Australian child care: from philanthropy to feminism/Deborah Brennan.
Includes bibliographical references and index.
1. Child care – Australia – History. 2. Child care – Government policy – Australia. 3. Child care – Australia – Public opinion. 4. Public opinion – Australia. I. Title.
HQ778.7.A8B74 1994
362.7'0994–dc20   94–8232
                                                                 CIP

A catalogue record for this book is available from the British Library.

ISBN 0 521 41792 9 Hardback

For Murray, Anna and Timothy –
who know the whole story

Contents

List of tables viii
List of abbreviations ix
Acknowledgements xi

Introduction: Women, the State and the Politics of Caring for Children 1
1 The Kindergarten Movement and Urban Social Reform 13
2 For the Sake of the Nation 32
3 A Mother's Place ... ? 52
4 Hitching Child Care to the Commonwealth Star 70
5 Playing Beneath the Sword of Damocles 96
6 For Love *and* Money 119
7 Child Care – an Industrial Issue 141
8 New Players, New Rules 164
9 Equity and Economics 186
Conclusion 205

References 215
Index 233

Tables

1	Foundation dates of major voluntary organisations and training colleges	18
2	Expenditure trend in Children's Services Program, 1973–74 to 1982–83	130
3	Possible fiscal gain to the commonwealth from working mothers with 0–4-year-old children in commonwealth funded services	199
4	Growth in expenditure and number of places, 1974–93	203
5	Number of operational child care places, states and territories, 1993	208

Abbreviations

AAP	Australian Assistance Plan
AAPSCD	Australian Association for Pre-School Child Development
ABS	Australian Bureau of Statistics
ACCA	Aboriginal Child Care Agency
ACER	Australian Council for Education Research
ACOA	Administrative and Clerical Officers Association
ACOSS	Australian Council of Social Service
ACSPA	Australian Council of Salaried and Professional Associations
ACT	Australian Capital Territory
ACTU	Australian Council of Trade Unions
AECA	Australian Early Childhood Association
AFR	*Australian Financial Review*
AGPS	Australian Government Publishing Service
ALP	Australian Labor Party
APA	Australian Pre-School Association
APC	Australian Pre-Schools Committee
CAE	College of Advanced Education
CCAW	Child Care at Work
CCC	Community Child Care
CKA	Creche and Kindergarten Association of Queensland
CPD	*Commonwealth Parliamentary Debates*
CSP	Children's Services Program
DEET	Department of Education, Employment and Training
DSS	Department of Social Security
FACSA	Family and Children's Services Agency
FAUSA	Federation of Australian University Staff Associations

ABBREVIATIONS

FKA	Free Kindergarten Association
FKU	Free Kindergarten Union
HFKA	Hobart Free Kindergarten Association
HHLGCS	Health, Housing, Local Government and Community Services
HR	House of Representatives
ICCC	Interim Committee for the Children's Commission
ILO	International Labour Organisation
INAC	Interim National Accreditation Council
JET	Jobs, Education and Training
KUNSW	Kindergarten Union of New South Wales
KUSA	Kindergarten Union of South Australia
MUP	Melbourne University Press
NACBCS	National Association of Community Based Children's Services
NCOSS	New South Wales Council of Social Service
NSW	New South Wales
NT	*National Times*
NWAC	National Women's Advisory Council
OECD	Organisation for Economic Co-operation and Development
PRS	Priorities Review Staff
SDN & NSA	Sydney Day Nursery and Nursery Schools Association
SDNA	Sydney Day Nursery Association
SMH	*Sydney Morning Herald*
SNAICC	Secretariat of National Aboriginal and Islander Child Care
SUPS	Supplementary Service Grants
SWC	Social Welfare Commission
VADN	Victorian Association of Day Nurseries
VCOSS	Victorian Council of Social Service
VICSEG	Victorian Co-operative on Children's Services for Ethnic Groups
WEB	Women's Employment Board
WEL	Women's Electoral Lobby
WTUC	Women's Trade Union Commission

Acknowledgements

Over the years that this book has been in preparation many friends have given me support and encouragement and sustained my belief in the worth of the project.

I would particularly like to acknowledge the generous assistance, encouragement and inspiration provided by Professor Bettina Cass who supervised the thesis from which this book emerged. Associate Professor Trevor Matthews supervised my early work in this area and I would like to record my thanks for the interest he showed in an unfamiliar policy area.

Many other friends at the University of Sydney have given friendship and support, and have helped me to keep the task in perspective. I would especially like to thank Bob Howard, Louise Chappell, Liz Kirby, Diarmuid Maguire, Lisa Hill from the Department of Government, and John Freeland, Jude Petruchenia and Lindsey Napier from the Department of Social Work and Social Policy.

Many of the ideas in this book have been discussed with friends in the women's movement, trade unions and community child care groups; some of the events are ones we have lived through together. These links with people working in children's services have been extremely valuable in developing my analysis. I would particularly like to acknowledge the friendship and assistance of Chris Baxter, Marie Coleman, Eva Cox, Jan Craney, Ros Dey, Mary Dimech, Maureen Fegan, Judy Hill, Janet Johnson, Jan Kelly, Jen Levy, Lesley Osborne, Gae Raby, Jill Ruchel, Penny Ryan, Deb Sandars, Lynn Shoemark, Anne Stonehouse, June Wangmann, Lynn Wannan and Sue Young. Elizabeth

Reid generously made available a large volume of papers from her period as Women's Adviser to the Prime Minister. Russell Ross kindly calculated the adjusted outlay figures for Table 4 at the last minute. Kathy Dempsey compiled the index in a meticulous manner under very trying circumstances.

The directors of the six Lady Gowrie Centres around Australia provided me with access to fascinating collections of documents, photographs, newspaper cuttings and records. My research was also facilitated by several librarians. I would especially like to thank those at the Institute of Early Childhood Studies (Sydney), the Institute of Early Childhood Development (Melbourne), the Battye Library (Perth) and the State Library of Victoria. Elizabeth Dau, Dalma Dixon, Pam Cahir and Jean Gifford of the Australian Early Childhood Association in Canberra provided me with access to the records of this organisation and gave helpful suggestions at various points.

The importance of child care is something that I have experienced in a very personal way while writing this book and I extend my thanks to the staff at Boundary Lane Children's Centre and Phoenix Kindergarten who have provided superb care for Anna and Timothy. I thank them for their professionalism, their affection and their interest in my work.

I owe a particular debt to my friends Pauline Garde, Susan Johnston, Betty Hounslow, Chris Burvill, Judy Cole and Rod O'Donnell, all of whom have provided support and friendship in numerous ways.

Finally, my thanks to Murray Goot, who has lived with this work for as long as I have, who has encouraged me at every stage and has supplied ideas, meals, intellectual stimulation, and valuable editorial comments as well as sharing the joys and responsibilities involved in child care on the home front.

Introduction:
Women, the State and the Politics
of Caring for Children

Over the past century, child care in Australia has moved from being a peripheral matter – of interest mainly to charitable groups comprised of upper-class women and a few progressive educationalists – to a high profile, vigorously debated political and public policy issue. In the 1990s, child care is widely regarded as central to the economic and social goals of the nation. This book concerns the processes by which that transition has come about. Its underlying theme is the shift in the construction of child care from a philanthropic issue to one which is firmly located on the mainstream agenda of Australian politics.

In recent feminist scholarship, two approaches to child care provision have held centre-stage: the systems of extensive, state-funded provision exemplified by the Nordic countries (especially Sweden, Finland and Denmark); and the 'hands off' approach of the British and American governments which effectively have no national policy in this area. Scandinavian, British and American writers have provided a number of excellent analyses of the history and politics of child care provision in their countries and some illuminating comparative studies (Borchorst 1990; Cohen 1988; Leira 1992; Ruggie 1984; Siim 1990; Ungerson 1990). An analytical framework which focuses on Britain and Sweden as the polar opposites of child care policy is employed in a recent discussion of child care in the OECD countries. Here, Sweden, Denmark and Norway are presented as instances of 'maximum public responsibility', while Britain and the United States exemplify the trend of 'maximum private responsibility'. Australia is one of several countries lumped into a third category of 'other cases' (OECD 1990). In another account, this time by the well-known American team Kamerman and Kahn (1991: 201),

Australia is linked with Britain and the United States in a category described as 'major laggards'.

The Australian experience repays more careful analysis. Since the early 1970s Australian feminists have made use of the state to achieve reforms in a range of areas: sex discrimination legislation, equal opportunity programs, government-funded refuges, women's health and child care services are among the measures for which women have gained state support (Sawer 1990; Summers 1986). As was true of earlier social movements in Australia, the distinctive achievements of contemporary Australian feminism have been in the realm of bureaucratic innovation and public provision. Over the last fifteen years Australian women have created an extensive range of women's policy machinery and government-subsidised women's services said to be 'unrivalled elsewhere' (Sawer 1990: xv; Eisenstein 1991).

Although the demand for child care is a central goal of women's liberation, there are substantial national differences in how that demand has been translated into practice. Compared with Australians, British and American feminists appear to have been much more cautious about state-funded services and to have placed much greater emphasis on indirect strategies such as tax concessions for users and incentives to employers to establish work-based child care. This is, at least in part, a reaction to the terms under which publicly-funded child care has historically been provided in those countries. Jill Norgren (1982: 133) has characterised American child care policy as 'a stepchild to welfare policy for the poor and tax policy for the middle class'. The United States federal government provides direct child care assistance only for welfare recipients and families living below the poverty line. Better-off users receive indirect assistance through tax credits. Low income families in which both parents are labour force participants are very poorly served by this system. Most are ineligible for government-subsidised services and must either rely on commercial services or use informal, often substandard, care. Such families often find that their incomes are too low for them to benefit from the tax credit system.

In Britain, child care services funded by local authorities cater for less than one per cent of the relevant age group and are regarded strictly as a welfare service for children 'from deprived or inadequate backgrounds [who] have special needs that cannot otherwise be met' (Moss 1982; Cohen 1993). Such policies and pronouncements are hardly likely to appeal to feminists as a basis for further expansion. Although there have been a few local campaigns and initiatives along the lines of the Australian community child care movement, the topic of child care does not seem to have captured the imagination of British feminists. Writing of the English scene, Denise Riley says:

the very term 'child-care' has a dispiriting and dutiful heaviness hanging over it which resists attempts to give it glamour or militance [sic] alike. It is as short on colour and incisiveness as the business of negotiating the wet kerb with the pushchair; and it has some of the awful blandness of the 'caring' voiced in the language of psychologised social work ... Like recommendations for anti-sexist behaviour, it makes the private heart sink a bit, while public socialist heads nod a half-automatic assent, as if recognising, these days, its inevitability. *(1983: 135)*

The approach of women in the Nordic countries has been different again. Sweden, as Joyce Gelb (1990: 138) notes, is frequently lauded as 'the nation in which equality has proceeded further than in any other Western country'. Sweden's extensive provision of high quality, low cost day care services is regarded by many observers as a model for women in other nations. In fact, Denmark and Finland both have more extensive child care provision than Sweden, but in the latter country child care services are embedded in an enviable range of supportive policies concerning parental leave, reduced working hours for parents, time off to care for sick children and to attend functions associated with school or day care.

Intriguingly, feminism appears not to have been particularly important in shaping Swedish child care policies. Kaplan (1992: 71) contends that Sweden has not really experienced a second-wave women's movement, largely because 'the demands that brought women together in other countries had actually been met' as a result of the initiatives of social democratic governments. Anette Borchorst (1990: 174–75) does not go so far as to argue the absence of second-wave feminism; she states, however, that 'the new feminist movement ... has not acted as a strong pressure group in relation to child care'. Her view is that the early feminist attack on traditional roles associated with motherhood led many second-wave feminists (themselves childless and economically independent) to ignore the problems of motherhood and child care. The Swedish 'sex equality' notion that came to dominate political debate in the 1960s focused on removing barriers to women's labour force participation although it was not specifically informed by feminist considerations. Consequently, policy matters which have a disproportionate effect upon women (notably child care) have usually been subsumed under family policy or labour market concerns (Gelb 1990: 157).

The demand for women's labour in Sweden from the 1960s onwards appears to have been the critical factor in promoting state support for child care (Ruggie 1984: 249). In contrast to their Australian counterparts, Swedish unions in the 1950s and 1960s saw the employment of local women as preferable to immigrant workers (Jonung and Thordarsson 1980: 109). The expansion of child care was motivated primarily by the desire to make the conditions of labour force participation more equal for men and women. Although the expansion of Swedish day care has occurred almost entirely under social democratic governments, the general direction of policy and the promotion of women's employment opportunities which it implies, have received broad support from all major political parties. In an extensive analysis of state provisions for working women in Britain and Sweden, Mary Ruggie (1984: 285) concludes that in Sweden the location of child care within the framework of labour market policy has been the critical factor in making this area of policy 'as ambitious, holistic, and successful as it is'.

The Australian women's movement's approach to child care has developed within a culture that places great reliance on state funding and provision. The goal of persuading governments to adopt and implement particular kinds of child care policies has been central to feminists' endeavours in this area. Indeed, for most of the key players, anxious to avoid the vagaries of the market and unwilling to accept the exploitation of women's labour that seems endemic to 'self-help' solutions, state provision has appeared to be the only realistic strategy. Eva Cox, a long-time activist in the child care arena, exemplifies this attitude:

> The possibilities women have of sharing the responsibilities for child care outside the immediate biologically-bonded group depend on acts of omission or commission by the state in providing certain types of services ...
> *(Cox, 1988: 190)*

Sawer (1990: xv) comments that the 'utilitarian attitude' of Australian feminists towards the state distinguishes them from feminists in the United Kingdom and the United States. In Australia, feminists working in the bureaucracy, especially those working on projects inspired by the women's movement and those whose positions require a demonstrated commitment to gender equity, have been labelled 'femocrats'. American and British visitors to Australia have recorded their surprise at the strength and vibrancy of the 'femocracy' in Australia. Hester Eisenstein, arriving from New York, notes:

> When I first got to Sydney, I was dazzled by the highly political feminists I met there. They seemed utterly at ease with the structures of power at state and national levels. They understood the mysteries of submission-writing; of applying for senior-level positions in government, including the magic language that unlocked the gates of appointment; of committee procedure; of lobbying at endless wine-soaked luncheons and dinner parties; and of the

(to me utterly impenetrable) rules of standing for pre-selection as a candidate for Parliament. These feminists were intensely practically minded, and they were immersed, too, in a kind of detail that I found overwhelming and mystifying. *(Eisenstein 1990: 89)*

Sophie Watson, coming to Australia from an under-funded university in Thatcher's Britain recalls a similar response:

I arrived in Canberra to find myself in the midst of a foreign and somewhat dazzling world. The feminists I met exchanged coded gossip about their ministers' plans for the following day, about the policies they were trying to 'get up', about the million-dollar budget they had won for women's research, about the interstate meeting they were flying to tomorrow. I was baffled. What relationship did these women have to the academic or community-based feminisms with which I was familiar? What kinds of feminism did they espouse? Why did everyone wear designer frocks and smart Italian shoes to work? *(Watson 1990: 3–4)*

The development of Australian child care thus represents a special case. It is not that the level of provision is particularly high: several European nations as well as all the Nordic countries have far more extensive provision. Rather, it is the particular model of child care that has been developed and the extent to which this model has been shaped by women, many of them feminists, that demands attention. In Australia, approximately two-thirds of the demand for work-related child care has been met and the Labor government is committed to completely meeting the need for work-related child care by 2001. The majority of child care services are provided by non-profit organisations managed by community groups (usually comprised of parents and child care workers). There is nationwide consistency in funding arrangments. Moves towards nationally consistent regulations are under way and, from 1994, all services will be required to become accredited in order to be eligible for certain subsidies. Publicly-funded services are not means-tested or restricted to those deemed 'needy'; rather, services accept users from a range of socio-economic backgrounds and charge fees which are related to family income. A system of subsidies is available to assist low and middle income earners in a range of commonwealth-supported services. Women have been crucially involved in this unique achievement – as lobbyists, bureaucrats and policy makers as well as users and providers.

The question of culturally appropriate, accessible and affordable children's services is a particularly acute problem for Aboriginal and Torres Strait Islander families. Since white settlement Aboriginal families have endured extremely high levels of government and police intervention in their lives. Policies such as the forced removal of children from their families and communities (which were pursued in some parts of Australia until the late 1960s) have left a legacy of suspicion and distrust of authorities – especially 'the welfare'. In the late 1970s, Aboriginal Child Care Agencies (ACCAs) were set up in several states in response to concerns about the large numbers of Aboriginal children being placed in institutions or with non-Aboriginal families. The Secretariat of National Aboriginal and Islander Child Care (SNAICC) was subsequently formed as the umbrella organisation for these groups.

Aboriginal and Torres Strait Islander people are disproportionately represented within the child welfare and juvenile justice systems as well as the adult prison population. The Royal Commission into Aboriginal Deaths in Custody found that, of the 99 people whose deaths it investigated, 43 had 'experienced childhood separation from their natural families through intervention by the State, mission organisations or other institutions' (d'Souza 1993: 42). SNAICC has called for national legislation to protect and safeguard the rights of Aboriginal children. It argues that Aboriginal children's services are currently 'fragmented and unplanned' and that proposals put forward by Aboriginal communities are not accepted on their own terms but 'squeezed into categories designed by white people' (Butler 1992: 13).

The extremely high levels of unemployment, poor health, and absence of basic infrastructure in many Aboriginal communities, mean that such families seek far more from child care services than do other Australians. Further, their needs are often different. For example, because of their high levels of unemployment, Aboriginal families are far less likely than others to require child care for work-related reasons. They may desire, however, to have services such as maternal and child health care, nutrition advice and counselling provided through a children's centre.

The agenda of the ACCAs has broadened considerably since their inception and they have worked hard to extend their influence beyond fostering and adoption. SNAICC has called for a national approach to policies for Aboriginal and Islander children and a new program which would bring together the entire range of services for Aboriginal children and their families.

Organisation of the Book

The starting point of this book is the establishment in the 1890s of voluntary organisations concerned with the care and education of young children. Chapter 1 explores the origins of the Australian kindergarten movement, documenting its 'child-saving' mission and its belief that the conditions of working class family life could be improved through voluntary, philanthropic activity. The establishment of day nurseries by separate, but related, voluntary organisations is also examined. The distinction between 'care' and 'education' services was institutionalised very early in the history of children's services in Australia. Day nurseries were intended to cater for the children of women who were 'obliged' to support themselves and their children. They were not intended to encourage women's participation in paid employment.

In Chapter 2, two early instances of commonwealth government support for children's services – the establishment of the Lady Gowrie child centres in the late 1930s and the limited program of commonwealth funding for children's centres which occurred during the Second World War – are explored. Both these initiatives were legitimated by appeals to a conception of 'national interest'; *women's* interests (apart from their roles as rearers of healthy children or contributors to the war effort) were not given any independent weight. The Lady Gowrie centres effectively represented a continuation of the philanthropic approach to children's services which had developed in the early decades of the twentieth century; with the difference that the Gowrie centres were underwritten by commonwealth funds. These centres were intended as 'model' centres, demonstrating optimum methods for the care of pre-school children in a period of intense public and official concern about the health of the poor. For the kindergarten unions, the Gowrie centres represented the high point of their influence with the commonwealth government.

During the Second World War, there was some break with the traditions of philanthropy and 'national interest'. As women's wage-earning activities gained more legitimacy, new groups sought commonwealth assistance for services which would assist those mothers who were contributing to the war effort through their labour market activities. The response of the commonwealth to the demands for child care was a strictly limited one. Rather than establish any new services (which might have set a precedent and encouraged further demands) the commonwealth made funds available to a small number of existing centres (mainly kindergartens) so that they could extend their hours, cater for more children and provide additional services such as care out of school hours. The funds provided for this purpose were made available only 'for the duration'. During the war, a range of new groups began to take part in public debate about services for young children and to challenge the hegemonic position of the kindergarten unions. Feminist groups, trade unionists and political radicals (including some members of the Communist Party) took part in wartime debates about child care and its purposes. Members of these groups also took part in running some of the wartime centres, and developed approaches to the control of services which differed from the traditional kindergarten and day nursery model, dominated by teachers and early childhood professionals.

Chapter 3 analyses the postwar debates about the most appropriate kinds of services for young children and the intensification of the split between 'education' and 'care' services. These developments took place against a background of increased labour force participation by women, especially by mothers. During the 1950s and early 1960s, the kindergarten unions, through their federal body, the Australian Pre-School Association, established an unchallenged position as public arbiters of young children's 'needs' and of the appropriate government responses. Key figures in the pre-school movement opposed the provision of child care services which would enable women to participate in the workforce. The kindergarten unions drew a sharp distinction between 'educational' services, which they promoted as desirable from the point of view of child development, and 'minding' services which, they claimed, served only the needs of mothers. From the early 1960s, some of the kindergarten unions, usually through local branches of the Australian Pre-School Association, exerted pressure on state governments to license and regulate child care services. This strategy was designed to limit the spread of profit-based child-minding services. Yet the kindergarten unions did little to modify their own services to cater to the children of mothers in paid work, or to lobby governments to establish publicly-funded child care. Rather, drawing upon the arguments of John Bowlby and others about 'maternal deprivation', they argued that the commonwealth should respond to the 'problem of working mothers' by introducing a mother's wage to encourage women to remain at home.

With the emergence of the second wave of feminism in the late 1960s, the pre-eminent position of pre-school educators in the early childhood field came under challenge. Feminists formed community child care lobby groups, questioned the notion of 'maternal deprivation' and called for the public provision of a range of child care services which would be run by parents and which families could use at their own discretion – not because (as the welfare model had it) they were deemed to be inadequate or 'needy'. Feminists expressed demands for new types of services which would be government-funded but managed and controlled by parents. In contrast to the early groups of kindergarteners, who had avoided government funding for fear that it might restrict their independence, these new groups sought government funding precisely because of the possibilities they believed it opened up for services to be controlled by mothers (and fathers), rather than by professionals. Feminists questioned the need for professionally trained staff to be employed in children's services and argued that parents and educators should work in partnership rather than in a hierarchical arrangement where teachers were 'experts' and 'professionals' and parents were seen as 'clients'. The demand for child care services was given further impetus when labour shortages led employers to call for measures which would assist women to enter the workforce. In 1972, as one of its last acts, the Liberal-Country Party government introduced the *Child Care Act*, to enable funds to be directed to non-profit organisations wishing to establish child care.

Community debate and government policy on child care were transformed by the incoming Whitlam government; developments of this period are the subject of Chapter 4. Labor came to power promising a year of pre-school education for every child – a policy commitment which had resulted, in part, from assiduous lobbying by the Australian Pre-School Association. Women's groups, however, sought the implementation of a much broader program of child care. Both the traditional pre-school organisations and feminist groups pressed their demands upon the commonwealth government with great energy and passion. The feminists (new to the business of policy making and implementation) directed most of their attention to achieving gains in the *political* arena. Although they gained some spectacular victories here (such as the adoption by the Labor Party of feminist-inspired child care policies), many of their endeavours were undermined by the skilful manoeuvrings of their opponents which often took place, behind the scenes, in the *bureaucratic* arena. Labor's period in government opened up possibilities for the establishment of new types of services and the implementation of parent control and community management. Probably the most significant aspect of this period in the long run was the legitimacy it gave to the idea of children's services being established and supported as a normal community service – not something which should be restricted to 'the needy'.

The changes to commonwealth child care policy which were implemented by the Fraser government are dealt with in Chapter 5. Committed to significant reductions in public expenditure and a return to 'traditional' family values, the incoming Liberal-National Party government substantially curtailed expenditure on children's services. Ironically, however, its determination to ensure that commonwealth assistance was directed to 'the needy' led it to embrace policies (giving priority to child care over pre-schools, for example) which, in many ways, were closer to feminist goals than the policies implemented by the Whitlam government. Pre-school and child care advocates, feeling that the gains they had made in previous years were threatened by continual funding cutbacks, formed a tentative alliance. As a result, towards the end of this period, there came into being a national organisation, the National Association of Community Based Children's Services, aimed at increasing commonwealth support for all types of children's services.

The industrial conditions of workers in children's services are discussed in Chapter 6. This chapter examines the development of industrial consciousness amongst pre-school teachers and child care workers, including home-based family day carers, and the gradual trend toward the unionisation and politicisation of these workers. From the late 1970s, child care workers played a significant role in political campaigns around government child care policies and their funding. These workers came to make direct links between government funding, their own industrial conditions and the quality of care received by children. In 1992, the Australian Council of Trade Unions took up the issue of the wages and working conditions of child care workers and sponsored a major test case which resulted in some important changes for workers in the industry.

Since 1983, under Labor, child care policies have been transformed. Child care has moved from a position on the periphery of debate about welfare, into the mainstream of social and economic policy making. The provision of places has more than trebled and child care has come to be regarded as an important component of the 'social wage'. Chapter 7 outlines the reasons why, and the processes through which child care has come to be more closely linked to other policies – especially social security and labour market policies. It also discusses the changes which have been made to child care funding arrangements, the guidelines concerning priority of access to publicly-funded services, and the industrial conditions of child care workers. The intense debate which has taken place concerning the economic benefits of publicly-provided child care is the subject of Chapter 8 which also details efforts by Labor's then Finance Minister to introduce a system of vouchers to replace the broader system of support for child care. The expansion of work-based and commercial child care and the general drift in Labor policy towards a child care system based upon private enterprise rather than community-based organisations is discussed in Chapter 9.

Terminology

Throughout this book both 'child care' and 'children's services' are used as generic terms covering a range of care and education services for young children. The following terms are used to denote particular service types.

Long day care centres, sometimes referred to as *child care centres* or *day nurseries*, are intended primarily for children whose parents are in paid employment or who are studying or training. They are open for a minimum of eight hours per day and usually operate for fifty weeks of the year. Non-profit services managed by parent committees are usually referred to as *community-based services*. Services run for profit are sometimes misleadingly referred to as 'private' services in Australia. Since there are a number of services which are non-profit but 'private' in the sense that they restrict their clientele to employees of a particular firm, hospital or educational institution, I have used the term *commercial* to denote services run as private, profit-making businesses. Most community-based long day care centres accept children from birth to school age and some also provide after-school care for young primary school children. Commercial centres are much less likely to cater for babies and toddlers. *Employer-sponsored* care in Australia is generally run on a non-profit basis, making it similar in some respects to community-based care. The element of parent or community control is less likely to be a feature of employer-sponsored care.

Family day care is a home-based service in which women are paid to provide child care in their (the carers') own homes, and are supported by regular visits from trained staff. Children from birth to primary school age may be catered for in family day care. A sponsoring agency, usually a local council, church group or other community organisation, takes responsibility for recruiting the caregivers and matching them with families seeking child care. The fact that each provider or carer is part of a broader network and has access to supports such as toy libraries, equipment and special playgroups, distinguishes this form of care from private childminding.

Pre-schools or kindergartens cater mainly for children in the year before they start school (around their fifth birthday in most Australian states). Pre-schools operate during school terms only and usually provide three to five half-day sessions per week. The short hours during which pre-schools operate and the fact that they are closed during school holidays make them inappropriate to the needs of parents who are in paid employment or who, for some other reason, need longer hours of care.

In several states, pre-schools are provided in conjunction with state primary schools and, like public education, are free. However, in New South Wales and Victoria (the two most populous states), most preschools are non-profit, community-based services run by parent committees whose efforts are supplemented by state government grants. In Tasmania, Western Australia, South Australia, the Northern Territory and the Australian Capital Territory, approximately 90 per cent of school beginners have attended pre-school. In New South Wales the proportion is much lower.

Multifunctional Aboriginal children's services provide a range of care, education and family support functions for Aboriginal and Torres Strait Islander families. Some pre-schools are provided by the states and territories as part of Australia's national Aboriginal educational policy.

Occasional or casual care centres provide a service for short periods, usually no more than three hours per week. These centres are intended to assist parents to do such things as visit the doctor or dentist, play sport, or simply have a break.

Multifunctional services provide a range of services for children in the same premises. The services usually include occasional care, full and part day care, playgroups and out-of-school hours programs. In some states, multifunctional services are provided through *neighbourhood centres*. Often run from converted houses, these tend to operate as 'drop-in' centres, as well as providing child care.

Playgroups involve groups of children meeting for play sessions under the supervision of their parents or other caregivers.

Mobile services operate in remote and isolated rural areas taking services such as pre-school sessions and play groups to children who live in dispersed communities.

Out-of-school hours care is a general term referring to services provided for young school children outside regular school hours. The main services are before-school and after-school programs and vacation care. Some centres provide *year-round* care, which combines before- and after-school care and vacation programs.

Informal care is care provided by friends, relatives and siblings of the children concerned. Such care is outside the scope of government policy and regulation, even though it is the most frequently used form of child care.

CHAPTER 1

The Kindergarten Movement and Urban Social Reform

> The Kindergarten Union stands for Formation, not Reformation, and if there were more Kindergartens and Playgrounds, there would be fewer gaols, fewer reformatories, fewer hospitals.
> *Kindergarten Union of NSW,* Annual Report, *1923*

The kindergarten movement in Australia emerged during the last decade of the nineteenth century and was firmly based in the tradition of women's charitable work. The late nineteenth century was a period of extensive philanthropic activity, much of it aimed at reforming working class family life and improving the living conditions of the inner-city poor. Reformers of the period established organisations which focused on such diverse areas as slum abolition, town planning, municipal playgrounds, child health and national parks. Governments, too, increasingly became involved in the regulation of family life and in areas hitherto regarded as 'private' (Sydney Labour History Group 1982). Between the 1880s and the 1930s state and federal governments passed laws concerning compulsory attendance at school, the care of neglected and delinquent children, divorce, the age of consent and child labour.

Kerreen Reiger, author of *The Disenchantment of the Home: Modernizing the Australian Family 1880–1940*, has described these years as 'a major formative period in modern Australian society'. During these decades:

> the material context of the family was rapidly assuming its twentieth-century features: the replacement of production centred on the home by that of industrial manufacture, the growth of suburbia and the introduction of technology into the domestic home. Demographic change ... was already altering the very shape of the family itself. Furthermore, a piecemeal but

coherent reforming effort was being directed at the interior of family life – at the patterning of family relationships – particularly the wife-mother role, the rearing of children and the management of sexuality. *(1985: 1)*

These years (especially the period around the turn of the century) were a time of ferment concerning women's place in society. From the 1890s onwards women were breaking into the public sphere and were actively campaigning for a range of legal and social reforms as well as for the vote (Allen 1979). In New South Wales, South Australia and Western Australia key figures in the suffrage campaigns – Maybanke Wolstenholme Anderson, Catherine Spence and Bessie Rischbieth, respectively – were also principal movers in the kindergarten movement.

Bourgeois Philanthropy and the 'Imminent Danger of Larrikinism'

The idea of the kindergarten first developed in Europe where it was particularly associated with the German educator, Friedrich Froebel (Denison 1978). Froebel differed from many of his contemporaries who regarded young children as 'ineducable' until the age of six or seven. However, he did not advocate that young children should be subjected to strict discipline or required to learn by rote. Froebel likened children to 'tender plants' which needed the right conditions in order to flourish. The teacher's role was, in effect, to be 'the gardener' (Edgar 1967: 214). Children who were provided with opportunities for play and rest, suitable educational equipment and the gentle direction of kindly teachers would grow like well-tended flowers (hence the term 'kindergarten' or children's garden).

Froebel did not evince any particular concern about the education of *poor* children. Families who were interested in having their children attend kindergarten were usually quite well-to-do. The kindergarten was, nevertheless, seen as a liberal concept and following the failure of the 1848 revolution it was banned in Prussia. At the same time, the reactionary governments set up in a number of German states led to the emigration of many liberal-minded Germans to England and America. In this way word of Froebel's 'new education' spread abroad. In England the first kindergartens were set up in London and Manchester, both centres of German immigration. Fees were charged at these kindergartens, effectively ensuring that only children from the middle and upper classes were enrolled; the idea of providing free kindergartens for working-class children came later. In 1872 William Mather established the first such kindergarten in the industrial city of Pendleton. Over the next few years free kindergartens were also opened in London and Edinburgh. By 1912 the London–based Froebel

Education Institute claimed that the kindergarten movement was active 'in most poverty-stricken and deprived districts of large towns'. Whilst the movement may have been active, it does not appear to have attracted much support from wealthy patrons. The English free kindergartens were beset by financial problems. In 1919 all were subsumed into a system of nursery schools financed by local authorities (Whitbread 1972: 56).

In contrast, the idea of the free kindergarten provided as a charitable endeavour found fertile soil in America. There, too, the earliest kindergartens were restricted to the children of wealthy families but free kindergartens for the poor were soon established in Boston, New York City and San Francisco where they were seen as a powerful means of assimilating immigrant children. The kindergarten, wrote the editor of *Century Magazine* provides the 'earliest opportunity to catch the little German, Pole, Syrian, and the rest and begin to make good American citizens of them' (Lazerson 1971: 25).

In 1893 Margaret Windeyer, an Australian feminist, travelled to America to attend the World Congress of the International Council of Women. After the congress she stayed on in the United States visiting various women's organisations and projects. The Golden Gate Kindergarten Association was one project which particularly impressed her. On her return to Australia, in 1895, Windeyer circulated the association's annual report amongst her friends, including Maybanke Wolstenholme, who was then President of the Womanhood Suffrage League and an active member of the Women's Literary Society (Kingston 1979). Both Maybanke Wolstenholme, and her future husband Francis Anderson (philosophy professor at the University of Sydney) were prominent advocates of educational reform.

Several fashionable private girls schools in Sydney, including the College for Girls (later Redlands), Wesleyan (later Methodist) Ladies College and Maybanke College were at that time running fee-charging kindergartens for the children of wealthy families. In addition to these private ventures there had been some interest shown by the state government. A kindergarten organised according to Froebel's principles had been opened at Crown Street Public School in 1882 (Walker 1964: 129). The *Sydney Morning Herald* urged that more centres of this type should be opened in the densely populated inner suburbs in order to overcome the problem of very young children being sent to school 'as a sort of cheap and convenient nursery'. The *Herald*'s enthusiasm, however, does not appear to have been widely shared. In 1884 the Department of Education closed the Crown Street kindergarten on the grounds that it was unjustifiably expensive.

The Kindergarten Union of New South Wales

In 1895 a group of social reformers and educationalists, including both Maybanke Wolstenholme and Francis Anderson, formally inaugurated the Kindergarten Union of New South Wales. Miss Wolstenholme was the foundation president. It is clear from the objectives of the Union that its founders intended it to be a vehicle for the dissemination of knowledge about kindergarten principles as well as an organisation directly providing services for the poor. The objectives of the Kindergarten Union were: to set forth kindergarten principles; to endeavour to get those principles introduced into every school in New South Wales; and to open free kindergartens wherever possible in poor neighbourhoods (a'Beckett 1939: 13).

In Australia, as in the United States, the most enthusiastic supporters of the progressive educational ideas embodied in the kindergarten movement regarded it as an instrument of social reform. Through kindergartens these upper and middle-class women aimed to reach the families who lived in the unsanitary, overcrowded and poverty-stricken suburbs of the major cities and imbue their children with middle-class values such as cleanliness, courtesy, industriousness and thrift (Spearritt 1974). The purposes of educational reform and philanthropy were thus closely intertwined. As one of the leaders of the kindergarten movement was later to observe: 'A cry for reform in education would have been at that time unheeded, but it was comparatively easy to arouse interest in the conditions of neglected children and the imminent danger of larrikinism' (a'Beckett 1939: 13). As the kindergarten came into existence in the midst of an economic depression, many of these families were facing severe privations. With up to 30 per cent of skilled workers unemployed (and an even higher proportion of those regarded as 'unskilled'), thousands of families lacked the basic necessities of food, clothing and shelter (de Garis 1974: 225). The first free kindergarten in Australia was opened in the inner Sydney suburb of Woolloomooloo in 1896. The congested, working-class areas of Newtown and Surry Hills were the next locations.

In the debate within educational circles concerning the relative influence of heredity and environment, the early kindergarteners came down very firmly on the side of environment. They believed that attendance at kindergartens run by 'refined and womanly women' would counteract 'the bad habits and harmful things' learnt in the streets by the children of the 'poorer classes'.

> After the bustle and unceasing change in the streets, the Kindergarten was a place where the same lovely things were done in much the same way, day after day; where questions were answered, and where unity was always found.

In his new environment the child learned how to look up to God and how to look down on little children and pets, his ideals unconsciously became higher in an atmosphere of love and tenderness.

(quoted in Gardiner 1982: 17)

Attendance at kindergarten was regarded as having the potential to transform both the children and their families. Each kindergarten was to be a 'centre for social work' in the homes surrounding it and visits by teachers to the homes of the children were a regular feature of kindergarten work (Anderson n.d.: 3). To enable these visits to take place, kindergarten sessions were usually conducted in the mornings only. Student teachers attended classes of their own in the afternoon. Teachers often saw themselves as allies of other professionals intent on reforming working-class family life.

Kindergarten Unions in other states

By 1911, kindergarten unions (or their equivalents) had been established in all Australian states. In all states, except Tasmania, private training colleges for kindergarten teachers were also set up (Table 1). While each organisation shared similar aims, local factors and local personalities left their own particular stamp.

An important feature of the kindergarten movement in Victoria was the active involvement of the churches (Gardiner 1984: 8-24). In 1901 the first free kindergarten in that state was established in Carlton by a group of women connected with the Baptist Church. A few years later, in 1905, a Presbyterian group opened a kindergarten in the densely populated and poverty-stricken suburb of Burnley. The Methodist Church was the next to become involved with the opening of the Collingwood Free Kindergarten for Poor Children. Then, in 1906, a fourth kindergarten was opened in North Melbourne by the Church of Christ.

Thus, in Victoria, the establishment of individual kindergartens preceded the setting up of the Free Kindergarten Union. Other notable features of the Victorian movement included the involvement of senior members of the state education department and the involvement of prominent social figures. The original members of the Victorian Kindergarten Union included Dr John Smyth, the Principal of Melbourne Teachers College (and later Professor of Education at Melbourne University) and Mrs Alfred Deakin, wife of the Prime Minister. Another Melbourne resident, Lady Northcote, wife of the Governor-General, had been involved behind the scenes in encouraging the formation of the Kindergarten Union and she agreed to act as its patron (Norris 1978).

18   THE POLITICS OF AUSTRALIAN CHILD CARE

Table 1 *Foundation dates of major voluntary organisations and training colleges*

State	Organisation	Date formed	Training commenced
NSW	Kindergarten Union of New South Wales	1895	1896
	Sydney Day Nursery Association	1905	1932
Victoria	Free Kindergarten Union of Victoria	1908	1916[1]
	Victorian Association of Creches	1910	Not applicable
South Australia	Kindergarten Union of South Australia	1905	1907
Queensland	Creche & Kindergarten Association of Queensland	1907	1907
Tasmania	Hobart Free Kindergarten Association[2]	1910	Not applicable
Western Australia	Kindergarten Union of Western Australia	1911	1913

[1] Previously at State Teachers College.
[2] The Kindergarten Union of Tasmania was not formed until 1939.
Sources: Walker 1964: 452; Australian Pre-Schools Committee 1974: 15.

Whilst the development of the kindergarten movement in Victoria appears to have been relatively autonomous, the bodies formed in South Australia, Western Australia and Queensland were all linked more or less directly with New South Wales.

In 1905, the Reverend Bertram Hawker, an Adelaide Church of England Clergyman, visited Sydney and observed the work being conducted at the Woolloomooloo kindergarten. Impressed by what he saw, Hawker arranged for two of the leading lights of the Sydney movement (Miss Frances Newton and Miss Lillian de Lissa) to visit Adelaide in order to give lectures and to demonstrate kindergarten methods. Several demonstrations of kindergarten work were given at the Reverend Hawker's home and a third at Adelaide's Exhibition Building. Members of parliament, staff of Adelaide University and members of the public were invited to attend. Following these demonstrations a meeting was held at the university to consider the formation of a free kindergarten union. A motion that free kindergartens be established in the poorer parts of the city was proposed by

G. C. Henderson, Professor of English and History at the University. The motion was passed unanimously. Catherine Helen Spence, 'doyenne of Adelaide's emancipated, educated and articulate women' (Jones 1975: 129) became the first member of the Kindergarten Union of South Australia. Her niece, Lucy Spence Morice, who had helped the Reverend Hawker to organise the demonstrations, became its first secretary. The vice-regal seal of approval was given shortly afterwards when the state Governor, Sir George Le Hunte, became the patron of the union and Lady Le Hunte became its first president.

The expressed goal of the wealthy philanthropists who founded the Kindergarten Union of South Australia was nothing less than 'the betterment of humanity'. They believed that a 'kindergarten training' for children would lead to 'good citizenship' in later life and would counteract the 'evil habits' to which children living in the poorer parts of Adelaide were exposed. Like their counterparts in Sydney, they anticipated that in the long term the effect of kindergartens would be to reduce crime and reduce the cost to the state of prisons and reformatories (Kindergarten Union of South Australia 1980: 2).

Lillian de Lissa, writing in one of the early annual reports of the Kindergarten Union of South Australia, commented:

> People little know the odds we have to work against here in Adelaide, and would be appalled at the language which is fearful, and the habits which are of the worst, that a child of three knows and is slave to. Poor little mites! Where there is no kindergarten to help them, what misery and struggles are ahead. *(1908: 4)*

Yet even at this early stage she felt able to claim that, in the short period since kindergartens had been established, 'the language is better, the roughness has considerably decreased, and the carefulness and consideration for younger children has increased. Their games are more natural and wholesome, and the whole atmosphere purer'.

Initially, however, residents of the districts chosen by the Kindergarten Union as suitable for the establishment of a kindergarten showed considerable suspicion of their benefactors. Fifty years after she had set up the first kindergarten, Lillian de Lissa recalled her earliest attempts at enticing mothers to send their children along:

> Franklin Street was overflowing with children – they were all over the street! But when Bertram Hawker and I went round canvassing for children they were hurriedly swept indoors and the doors closed and we were regarded with considerable suspicion. *(de Lissa 1955: 26)*

No one had ever heard of a kindergarten. No one had ever heard of a play centre. Nobody had ever heard of people willing to have children who were not their own to come and play for the whole morning – and without paying anything! (de Lissa 1955: 27). Apparently these suspicions evaporated quite quickly, for within a few months of opening the kindergarten was filled to capacity. More than that, within a short time the mothers of Franklin Street were beginning to press for the setting up of a kindergarten in the nearby suburb of Bowden. Lillian de Lissa informed the women that the Kindergarten Union did not yet have the money to start a second kindergarten, adding: 'Besides, perhaps the mothers of Bowden would be as suspicious as you were and not want us.' Her account of the ensuing developments gives a strong indication of how highly the women had come to value the kindergarten:

> And so what the mothers did was to organise an arrangement whereby they went down and canvassed the women of Bowden themselves and offered to keep house and look after the children for a morning so that the Bowden mothers could come up and see what was happening in Franklin Street. And every day for a week or so, a group of Bowden mothers came up and watched in Franklin Street while the Franklin Street mothers went down and looked after the children and kept house at Bowden.

De Lissa continued:

> I was more stirred by this than by anything that had happened in my life up to that time, because I saw a vision of a new world; a world in which women, as women, would begin to think about children who were not their own and who would work for them and their well being though they themselves were getting nothing out of it. *(1955: 29)*

From South Australia the kindergarten movement spread to Western Australia. In that state an organisation known as the Children's Protection Society was already providing a creche service for the children of poor working mothers. Wishing to extend its service from the care of infants to the provision of a service for older children, members of the Children's Protection Society invited Lillian de Lissa to visit Perth. There she gave a number of public demonstrations of kindergarten activities. These proved so popular that they had to be moved to the Town Hall to accommodate all those who wished to observe. All the meetings were crowded and at the last one 'Miss de Lissa was cheered and cheered again' (*Australian Kindergarten Magazine* 1911: 5). Following these meetings and demonstrations the Kindergarten Union of Western Australia was established.

In Queensland the pattern of deveopment was slightly different. There an organisation known as the Creche and Kindergarten

Association was formed in 1907. The goal of the founders of this association was to combine the provision of creches for very young babies with kindergartens designed to serve older children. The emphasis in Queensland was more clearly on philanthropy than education. The person most directly concerned with setting up the Creche and Kindergarten Association was an American Congregationalist minister, the Reverend Loyal Wirt, who operated an 'Institute of Social Services' in the suburb of Fortitude Valley. Reverend Wirt acted in conjunction with Miss Celia Cooper, daughter of the Chief Justice of Queensland. In order to set up the association, Miss Cooper held a meeting at her home and invited the wives and daughters of prominent businessmen to attend. Lady Chelmsford, wife of the Governor of Queensland, was present at this meeting and became the first president of the association.

In Hobart the kindergarten movement began officially in 1910. The early reports of the Free Kindergarten Association are quite forthright in revealing the moral purpose and missionary zeal which characterised the founding kindergarteners. According to the first annual report of the association, in the days before kindergartens, many children had spent their days 'playing aimlessly in the streets'. Once kindergartens were established, however, 'they [spent] happy hours unconsciously acquiring moral, mental and physical training fitting them to take full advantage of the education provided by the State'. In terms reminiscent of the Golden Gate Kindergarten Association, the Free Kindergarten Association advised its supporters that kindergarten work was not a charity but 'a business investment for a business man' (KFA Hobart 1910: 2).

Women, Work and Child Care in the Early Twentieth Century

At the turn of the century, women from well-to-do families were increasingly likely to seek involvement in the world beyond the home. Young ladies of this period were not expected to earn their own living; they were supposed to pass from dependency upon their fathers to dependency upon their husbands. However, relatively low marriage rates, rising levels of education and the expectations generated by turn-of-the-century feminism led many to look beyond the confines of domesticity. One aspect of the establishment of kindergartens was that it provided an occupation (although not always remuneration) for young middle-class women who had open to them very few avenues of employment. As Graeme Davison has observed:

> By highlighting the physical and mental problems of the city-bred child the professions ... helped to create the need for a new range of professional or

> quasi-professional jobs for their sons, and especially their daughters, as kindergarten teachers, child welfare nurses, play leaders and so on.
>
> *(1983: 152)*

At the other end of the social and economic scale, there were untold numbers of poor and working-class women who were obliged by force of circumstance to earn a living for themselves and, frequently, to support dependants. The kinds of jobs which these women could do were also restricted, but for different reasons. The male-dominated labour movement actively excluded women from many occupations, refusing to allow them to enter into apprenticeships, denying them membership of unions and preventing them from gaining award coverage. As a result, women were frequently forced into the lowest paid and most exploitative forms of work – domestic service, outwork and prostitution. Other kinds of work that women did in order to maintain themselves and their families were often socially invisible. As Jill Julius Matthews has demonstrated, women have never occupied the 'commanding heights' of the economy and their labours have frequently been defined as 'non-work' (Matthews 1984). Over the decades, thousands of women have earned their own living or contributed significantly to the income of their families by undertaking such activities as music teaching, laundering, cleaning, producing and selling food, providing board and lodging and so on. Statistical records, however, make it very difficult to ascertain the number and proportion of women who combined responsibility for young children with some form of paid work, since home-based employment was routinely ignored. One estimate, however, suggests that at the turn of the century up to 20 per cent of all women in New South Wales (married and unmarried) who had responsibility for young children may have lacked a male income earner either because of death or effective desertion (Kelly 1988). Women in this situation faced formidable difficulties.

> The mother who was forced into the role of breadwinner was forced into occupations that were the most menial and ill-paid. She spent long hours doing arduous, heavy work. She was performing traditional female tasks within the home: sewing, cleaning, washing, minding children and keeping house, but she was doing it for others and was paid the merest pittance. The poorest women were left to pick up the dregs of work. Those without assistance from their extended family constituted one of the most vulnerable groups in the community. Their daily battle against destitution was unremitting. *(O'Brien 1988: 100)*

In addition to the lack of child care facilities and the exclusionary practices of the labour movement, the decisions of wage-fixing tribunals further cemented women's inferior position. In a series of judgments beginning in 1907 with the famous Harvester decision, Justice Higgins and other members of the Commonwealth Arbitration Court established the principle that *male* workers should be paid a minimum or 'living wage' sufficient to support themselves and a family. According to Higgins, 'A wage that does not allow for the matrimonial condition for an adult man is not fair and reasonable, it is not a "living wage" '. Hence, men, regardless of their actual domestic circumstances, were to be paid at a rate which (at least in theory) would enable them to support a family. Women, since they were assumed to be dependent upon men, were deemed not to be in need of the 'living wage'. Their wages were set at 54 per cent of the male rate.

The notion that wage rates should actually be related to the needs of the human beings who earned them (rather than the capacity of industry to pay) clearly had a strong humanitarian basis. Part of the motivation was a genuine desire to reduce poverty. But the living wage doctrine was inextricably bound up with the notion that most women did not work, or at least were not breadwinners. Women were *supposed* to be dependent upon men. They were not supposed to have others dependent upon them. The needs of women who might also have others to support were systematically denied. 'Fortunately for society', said Mr Justice Higgins, 'the greater number of breadwinners are still men' (Ryan and Conlon 1975: 95). As to the exceptional minority, those women who had to earn their own living and provide for the needs of others, their unusual circumstances could not be allowed to interfere with the principle of the male family wage.

Despite the difficulties and disincentives, thousands of women were engaged in paid employment. Domestic employment accounted for the largest proportion of women workers, but by the early years of the century factory employment was growing rapidly, especially in Melbourne and Sydney. Whereas in 1886 in Victoria, one in five members of the industrial workforce was female, by 1907 this figure had risen to one in two. Similarly, in New South Wales in 1886 one in seven industrial workers was female; by 1907, the figure was one in three. By 1911, the year by which kindergarten unions had become established in all six states, almost 110,000 female industrial workers were classed as breadwinners (Kingston 1975: 60).

The situation of women with very young dependent children was especially precarious. How did these women cope? Some evidence suggests that it was not uncommon for women to work with their babies alongside them. As early as 1905 it was deemed necessary to introduce legislation banning the employment of mothers for at least four weeks after confinement (Kingston 1975: 70). In Louis Stone's famous novel

Jonah (set in Sydney in the early 1900s and published in 1911), the young, unmarried Ada returns to work a few months after giving birth to her illegitimate child. Back at the factory 'her disaster created no stir. Such accidents were common'. Nevertheless, at least in real life, the long hours of work and the conditions within factories would have made it impossible for women to exercise this so-called option for more than a few months.

Domestic service was still the major form of employment available to women around the turn of the century. However, a single woman accompanied by an infant would have had difficulty securing decent domestic employment. The courses of action open to women with sole responsibility for babies and young children were pitifully limited. Often they resorted to drastic solutions.

The practice of baby farming appears to have developed during the nineteenth century as one response to the plight of unmarried mothers. Baby farmers accepted responsibility for the care of children on a semi-permanent basis. Generally they received a lump sum payment in advance and, in some cases, further regular payments. In the absence of other forms of child care provision, many desperate women availed themselves of the 'service' offered by baby farmers in the hope that they would some day be reunited with their children.

It appears that some baby farmers made their living by disposing of the infants entrusted to their care and pocketing the money which had been provided for their maintenance (Sumerling 1983; Burton 1986). Some observers, in fact, regarded this as the unspoken nature of the contract between the parties. Others have suggested that, given that most caregivers were 'inexperienced and uneducated women scratching out an income', the chief causes of the loss of infant life may have been 'misguided nursing, neglect and poverty' (Laster 1985: 150). Whatever the truth, it is clear that handing over one's baby into the care of such a person was likely to have been an act of desperation. Women who, for one reason or another, found themselves responsible for babies or young children did indeed resort to desperate measures. Judith Allen has shown that in the early years of this century it was not uncommon for dead babies to be found in public places, often simply wrapped in newspaper. Between 1881 and 1939 over 800 unidentified babies were taken to Sydney City morgues. Even more babies may have been disposed of in rural areas where such actions were likely to have been more easily concealed (Allen 1982: 115).

Baby farming appears to have been fairly widespread in nineteenth-century Melbourne and Sydney. In 1890 the Victorian government attempted to regulate the practice through the introduction of the *Infant Life Protection Act,* which provided for the licensing of baby minders. Yet it is obvious that in the absence of legitimate means by which to support themselves and their children, hundreds, perhaps thousands, of women were forced to resort to criminal ways of disposing of their babies. Frances Knorr, a twenty-six-year-old Melbourne woman, was hanged in 1894 for the murder of three infants left in her charge. The previous year, John Makin, a New South Wales baby farmer, had been executed for the murder of eight infants. Immediately before his death he remarked indignantly: 'That's what a man gets for obliging people' – a macabre recognition of the desperate necessity of the women who had given their children into his care (Tiffin 1982). Clearly the stigma of being an unmarried mother contributed to extreme action this of type, but the systematic blocking-off of other means by which women could support themselves and their dependents was no doubt the principal cause.

Use of Schools as Child-Minding Centres

One of the most significant changes in the period preceding the kindergarten movement was the introduction of state-funded schooling. Education, which hitherto had been the preserve of those who could afford to pay fees, was made available – indeed compulsory – for all children. One consequence of this new system was that it removed from the home young girls who had previously been responsible for the care of younger siblings. Many families, in order to overcome the difficulties caused by the loss of their resident child minders, responded by enrolling very young children in the newly-established schools. Thus, in the years immediately following the passage of the *Public Instruction Act* in New South Wales there were numerous reports of elementary schools being 'embarrassed with infants'. In 1881, a survey of the ages of children attending school found that almost 20 per cent of them were below the official age for starting school (Walker 1964: 62).

In an effort to cope with these large numbers of young children, infant schools were set up in several areas. These schools were not based on the newly emerging principles of early childhood education. Instead, groups of children were 'housed in a corner of the primary class room ... and taught the 3Rs by anyone available to do so, frequently the "master's wife" ' (Walker 1964: 63). The Department of Education tolerated the presence of such young children in its schools, but set its face against the direct provision of kindergartens within the schools. At the time this decision was made (in the mid-1880s), the department decided to try to incorporate 'kindergarten principles' into the existing infant schools and, in areas where the latter were established, to accept children from the age of four years. For about another decade young children were permitted to attend school if their parents wished but during the depression of the 1890s, a sharp reduction in education expenditure resulted in a decision to exclude children below the compulsory attendance age of six.

Establishment of Day Nurseries

While the kindergarten movement eschewed the provision of services which would enable mothers to improve their material circumstances through paid work, in both Melbourne and Sydney the day nursery movement grew up alongside the kindergarten unions with the aim of providing just such a service. In England and several European countries there had been earlier instances of nurseries being provided in conjunction with factories and other places of employment; Robert Owen's 'Infant School', for example, opened at the New Lanark cotton mills in 1816 (Denison 1978: 47–64). But in Australia there was no history of this type of employer-sponsored provision. The day nursery movement in this country was an offshoot of the kindergarten movement, although the movements differed in a number of significant respects.

The Sydney Day Nursery Association was formed in 1905 and the Victorian Association of Day Nurseries in 1910. The establishment of the Sydney Day Nursery Association was precipitated by a decision made by the New South Wales Kindergarten Union in 1903 not to admit children under the age of three years. (Children as young as eighteen months had previously been accepted into kindergartens.) The reason given for this decision was that 'the kindergarten students attended to be trained as teachers not nurses' (Kelly 1988: 55). The possibility of having to carry out such low status, 'nurse-maidish' activities as nappy-changing and spoon-feeding was apparently a deterrent to some of the young women who might have considered kindergarten teaching as an occupation. Significantly, the Kindergarten Union was prepared to put the wishes of these potential student teachers ahead of the interests of the poor children and families it was avowedly intended to serve.

Whatever the reason, kindergartens and day nurseries were to follow quite different paths. Kindergartens would continue to present themselves primarily as an educational service. Although they obviously provided a limited childminding service for the mothers of their charges this was regarded as purely incidental; kindergartens, as their proponents never tired of saying, were not in the business of relieving mothers of *their* responsibilities. Day nurseries were different. They were specifically intended to meet the child care needs of women who had to undertake paid employment in order to support themselves and their children. As the Sydney Day Nursery Association explained in its first annual report:

> There are in Sydney, as in every city, many poor working women who, through sad circumstances, are forced to fill not only the places of both mother and father, but in addition to be the breadwinner of the family ... These mothers are forced to leave early in the morning to pursue their work in shop, factory or steam-laundry, and their babies, often two or three in number, ranging from a few weeks to a very few years, are left in the care of a child, little more than a babe herself, and failing her, to any one of the neighbours who will undertake the charge ... It is [to enable these mothers] to keep their home and family together, and to supply their little ones the wholesome and loving care of which they are deprived ... that the 'Sydney Day Nursery Association' has been formed. *(Quoted in Spearritt 1979: 18)*

The day nursery movement prided itself on being an 'institution which helps a woman to help herself'. In order to prevent any 'abuse' of the service, women seeking admission for their children had to present a letter from their employer (Sydney Day Nursery Association 1924: 8). The day nursery associations were very proud of the service they offered and did not appear to feel that the children for whom they cared were disadvantaged in any way by being in the nursery rather than in the care of their mothers:

> At the day nursery the child may be left in pleasant and healthy quarters at 7 am and fetched again at 6 pm. It will be under the care of skilled and kindly women who will see to its bathing, dressing and feeding. If over two years old, it will be taught in the kindergarten among other little playfellows; if ailing, it will obtain prompt medical advice.
> And all this for 6d a day! *(Sydney Day Nursery Association 1921: 4)*

The Development of Teacher Training

One of the earliest initiatives of the kindergarten unions in most states was to establish training programs for kindergarten teachers. Indeed, it is a measure of the importance which the pioneers of this movement attached to trained staff that they set up these training courses with such speed. From the earliest days trained teachers ran the kindergartens. Teachers were brought in from America and Britain until the colleges were established here and Australian women could undergo training. In Sydney and Melbourne some private girls schools which ran kindergartens provided practical experience and educational courses to girls who were interested in this type of work. However, separate institutions for the training of kindergarten teachers did not come into existence until the kindergarten unions were established. In Sydney, the Kindergarten Union began training teachers in 1896, just one year after the union itself was formed. Sydney Kindergarten Teachers College opened in 1900. By 1916 similar colleges had been established in every capital city.

Day nurseries adopted a different approach to staffing. Their main model for the congregate care of babies and toddlers was the hospital or orphanage. Concern for the physical health and wellbeing of the children was uppermost. Accordingly, nurses were seen as the most appropriate staff. Day nurseries were headed by a matron, staff wore uniforms (including veils) and a strict regime of health procedures (nutrition, fresh air, regular medical and dental checks) was implemented. However, from the early 1930s, the day nursery movement began to focus its attention on children in the two-to-five-years age bracket (rather than on babies) and to increase its educative role (rather than 'merely minding' the children). In 1932, a Nursery School Teachers College was established in Sydney under the auspices of the Sydney Day Nursery Association (Spearritt 1979: 20).

Setting up independent training colleges outside the state education system was a bold decision for these voluntary groups. It was also a statement of their desire to retain their status as independent organisations, offering a service that was not governed by politicians or bureaucrats. In at least two states, South Australia and Victoria, the Education Departments were keen to provide kindergarten teacher training directly or to offer courses in co-operation with the relevant kindergarten union. In Adelaide, in 1906, the state Labor administration offered to train kindergarten teachers in the University Training College, alongside primary teachers. Lillian de Lissa, then principal of the kindergarten college, vehemently rejected the offer. She argued that:

> It would be a decided disadvantage for the kindergarten students to mix with the State teachers who were imbued with such a different spirit. It would be unwise for the girls to work with them until they had learned to regard their duties in a true missionary spirit – not as a profession but as a religion.
>
> *(Jones 1975: 141)*

The first duty of kindergarten teachers, according to de Lissa, was 'not to obey like dumb-driven cattle' – her image of the primary school teachers – 'but to think out problems for themselves'. De Lissa argued that 'the Government Training College was purely intellectual' and that if teachers were trained there, 'kindergartens would become merely places of instruction like the infant schools, instead of places for the development of character ... [They] would be crushed under departmental routine and red tape' (Jones 1975: 141).

In Victoria, the Education Department and the Free Kindergarten Union conducted a joint training program from 1910 to 1914. Under this arrangement the union's students attended the State Teachers' College for lectures in sub-primary education and, in turn, the union's supervisor of kindergartens gave lectures to both departmental and union students on kindergarten methods. Relations between the two bodies deteriorated however, for, while the union was content for its students to obtain their sub-primary practical experience in the infants departments of state schools, it was not happy about the placement of departmental students in union kindergartens. Some members of the Education Department had played a vital role in founding the Free Kindergarten Union of Victoria and were deeply distressed by the union's reluctance to co-operate in the training scheme. According to Lyndsay Gardiner, John Smyth, the principal of the State Teachers College and an active member of the Free Kindergarten Union, and Frank Tate, the Director of Education,

> had seen the free kindergartens as the first rung on a splendid ladder of total education for children; now the Union was refusing to play the part assigned to it. The situation, Smyth felt, was intolerable. The Union, he wrote to Tate, should never have meddled in teacher training. For Smyth there was a deeper grief, too. He loved his state training college, indeed, it was ... virtually his creation. Smyth saw it as *the* formative influence in the professional training of teachers – all teachers; but for Union students it was not the only, nor even the major, influence. They came as passers-through; their theory there was divorced from their theory under their own supervisor, and from their practical work in the free kindergartens. This made a mockery of the concept of one educational edifice. *(Gardiner 1982: 29)*

The Free Kindergarten Union of Victoria completely severed its connection with the Education Department in late 1914, and thereupon set up its own independent training course.

These events in South Australia and Victoria are indicative of the way the kindergarten unions viewed themselves and their students. They clearly could not accept that the philosophy and methods of kindergarten teaching could be passed on within a state-run training college. No doubt, too, 'they saw kindergarten teachers as young women of their own background who shared their own values and whose parents could pay substantially for their training' (Gardiner 1982: 30). In any event, their decision to set up private colleges ensured that kindergarten teaching remained an occupation open only to girls from well-off, middle and upper-class families. Since the colleges operated as private institutions and received no government assistance (or only a token contribution), fees had to be charged. This requirement excluded girls whose families were unable or unwilling to support them financially while they prepared for an occupation which would earn them no more than a pittance even when they were fully qualified. The entrance requirements set by the colleges, although portrayed as objective criteria designed to ensure high standards, also constituted an unofficial barrier against the less well-off. At Melbourne Kindergarten Teachers College, for example, the entry requirement in 1925 was an Intermediate pass in six subjects. The school leaving age at the time was fourteen and most public schools did not offer instruction beyond the eighth grade (that is, the year before the Intermediate). Thus, only those who attended private schools were likely to have the required qualifications.

Community and Government Support

Both the kindergarten and day nursery associations operated largely through the voluntary efforts of women who resided in prosperous suburbs. These women formed committees, or 'circles', and usually took responsibility for a particular kindergarten or nursery – often miles away from the objects of their concern; for example, a circle of Manly women (from Sydney's Northern beaches) supported the Forest Lodge day nursery (in Sydney's inner west), while the Ravenswood Old Girls raised money for the children of Surry Hills. The women in these circles often became directly involved with the work of the kindergarten or nursery. They visited the children, organised outings for them and performed many of the day-to-day tasks, such as laundering, cooking, sewing and decorating.

While the social origins of these organising committees were very similar, the class bases of their support were quite different. Nothing better illustrates this than the types of fund-raising activities which each undertook. The kindergarten movement was able to organise events such as fêtes at Government House, fashionable balls, displays of antique furniture and other *objets d'art* belonging to committee members, concerts by Dame Nellie Melba, and other grand 'society' occasions. The day nursery associations, by contrast, were forced to resort to much less glamorous means of support. The Victorian Association of Day Nurseries adopted the novel method of laying a sheet in the centre of the Carlton football ground at half-time so that the spectators could throw in their pennies. The Sydney Day Nursery Association, frustrated by its inability to attract large donations, had special stamp books printed in the 1920s to encourage 'people with small incomes' to make regular contributions; each square in the book represented sixpence and the total value of the book was one pound. Other forms of assistance recorded by the day nurseries suggest that they had a measure of direct support from working-class men. Patrons of the Forest Lodge Hotel in Sydney, for example, instituted a system of fines for swearing – the proceeds going to provide treats for the children at the nearby Forest Lodge Day Nursery. Men employed at the Eveleigh Street railway workshops promised to make regular donations to a day nursery in their area if one could be established.

In all states the kindergarten unions and the day nursery associations sought assistance from government – provided no strings were attached. By the second decade of the century, all state governments were providing some assistance to kindergartens, although the level of assistance varied markedly. The two largest states, Victoria and New South Wales – the only states with day nursery associations as well as kindergarten unions – were much less keen to provide financial assistance for day nurseries rather than for the more respectable form of care. Although the Sydney Day Nursery Association received a small grant from the time of its inception, no state government assistance was given to the Victorian Association of Day Nurseries until 1943. The disparities between the assistance given to kindergartens and that given to day nurseries undoubtedly reflected the widespread suspicion that day nurseries threatened the bond between mother and child.

CHAPTER 2

For the Sake of the Nation

> It is the Nation's responsibility to turn out men and women who are A1, not C3. Men and women who are fit to live a full life ... for the service of the Nation.
> *Ada M. a'Beckett, First President of the Australian Association for Pre-School Child Development, 1939*

> While these wartime Children's Centres cater for the children of mothers who are already engaged from economic necessity on war work, they deserve some financial assistance from the Commonwealth. If, however, they are to be used as a means of encouraging mothers to avoid their responsibilities to their children, the Commonwealth should not render any aid.
> *J. Brophy, Acting Assistant Secretary of the Treasury, 1943*

The provision of pre-schools and day nurseries remained within the sphere of voluntary activity, supplemented by small grants from the state governments, until the late 1930s. Before this, in keeping with the prevailing view that 'welfare' matters were most appropriately dealt with by the states and philanthropic organisations, no consideration appears to have been given to the potential role of the commonwealth government in children's services. In the brief period from the late 1930s to the mid-1940s, however, several developments took place which challenged the assumption that there was no role for the commonwealth in this field. In 1938 the commonwealth Department of Health, in response to mounting concern about the health of working-class children, announced its intention to establish demonstration 'child study centres' in each of the state capital cities. These centres were opened in 1940 under the auspices of the newly-established Australian Association for Pre-School Child Development – a national body formed by the state-based kindergarten unions. Three years later, the commonwealth government again became involved in a limited way in children's services, this time as a result of concern about the care of children whose mothers were involved in the national war effort. The 'wartime children's centres' program was a short-term measure, quickly wound down at the end of the war. The Gowrie centres and wartime children's centres were both justified by notions of 'national interest'. The nature of these initiatives in children's services, the structures devised to implement them and the ideology behind commonwealth involvement ensured that each was a very circumscribed event.

Maternal and Child Health in the 1930s

The 1920s and 1930s saw intense debate about the health and welfare of mothers and children. The debate was fuelled by a variety of concerns ranging from fears of 'race suicide' to humanitarian concern for the plight of the poor. Between 1924 and 1933 the birth rate in Australia fell below the level of population replacement for the first time in the country's history (National Population Inquiry 1975: 193). At the same time, there was mounting evidence of the poor health of children and mothers in working-class families, particularly those without a male breadwinner. During these years, maternal and child health came increasingly to be regarded as issues of national significance.

In the course of a Royal Commission into the adequacy of the basic wage, conducted in 1920, extensive and detailed information had been gathered about the daily struggle of poor families to survive. Then, in 1927, the commonwealth government established a Royal Commission on Child Endowment. The evidence presented to the commission provided further information about the struggles of the poor (particularly women who, for one reason or another, did not have a male wage-earner to contribute to the family's income) to maintain themselves. One detailed submission relied extensively on the records of the Sydney Day Nursery Association. The Minority Report of the Royal Commission drew particular attention to the effects of poverty and inadequate housing on the health of women and children living in the industrial suburbs. These issues had also been the subject of a *Report on Maternal and Child Welfare* commissioned by the commonwealth Department of Health from Dame Janet Campbell (senior medical adviser for maternity and child welfare with the Ministry of Health in London) and published in 1930. Campbell's report (1930) showed that the maternal death rate in Australia had risen consistently from 1922 to 1928 and was even higher than the rate in England and Wales. She also showed that the rate of neo-natal mortality (the death rate for children under one month) had fallen very little over this period and that there had actually been an increase in the death rate for infants under one week. Campbell recommended the development of infant and child welfare services and an increase in the level of government funding provided to the voluntary organisations which offered these services. She also advocated increased government intervention, at both commonwealth and state levels, into all aspects of maternal health. Campbell expressed particular concern about the absence of supervision of the health of children between the age at which mothers ceased to take them to the infant welfare clinic (around 18 months) and the age at which they started school and once again came under some kind of supervision by medical authorities.

In the same year that Dame Janet Campbell's report was published, the Federal Health Council (which had come into existence in 1926 as a result of an earlier Royal Commission on Health) expressed serious concern about the health of children below school age. At its fourth session, held in Canberra, the council recommended that each state should attempt to identify the factors impinging on the 'problem of the pre-school child' in order that a national approach might be devised.

Throughout this period, issues of maternal and child health were widely debated in public, academic and governmental circles and the lack of attention to children in the years before school came in for much critical comment. In 1925 Dr Harvey Sutton, Principal Medical Officer of the New South Wales Education Department, estimated that 35–40 per cent of school beginners had health problems which could have been remedied had they been detected between the time the children ceased attending baby clinics and the time they began school. Ten years later, as Professor of Public Health and Tropical Medicine, Sutton sparked a controversy when he claimed that significant proportions of children starting school showed evidence of having suffered from rickets and malnutrition. In 1930 the medical branch of the South Australian Department of Education estimated that 15 per cent of children in that state were suffering from malnutrition (Thame 1974: 226–8).

Kindergartens and day nurseries played a crucial role in safeguarding the health of children in the densely populated areas of Australia's major cities, particularly during the Depression of the late 1920s and early 1930s. The Depression had a catastrophic impact on the poor, many of whom had been living in conditions of severe deprivation well before its onset. The annual reports of the kindergartens and day nurseries refer poignantly to the hardship suffered by poor families (especially the children in these families) at this time and the distress caused by unemployment in a society which made no provision for such things. Poor families endured a range of deprivations including inadequate shelter and clothing, chronic illness and hunger. Many families left their homes either because they were evicted or because they needed to move on in search of work. Others were forced to take in boarders or to provide accommodation to members of their extended families, often leading to gross overcrowding. Of the 56 children enrolled at Paddington kindergarten in 1929 only two came from homes occupied by one family. The majority had lodgers or boarders and in some cases three or four families occupied one tiny house (Kindergarten Union of NSW 1929: 47).

Approximately 70 per cent of the mothers of children attending day nurseries in Sydney were in domestic employment; most of the others worked in factories or as waitresses. As the Depression deepened many of these women lost their jobs. In the case of domestic servants this was because reductions in public transport made it impossible for them to get to the North Shore and Eastern Suburbs homes in which they were employed. In 1929, 'so far-reaching [was] the distress due to unemployment', that the Sydney Day Nursery Association waived its rule which prohibited children whose fathers were capable of work from being accepted into the nurseries. Contagious diseases were an ever-present fear for staff working in the day nurseries and kindergartens. Illnesses could spread extremely rapidly amongst children who were not robust to begin with and who came from homes with no running water, poor sanitation and inadequate food. In its annual report for 1929–30, the Sydney Day Nursery Association reported that there had been forty-three cases of measles, forty-one of whooping cough, twenty-three of chicken pox, ten of scarlet fever, ten of gastroenteritis (three of whom died) and four of pneumonia (one of whom died). This level of illness was described in the report as 'reassuringly small' (Sydney Day Nursery Association 1930: 8).

During the Depression many kindergartens added a 'meal and sleep' program to the traditional morning session in order to ensure that children had at least one good meal and a rest each day. Average weight gains of one to one-and-a-half pounds per month were reported after the children commenced this program which provided them with wholemeal bread, salad, fruit, cocoa, figs and dates. Of course, relatively few children attended the kindergartens and day nurseries and the scale of the problem was vast. In 1930 the *Sydney Morning Herald* reported that in the suburb of Balmain alone there were 2,000 children who were 'so seriously under-nourished as to be in a state of semi-starvation' (Wheatley 1988: 223). The annual report of the Free Kindergarten Union of Victoria, for the same year, records that a doctor who examined all the children attending Melbourne kindergartens estimated that one-third of them were suffering from malnutrition. The doctor regarded this level of malnutrition as 'appreciably less' than that suffered by children in the same districts who were not attending kindergarten.

The reports of the visiting dental officer present an equally grim picture of the health status of inner-city working-class children and also suggest the importance of the assistance provided through the kindergartens. The dental officer who examined 600 children attending Melbourne kindergartens in 1930 extracted 172 teeth and filled a further 987. A staggering 111 children were sent to the dental hospital for treatment under general anaesthetic and these children had an average of six teeth extracted. Less than five per cent of the children were considered to be 'dentally fit' (Free Kindergarten Union of Victoria 1930: 12).

Staff and voluntary assistants in the kindergartens and day nurseries worked under extremely difficult conditions during these years. All the kindergarten unions and day nursery associations had their government grants reduced and donations from the public also dried up. In New South Wales a benefactor, Florence Sulman (daughter of the well-known architect and town planner Sir John Sulman), paid for each kindergarten to take on an additional teacher (at assistant's wages) so that some teachers who would otherwise be unemployed could at least remain in touch with their work. An Adelaide kindergarten teacher interviewed by Wendy Lowenstein for her oral history of the Depression, *Weevils in the Flour*, recalled working in a centre attended by twenty two-year olds and forty older children and staffed by only two teachers. When the hours of attendance at this centre were extended beyond the morning to include a 'meal and sleep' program, the teachers were required to attend for the extra hours and also to do the cooking themselves. These were not the only extra services required of the teachers. Because of the very tight financial situation staff often had to make furniture and play equipment themselves. Some teachers attended carpentry classes so that they could learn to make wooden toys and equipment. Others improvised dolls from papier-mâché (Lowenstein 1978: 341-4). In some Sydney kindergartens teachers cut their own hair to make paint brushes for the children.

Formation of the Australian Association for Pre-School Child Development

Professional women's organisations took a keen interest in the discussions about maternal and child health and debated a number of solutions – almost always involving an extension of the educational and supervisory roles with which they were becoming increasingly identified. In 1936, celebrations were held in Adelaide to mark the centenary of the city. As part of these celebrations, the Women's Centenary Council organised a Maternal and Child Welfare Congress which was attended by both overseas and local experts. The keynote speaker on the first day, a Professor Winifred Cullis, addressed the topic of the wellbeing of children in their pre-school years and stressed the role of nurseries and kindergartens in maintaining children's health. Parallel to the main congress, the kindergarten unions held their own meeting, taking advantage of the fact that the centenary celebrations had brought together representatives from all over Australia. This meeting was organised by the Kindergarten Union of South Australia and opened by Lady Gowrie, the Patroness-in-Chief of the Free Kindergarten Union of Victoria. A meeting held in Melbourne the following year (at which Lady Gowrie again played a key role) resolved to call an interstate conference in 1938 and to discuss the formation of a national body.

Further community interest in the welfare and education of young children was generated in 1937 when an international conference of the New Education Fellowship was held, also in Adelaide. Pre-school education was an important focus at this conference, which featured figures of international renown such as Susan Isaacs and Beatrice Ensor (Burgess et al. 1975: 20). In 1938 representatives of the kindergarten unions of each state assembled once again and this time, 'almost entirely due to Lady Gowrie' (Rudduck 1966: 4), formally resolved to form a federal organisation to be known as the Australian Association for Pre-School Child Development. (The AAPSCD changed its name to the Australian Pre-School Association in 1954 and, in 1979, became the Australian Early Childhood Association.) The aims of the federal organisation, outlined at its inauguration, were: to co-ordinate the work of the six kindergarten unions; to set standards for the guidance of young children in nursery-kindergartens; to set standards for the training of kindergarten teachers; to establish a bureau of publications relating to pre-school work; and to organise a conference biennially (Spearritt 1980: 4).

These aims encapsulated the fundamental purposes which the organisation envisaged for itself: standard-setting (the AAPSCD swiftly came to regard itself as the guardian of standards in relation to *both* kindergarten and day nursery services), public education and encouraging the employment of trained staff. Significantly, the day nursery associations were not invited to join this new association – a reflection, no doubt, of the fact that most kindergarten enthusiasts regarded full-day care for children as undesirable. Political considerations may also have played their part. The kindergarten unions relied significantly on state government assistance and some ministers of education were known to be extremely hostile to out-of-home care for young children. The New South Wales Minister for Public Instruction, Country Party member David Drummond, although accepting that sessional kindergarten programs could be of benefit to poor children, was vehemently opposed to day nurseries. He regarded the care of children in group settings on a full-day basis as the beginnings of a 'state hatchery'. His Victorian counterpart, Country Party Minister for Public Instruction Dr John Harris, was sceptical even of kindergartens. He believed that they had the potential to break up the family and that, because of their 'collective' approach to child-rearing, they were likely to be breeding grounds for socialists (Spaull 1982: 240).

In 1936 the commonwealth Minister for Health, United Australia Party member W. M. Hughes, opened the first session of the National Health and Medical Research Council (which superseded the former Federal Health Council). In his speech, the minister emphasised that the first objective of the council should be to raise the standard of health of the Australian community:

> By health I do not mean a negative condition, mere freedom from active disease; but that state of bounding energy and vitality that makes one rejoice and be glad to be alive ... Surely we can with great profit devote much more detailed attention to the care of the infant and the growing child of pre-school age; in Kindergartens or its own home, following this up right to the end of school age, and even beyond it. In this way, ill-health amongst adults and in early middle age would be very considerably reduced.
> *(National Health and Medical Research Council 1937–38: 4)*

The following year the Treasurer announced in the budget speech that 'an amount of £100,000 is being provided in respect of public health projects, especially in relation to the health of women and children' (Rudduck 1966: 8). Soon after this, the Director-General of Health, Dr J. H. L. Cumpston, wrote to all state health departments asking for suggestions for projects in relation to the pre-school child which would 'recognise, extend and make full use of the kindergarten system'. Cumpston also requested Dr Vera Scantlebury Brown, Director of Infant Welfare in Victoria, to prepare a memorandum on the care of the pre-school child which could be presented at the meeting of the National Health and Medical Research Council to be held in Sydney later that year. Dr Scantlebury Brown's memorandum (which was prepared in conjunction with members of the Free Kindergarten Union of Victoria) was considered in detail at that session and, subsequently, Dr Cumpston asked her to estimate the cost of setting up a demonstration pre-school. The Free Kindergarten Union of Victoria began to lobby the commonwealth government intensively for funds to establish a model pre-school in Melbourne.

Establishment of the Lady Gowrie Child Centres

Just one month after the AAPSCD was formed, the Prime Minister, J. A. Lyons of the United Australia Party, informed the state premiers that the commonwealth had decided, 'without intruding upon fields already occupied by State Governments', that:

> a Demonstration Centre should be established in each capital city at which not only will the methods for the care and instruction of young children be tested and demonstrated, but also problems of physical growth, nutrition and development will be studied. *(Cumpston and Heinig 1944: 2)*

On the day of this announcement, Mrs a'Beckett, the President of the AAPSCD, was visited by the commonwealth Minister for Health, Earle Page, who informed her that the government wished to enlist the assistance of the AAPSCD in this new venture. The AAPSCD was asked to take on responsibility for the administration and supervision of these centres for a period of five years. Mrs a'Beckett told the press:

> I have no doubt that the formation of the AAPSCD has commended the movement to the Minister for Health, showing as it does that we are not isolated units in each State, but groups endeavouring to work together for the good of the whole. *(Argus 22 March 1938)*

Mrs a'Beckett was no doubt correct in her assessment of the importance of having a *nationally* organised body. As a friend of Lady Gowrie she would also have been aware that the Governor-General's wife had personally put pressure on commonwealth ministers to allocate the entire £100,000 set aside for maternal and child health projects to the kindergarten unions; she may have been quietly advised by Lady Gowrie to encourage the formation of such a body. Lady Gowrie's energetic endeavours to assist the state-based unions to set up a federal body may be explained, at least in part, by her knowledge that this would make the proposal more attractive to the commonwealth. It is not surprising that the AAPSCD decided to honour the architect of their success by naming these demonstration centres the Lady Gowrie Child Centres.

The Gowrie centres generated controversy from their inception. The government's decision to spend the entire £100,000 on demonstration centres to be supervised by the kindergarten unions was a bitter blow to many other organisations throughout the country. According to a commissioned history of the Australian Early Childhood Association:

> During the next few months the Prime Minister, the Minister for Health, the Director-General for Health, the State Premiers, the State Health Ministers and local members were all inundated with letters from irate organisations who were already long established and devoting voluntary and professional time and money to the care and welfare of children under six.
> (Jackson-Nackano n.d.)

Another aspect of the Gowrie centres which caused some tension was their level of staffing and the relatively high salaries they paid. By any standards (especially by those of Australia in the late 1930s) the centres were well staffed. Each had a director, a minimum of five assistant teachers, a social worker, an infant welfare nurse/dietician, a part-time medical officer, a secretary and a caretaker and a cook-housekeeper. The salaries paid to the director (£300) and first assistant teacher (£200) were determined by the commonwealth and were well above those that other pre-school teachers received. The high wages engendered some resentment; fears were expressed that these lavishly funded centres might entice staff away from other kindergartens. At the inaugural AAPSCD conference Alice Creswick (Convenor of the conference Garden Party Committee as well as the Finance Committee) voiced the concern that 'the best and most highly-qualified girls will leave our local kindergartens to take up these posts; and though we do not grudge them the promotion, they can ill be spared' (Creswick 1939: 178).

A study of the records of children enrolled at the Perth Gowrie centre between 1940 and 1945 suggests that there were also a number of tensions and difficulties between the staff and the children's families. Since these were generated by the philosophy and objectives which underpinned *all* the Gowrie centres, similar problems were almost certainly experienced elsewhere. As Reiger has demonstrated, by the 1920s and increasingly through the 1930s, the child-saving mission of the early kindergartens was being replaced by the idea of the kindergarten (or pre-school) as an educative and social environment. The new emphasis was on the scientific principles of child development, on gathering data, on measurement and professionalism (Reiger 1985: 164–5). The Lady Gowrie centres epitomised this approach.

The Gowrie centres, conceived in a context of intense public and official concern for the health of children, were not intended merely to provide the kindergarten unions with an opportunity to demonstrate their own methods of care and education; they were also seen as research centres where problems relating to the health and wellbeing of children could be studied. Among their purposes were 'the testing and demonstrating of methods for the care and instruction of the young child' and the 'study [of] problems of physical growth, nutrition and development' (Cumpston and Heinig 1944: 3). The centres were to be established in 'densely populated' areas – a euphemism, no doubt, for the type of congested inner-city, working-class suburbs in which charitable kindergartens had been traditionally located.

In line with their function as research centres, measurement and observation of the children's physical growth and development was a major preoccupation of the staff at the Lady Gowrie centres. Each centre enrolled one hundred children who, in order to conform to the research requirements of the commonwealth Department of Health, were supposed to be 'Australian born children of Australian born parents' (Terrey and Ponsford 1966: 20). In practice this meant excluding Aboriginal children and children born to parents who were non-English-speaking migrants. The children were also supposed to be 'normal' – without psychological, physical or mental defect. Enrolment at a Lady Gowrie centre was regarded as a serious commitment. Parents had to provide detailed information about their children. They were also required to sign an agreement promising that their children would attend regularly and that they would co-operate with the staff 'in the proper guidance of the child'.

The intense focus on the physical habits and bodily development of the children was one of the features of the Gowrie program which caused difficulties with some of the children and their parents. According to Patricia Crawford, who made a detailed study of the records of the Perth centre between 1940 and 1945, 'the staff were obsessed with the children's physical development'. Every child who attended a Lady Gowrie centre was examined by a nurse each day and detailed notes were taken about his or her health. Elaborate record forms were devised and parents were asked to give the staff detailed information about their children's sleeping and bathing routine, bowel habits, eating patterns and behaviour at home. Once a month each child was stripped, weighed and measured. Many children objected strongly to this and, on this issue, parents were often prepared to support the children against the staff. Another aspect of the Gowrie program that caused difficulties (at least in Perth) was the fact that staff members – acting, as they saw it, in the interests of the 'overall health and well-being' of the children – frequently made inquiries from neighbours about the children and their families. All kinds of comments and observations made by neighbours about parents' drunkenness, swearing and overnight visits by non-family members were recorded. Neighbours' opinions about whether a child's absence from the centre was genuinely due to illness or whether the child had been 'truanting' were also sought and recorded. On one occasion, when neighbours reported to the Gowrie staff that a mother had left her young children alone at night, staff alerted the police (Crawford 1988).

Conflicts also occurred between staff and mothers when the former offered 'guidance' about the rearing of their children. Such 'guidance' often came in the form of adverse judgments about the current practices of the household, particularly if the practices included mothers having any kind of paid employment. As Crawford has commented:

> It was not [the Gowrie's] intention to provide child care so that [the mothers] could pursue their own interests. Rather, the staff's ideal mother was one who was fully involved in the daily working of the centre, under their direction. *(1988: 192)*

The teachers and social workers were particularly critical of those working mothers whose employment required them to spend long hours away from home. They seem to have had little understanding of the fact that long hours were often necessary because the kind of work available to these women was poorly paid. One woman, whose records were examined in Crawford's study, was constantly rebuked by the Lady Gowrie staff for her long absences from home; usually from seven o'clock in the morning until after dinner in the evening. For these hours of work she earned thirty shillings per week. The constant admonitions of the staff that the woman's two young children 'needed her at home' can have done little to ease her situation. As late as 1956, the Director of the Perth Lady Gowrie Centre publicly stated that 'the first cause of stress in children is a mother's employment for gain' (Crawford 1988: 200).

The Gowrie centres, backed by vice-regal patronage, staffed by young, childless women from the 'better' suburbs and supported by generous commonwealth funding to facilitate systematic study of the poor, represented the high point of influence of the traditional, philanthropic kindergarten movement. The demonstration centres epitomised the class divisions embedded in children's services: the women who had instigated the establishment of the centres, who negotiated with politicians and bureaucrats over their structure and purposes, and who worked in them were solid, middle and upper-class citizens. The recipients of the services were respectable battlers at best, at worst, pathetically poor.

Despite the reality of the lives of many of the children, the centres were based on a model of family functioning in which a male breadwinner provided financial support while the women cared for children and home. The staff pointed out to families the ways in which they failed to live up to this ideal and attempted to 'educate' them about the 'proper' ways children should be reared. There is little evidence that the staff had any understanding of the larger social problems which beset these families, problems such as inadequate wages, poor housing and lack of child care.

Women's Work and Child Care during World War Two

The Second World War saw new pressures brought to bear on the commonwealth government regarding its role in children's services. During the war, a number of newly formed groups began to take part in public debate and lobbying around the child care issue. For the first time, the commonwealth government came under sustained pressure to take direct responsibility for the provision of child care for the children of working mothers. There were, however, strong countervailing pressures. Lynne Davis, in her detailed account of women's work and child care provision during the war and postwar reconstruction periods, lists these as 'defence of the family as the basic unit of society, anti-communism, concern for proper child development, and cost-benefit analysis' (Davis 1988).

During the Second World War there were significant changes in the extent and nature of women's workforce participation. The war signalled a shift for women away from 'private' and into more 'public' forms of employment. Female self-employment and private domestic employment fell, while women's employment as wage-earners, members of the defence forces and rural workers grew (Kramar 1982). The increase in the workforce participation of married women was particularly pronounced. Whereas in 1933, married women represented only 11 per cent of the female workforce, by 1943 they accounted for 25 per cent (Faro 1983: 35). The war gave new legitimacy to the employment of married women and opened up a range of possibilities for them. Some of the opportunities generated by wartime mobilisation (such as opportunities to work in 'masculine' jobs like vehicle-building and metal industries) were short-lived. Others were longer-lasting. From 1933 onwards, tens of thousands of women – attracted by the higher wages that could be earned in secondary industry as well as the more regulated conditions there – left private domestic employment. After the war, most women who held jobs worked in shops, offices and factories; few remained in domestic employment. A significant and permanent change had occurred in the everyday lives of large numbers of women.

Early in 1942, the commonwealth government established the Women's Employment Board, an independent tribunal whose purpose was to regulate the wages and conditions of women employed in occupations usually performed by men. The rulings of the WEB were, on the whole, very beneficial to those women to whom they applied. While few of its decisions granted women equal pay, most gave them 90 per cent of the male wage; as most women outside the scope of the WEB's jurisdiction were still receiving 54 per cent of the male rate, this was a considerable advance. The WEB contributed significantly to altering and enlarging the scope of women's work and played an important part in educating the community about the actual and potential contribution of women to the nation's productive effort. The Chairman of the WEB, Judge Foster of the Victorian County Court, took every opportunity to express his admiration for women's role in war production (Larmour 1975: 50).

There does not appear to have been any significant pressure for increased child care provision before 1942. In the early stages of the war, single women could be employed but married women were regarded by the commonwealth government as 'non-employable'. In July 1941, permission was given for married women to be employed in munitions factories and early in 1942 the Department of Labour and National Service officially sanctioned their employment in a much broader range of occupations. Only after this had occurred was it possible for the care of the children of women war workers to become a public issue. In the second half of 1942 public meetings were held in all state capital cities, followed in most cases by the establishment of groups whose purpose was to campaign for child care provision.

A conference on 'Child Care and the War', held in Sydney in December 1942, called on the commonwealth government to provide funds for child care for pre-school children and those of school age. It also urged the establishment of a commonwealth Child Care Department. As a result of this conference, a 'Care of the Child in War-time' Committee was established. Another Sydney group, based round the National Council of Women, also worked for child care as did the Child Welfare Advisory Council.

Some months before this the commonwealth Minister for Health and Social Services, E.J. Holloway, had met with representatives of the Melbourne-based Council for Women in War Work to discuss day nursery provision for the children of women war workers. Holloway informed the women that the Department of Labour and National Service had considered such a scheme but had found it to be impracticable; the Department of Health and Social Services had also rejected the idea, principally on the grounds that women with young children did not wish to work and were not compelled to do so. The Minister also argued that such a scheme would require the diversion of labour and materials from other urgent projects such as hospitals and that, in any event, there were unlikely to be sufficient trained personnel to staff an expanded program of child care services.

The women suggested that existing facilities could be expanded in order to provide for a greater number of children without incurring capital costs or substantially greater salary costs. The Minister considered this to be a constructive proposal and agreed to give consideration to a practical scheme along these lines. The following month the Co-ordinating Committee for Child Care in War-time was established in Melbourne. The committee included representatives of child care organisations, trade unions, and representatives of the medical and social work professions. Ruth Crow, an active member of the Communist Party, who was involved in this committee, recalls that there was 'a considerable clash of values' amongst its members.

> The differences revolved around the philosophy that 'the child's needs are paramount' and that 'we must not make a need for child care'. Thus, the traditional child care organisations ... were strongly opposed to mothers being in paid employment. On the other hand, the experience of these organisations was a great asset in many ways. *(Crow 1983: 5–6)*

The Co-ordinating Committee undertook to establish a project that would demonstrate the type of provision needed for the care of children of women war workers. The centre which arose from this commitment was the Brunswick Children's Centre. Located in the middle of an industrial suburb employing thousands of women (including several hundred making parachutes at the Holeproof factory), this centre was financed by the commonwealth and state governments and the local council. It provided a comprehensive program catering for babies, toddlers, pre-schoolers and school age children. A committee of management comprising users, local residents and two representatives of the Co-ordinating Committee was to oversee the operation of the centre. Ruth Crow, who was appointed secretary/organiser of this centre, observes that one of the most significant features of this and other wartime children's centres was the involvement of working-class women:

> Traditionally, children's services (kindergartens and infant welfare centres) had relied on voluntary helpers but these were nearly all recruited from the more affluent suburbs and were mainly older women ...
> Exciting new forms of organisation were developed in the collectives at the Brunswick centre and at the other wartime day nurseries. *(Crow 1983: 7)*

Although the Brunswick centre was widely regarded as successful and was seen by many as a model for the development of children's services, no other centre seems to have matched either its comprehensive program or the wholehearted efforts of its staff to co-operate with the parents in running the centre and caring for the children, rather than regarding them as the objects of professional intervention (Davis 1987a).

The main public service support for an expanded role for the commonwealth in child care provision came from the Department of Labour and National Service. In March 1942, Constance Duncan (employed in the Industrial Welfare Division of the department) suggested that existing creches, day nurseries and kindergartens be brought into a national scheme and offered financial assistance on condition that they complied with certain guidelines regarding the type of service they offered, hours of operation, employment of trained staff and physical standards. She also suggested that additional centres be developed in areas nominated by the department based on surveys of potential women workers. The Department of Labour and National Service advised the Prime Minister's Department that it was 'convinced that the children of married women already in industry are in many cases being neglected, and, where satisfactory private arrangements are made for their care, the occasional breakdown of such arrangements involves their mothers in increased domestic difficulties and contributes to absenteeism'. The Department declared itself willing to 'co-operate enthusiastically in any comprehensive scheme which may be put forward for the solution of this problem' (quoted in Davis 1988: 111). It suggested that the administration of such a scheme be entrusted to the Department of Health, partly because of its existing commitment to the Lady Gowrie child centres. However, the Director-General of Health, Dr J. H. L. Cumpston, was not interested in the proposal and the Minister for Health was adamantly opposed to it.

Following continued representations on the subject, Dr Cumpston appears to have changed his mind. At the end of 1942, he and the Director of the Industrial Welfare Division in the Department of Labour and National Service discussed with the Treasurer, J. B. Chifley, the question of care for the children of women war workers. Chifley's view was that this area was best left to the states. Subsequently, however, after consultations with the Prime Minister, Chifley approved the expenditure of £25,000 for an 'experimental' program. This initiative had less than the wholehearted support of the government. According to Davis (1988: 112), the commonwealth Health Minister's reservations regarding child care were still such that he declined to issue any press releases about the experimental program.

The money made available was not, as had originally been proposed, to fund a scheme of commonwealth child care centres, but to encourage the existing child care organisations to extend their services to cater for the children of women war workers. In January 1943, the commonwealth government formally invited the kindergarten unions, the Victorian Creche Association and the Sydney Day Nursery and Nursery School Association to expand their existing services. The purpose of this scheme was twofold:

> (i) to estimate the extent of the demand and the response which has been made by the women employed in industry and possible future needs; (ii) to determine the best policy in relation to assisting women engaged in war industry, by relieving them of the care of their children during working hours and to gain sufficient experience to enable a larger scheme to be most effectively planned. *(Heinig and Duncan 1943)*

The commonwealth's decision to respond to pressures for wartime child care by providing additional funding to voluntary organisations rather than by establishing its own administrative mechanisms meant that there was no significant break with the philanthropic tradition.

The program was indeed an extremely limited one. It involved just fourteen centres in three states. Nine of these were in Victoria – five sponsored by the Free Kindergarten Union and four by an organisation known as the Women of the University Patriotic Fund. Two Free Kindergarten Union centres in South Australia took part in the scheme and three Sydney Day Nursery centres in New South Wales. Use of the centres was strictly controlled. The women were questioned regularly as to whether (and where) they were going to work. Employers were also asked to report on the women's attendance. In some instances children whose mothers' employment was not regarded as 'essential war work' lost their places at the kindergarten. In total the commonwealth's program provided for 750 pre-school children and 100 children of school age. Funding to these services ceased shortly after the war. By early 1946, total expenditure on the program had amounted to approximately £40,000.

The Australian experience was very different from that of England or the United States. In England, the number of day nursery places expanded from 4,000 in 1938 to 72,000 in 1944 (Ferguson and Fitzgerald 1954: 181–203). In America, under the *Community Facilities Act*, more then $50 million was spent on day care between 1941 and 1945 and more than a million and a half children were attending day care centres by the end of the war (Steinfels 1973: 647). In Australia, however, as Davis shows:

> In spite of much public discussion and lengthy canvassing of the issues within the Commonwealth Departments of Labour and National Service, Treasury and Health, very little ever came of the child care proposals. Such decisions as were taken were half-hearted and inconsistently publicised, and there seems always to have been considerable ambivalence about both the desirability and the objectives of the programme. The amount of money allocated to it was derisory, and the amount actually expended even more meagre. *(1988: 139)*

In Australia, both the Catholic church and the trade union movement powerfully influenced the government's response to the child care issue.

> The labour movement was sensitive to any possible undermining of the privileged status of male labour. The Roman Catholic Church (whose members made up a significant proportion both of the membership of the Australian Labor Party and of its constituency) opposed any policy which might undermine the sexual division of labour within the family, which the church so strenuously defended, or which might open up the years of early childhood to secular influences. *(Davis 1988: 236–7)*

The cold war atmosphere which developed from the late 1940s onwards had an impact within child care organisations. The limited co-operation which had occurred in organisations such as the Co-ordinating Committee for Child Care in War-time did not continue past the end of the national emergency. In 1948, Ruth Crow was asked to take part in a delegation of the Victorian Association of Creches to meet the Premier. The Premier refused to meet the delegation while it included a communist. The association responded by asking her to resign from the organisation. Crow claims that many others who were thought to be communists or to have associations with communists were asked to leave nursery and kindergarten committees at this time (Interview, 1983).

Planning for the Postwar Period

The postwar period saw a reassertion of traditional views about gender and the division of labour within the paid workforce and the home, although such views did not reflect the reality of many women's experience. The women's labour force participation rate dipped briefly following the war but thereafter climbed fairly steadily (Faro 1983: 15). Women's organisations, however, were increasingly preoccupied with the working conditions of women in the home. Aside from equal pay, little attention was given to the treatment of women in paid employment.

In planning for postwar reconstruction, a great deal of attention had been paid to the expansion of social services and the need for additional child care services was frequently noted in government reports as well as in popular debate. In 1943, H.C. Coombs, the Director-General of Post-War Reconstruction, argued that kindergartens and creches (amongst other things) were necessary for 'a full and complete life' (Faro 1983: 64). Even the Joint Parliamentary Committee on Social Security strongly recommended the provision of services for young children in its eighth interim report presented in 1945 (Joint Parliamentary Committee on Social Security 1945–46: 1208).

In her discussion of 'state construction of domestic life' in relation to population policies and family policies, Bettina Cass demonstrates how 'the family' was constituted as 'the legitimate recipient of the rewards of the post-war reconstruction state' (Cass 1988a: 171). There were some limited exceptions to this. In 1942 the National Health and Medical Research Council established yet another inquiry into the decline of the birth rate. No less than six expert committees were set up to investigate the birth rate 'problem'. One of these – charged with the task of inquiring into what would constitute a 'Fair Deal for Mother, Infants and Young Children' – was headed by Constance Duncan (whose role in promoting a scheme of commonwealth-funded child care centres was noted earlier). Duncan's committee advocated a range of measures to help mothers with housework, child care, infant and maternal welfare services. Likewise, a 'Memorandum of Some Aspects of Decline in Birth-Rate and Future of Population in Australia' prepared by experts from the Departments of Post-war Reconstruction, Labour and National Service and the Bureau of Census and Statistics also placed considerable emphasis on the importance of social services including kindergartens and day nurseries, communal laundries, assistance in times of domestic crisis and family holidays.

In most of this planning, however, there was no appreciation of the distinction between kindergartens and day nurseries and no attempt to locate child care in relation to women's employment. Very often services for children were presented as a means of reinforcing traditional conceptions of the family or of encouraging women to bear more children. The Joint Parliamentary Committee on Social Security, for example, stated:

> We are convinced that with the development of a system of creches and day nurseries, and of home 'minders', the lot of the mother with young children could be greatly eased. There would be a restored encouragement of family and happier home life if mothers could be assured of regular relief at home for shopping or visiting excursions, and the young married couple could be released together for an occasional evening at the pictures or a dance.
> *(1945–46: 1208)*

Even some feminists conceived of child care as a way of encouraging the birth rate, rather than as a means to women's independence and autonomy.

> The answer, to my mind, is simple – CRECHES – government-sponsored, government-run, clean, healthy creches where we may *sometimes* leave our babies, knowing they are being well cared for, while we go on our way gathering stimulation from our contacts with our free fellows. Then watch the birthrate increase ... *(de Coney 1945: 31)*

In 1943, 200 delegates from over 90 organisations throughout Australia attended a National Women's Conference for Victory in War and Victory in Peace. The resolutions from this conference, several of which related to child care, were put together to form an Australian Women's Charter which was presented to the Prime Minister in March 1944. The charter called for the commonwealth government to 'establish a National Children's Bureau to disseminate information and formulate a program for the welfare of children' and 'to subsidise the establishment of a network of child centres to be developed and administered by a combination of State and local governments and elected citizens' bodies'.

Children's services also figured prominently in the debate which took place concerning the types of general community facilities that governments should provide. Most women's organisations favoured the establishment of kindergartens as part of the normal infrastructure of 'new communities'. The Kindergarten Union, the Women's Services Guild, the United Associations of Women and the Care of the Child in War Time Committee also urged the commonwealth government to take responsibility for the pre-school child and to increase expenditure on facilities for this age group (Allport 1984: 141).

However, the idea of establishing such facilities roused considerable opposition from several quarters, especially from the churches. When the Community Facilities Committee (established by the Department of Post-war Reconstruction) published its report on the basic facilities which should be located within a reasonable distance of every home, it recommended that kindergartens should not be included amongst the basic requirements of local communities but that 'a demand for this facility by the community should determine the need' (Allport 1984: 182).

The establishment of the Lady Gowrie centres and the wartime experiment with children's centres have a number of common features. Both were instances of limited commonwealth intervention into child care in support of national goals. In neither case were women's *own* interests (independent of their role as rearers of healthy children or workers for the war effort) accorded legitimacy. Indeed, in both cases, every effort was made to ensure that women did not make use of the service merely to pursue their own interests, even (in the case of the Lady Gowries, especially) if 'their own interests' were earning a living.

The Gowrie centres combined a modified version of the philanthropic model of the early kindergartens with 1930s ideas about 'proper', 'scientific' ways of monitoring children's development. Their major purpose was not to offer 'child care' but to provide opportunities for trained teachers to 'educate' working-class parents in the right ways of rearing children. There was no acknowledgment of the possibility that the problems faced by these families (including the poor health of the children) could only be addressed by an improvement in their material conditions and that this, in turn, required child care services so that mothers would be able to participate in paid employment.

The official response to the needs of employed women during the Second World War was a similarly narrow and prescriptive one. The commonwealth government went to great lengths to ensure that the wartime children's centres benefitted legitimate war workers. There was a determination on the part of all concerned to ensure that these services were not regarded, or used, 'as a means of encouraging mothers to avoid their responsibilities to their children' (Davis, 1987: 21). Despite their undeniable limitations, however, both of the commonwealth's initiatives were important in focusing attention on the commonwealth as a potential source of funding and national planning for children's services.

CHAPTER 3

A Mother's Place . . . ?

> In our society, the nuclear family (read 'mother') has been held to be fully responsible for the development and socialization of the child under school age. Women's Liberation holds this to be an unreasonable and unsatisfactory method of childrearing. The recently formed Women's Liberation 'Community Controlled Child Care' action group ... denies the assumption that the ideal environment for the small child is home with mother, all day everyday ...
>
> *Winsome McCaughey,*
> Founder of Community Child Care, Victoria 1972

In keeping with the strong re-assertion of women's traditional roles which occurred in the postwar period, the children's services which received most attention and which expanded most rapidly were kindergartens. The various kindergarten unions and the AAPSCD returned with relief to providing and supporting educational programs, mainly for three- and four-year-old children; at every opportunity they distanced their project from 'child minding'. Kindergartens, as we have seen, assumed a model of family life in which roles and responsibilities were sharply divided along gender lines: father performed the role of breadwinner, mother that of nurturer and homemaker. As the decades wore on and kindergartens were increasingly regarded as the first rung of the educational ladder, they began to assume some of the features of the school system; closing during school holidays, for example. At the same time, the term 'pre-school' became popular with parents, presumably because of its clear educational connotation and the fact that it was not associated with 'charity'. This change in terminology was resisted (largely unsuccessfully) by many professionals in the field who were keen to retain a clearly-defined arena of 'early childhood education' based on a philosophy and set of methods which differed from those used in primary schools. While none of the Kindergarten Unions chose to include 'pre-school' in their title, the Australian Association for Pre-School Child Development retained the term when it became the Australian Pre-School Association (APA) in 1954.

Pre-schools were transformed in a number of ways during the 1950s and 1960s. Increasingly they became the preserve of children from middle-class families which fitted the prescribed mould of the nuclear family. Families who needed child care services in order that the mother could undertake employment, were excluded by the very structure of pre-schools. Not many jobs available to women could be fitted into the half-day sessions offered by pre-schools and few employers would have countenanced women's absence during school holidays. In any case, pre-school teachers expected mothers to be available on a regular basis for 'morning tea roster' and other activities conducted under the supervision of the teacher.

With the steady increase, during the 1950s and 1960s, in married women's workforce participation, the need for child care services expanded. Needs however do not automatically translate into demands and certainly not into demands on the state. While there was some response from the market (a number of women set themselves up in their homes as child minders and in some states commercial centres began to proliferate), most women appear to have coped with the lack of child care services by calling upon friends, neighbours and members of their extended family to provide help. They managed in private, individualised ways. Women with young children were not supposed to be employed outside the home, and if they 'chose' to do so, dealing with the ensuing tensions was their own responsibility. Only as the post-war economic boom reached its peak in the late 1960s and employers began to complain of a shortage of female labour, did the commonwealth government take some limited action to encourage and subsidise the provision of child care facilities for the children of working mothers.

Kindergartens: the Transition from Philanthropy to Education

A notable feature of the expansion of kindergartens from the 1940s onwards, was their spread to the more prosperous suburbs of the major cities. This development had in fact begun during the war. In New South Wales the first locally-sponsored kindergartens were in the comfortable Sydney suburbs of Cheltenham (1942) and Killara (1944).

Women who previously might have formed 'circles' to support a kindergarten in an inner city area now began to work for the establishment of kindergartens in their own areas. In Victoria, a parallel development occurred; by the mid-1950s approximately three-quarters of the kindergartens affiliated with the Free Kindergarten Union were run by local parents rather than non-resident philanthropists. Interest in kindergartens in Victoria was reported to be growing rapidly with 'almost daily' enquiries concerning the establishment of new centres. The enquiries came from 'industrial suburbs, middle class suburbs, large country towns and cities and small country towns'. The Victorian Department of Health, at the instigation of Dr Vera Scantlebury Brown (Director of Maternal, Infant and Pre-School Welfare), actively encouraged the development of pre-schools. It provided a contribution towards the capital costs of new centres and an annual subsidy towards running costs. These subsidies, however, were dependent upon substantial voluntary effort by parents. By 1947, more than 3,000 children were on waiting lists (FKU 1946–47: 16). In Queensland, the Creche and Kindergarten Association reported in 1951 that 'never before [had] the need for kindergartens and creches been more pressing' (CKA 1950–51: 4).

Professionals in the field maintained a strong emphasis on the pre-school as a place where mothers could be educated about proper child development and appropriate ways of rearing children. According to the Chief Pre-school Educational Supervisor of Victoria, Helen Paul, 'far from being an opportunity of avoiding parental responsibility' a properly run pre-school would actually set new goals and standards for parents: 'the pre-school centre may act as a school for parents. A centre where through informal observation, conference with the teacher, discussion groups, &c., the principles of wise child-management may be observed, and where parents may learn to better understand their own children' (1945: 2212).

Key figures in the pre-school movement were strongly of the view that while short periods spent in a kindergarten were beneficial to the child, attendance at day nurseries was undesirable – perhaps necessary for a few unfortunates, but certainly not to be encouraged. Thus, in advocating an extension of what she described as 'the normal kindergarten' which would assist the mother at home, Helen Paul asserted:

> It cannot be stressed strongly enough ... that it is an undesirable experience for a pre-school child to be away from home care for such long periods. Such centres are only justified by the plight of the mother. The correct way to assist her for the good of the child would be to make it economically possible for her to stay at home at least during the child's tender years, and give him the care he needs. *(1946: 2241)*

In her evidence to a Western Australian Royal Commission on Kindergartens, Edith Bailey, the President of the AAPSCD, stated that 'the feeling of the kindergarten unions and training colleges is that it is undesirable for children under three years of age to be in groups'. Whilst acknowledging that it could be necessary in some limited circumstances for women to work, she also stated that 'the situation would be far better met by a subsidy for the mother'. She also agreed with the Royal Commissioner that women who worked when it was not essential for them to do so were 'shirking responsibility' (Bailey 1952).

In 1954 the Advisory Board of the Western Australian Kindergarten Union reported that parents in poorer areas were not always willing to support the local kindergarten, and speculated that perhaps kindergartens in these areas should be closed in order that others could be opened in areas where parents showed greater commitment. Reflecting the belief that postwar affluence was rapidly creating a classless society, the report of the Advisory Board continued: 'It is doubtful whether the parents in any particular suburb have any less money than in any other suburb under present day conditions' (Kindergarten Union of Western Australia 1954).

In all states, demand for the establishment of pre-schools rapidly outstripped the number of trained teachers available to staff them and the shortage of staff proved to be a major impediment to the expansion of services. In 1944 New South Wales reported 'an acute shortage of teachers', while in South Australia in the mid-1940s it was estimated that there would need to be a trebling of enrolments at the college just to maintain the centres that had already been opened. In 1945, Melbourne Kindergarten Teachers College was turning out twenty trained teachers per year, but estimated that two hundred would be a more appropriate number (Paul 1945: 2214).

There was little that the colleges could do about the shortage of teachers. Their space and facilities were very limited – most were still being conducted in converted private homes. Pre-school teaching also suffered from what was referred to as a 'high marriage mortality rate' – meaning that many young women abandoned their careers upon marriage.

The phasing-in of equal pay for male and female teachers in primary schools was another factor which drew teachers away from working with pre-school age children. As late as 1971 a three-year-trained pre-school teacher working as the director of a Queensland pre-school received a lower salary than a two-year-trained primary school teacher in her first year out of college. In Western Australia and South Australia a pre-school director had to have six years' experience before her salary reached parity with that of a two-year-trained teacher in her first year on the job (Fitzgerald and Crosher 1971: 14–15). The pay reflected a career closely linked in the public's mind with 'mothering'.

Young women who decided to undertake pre-school work in preference to teaching in primary or secondary schools were disadvantaged in terms of scholarships, salary rates, and career progression:

> The cleavage starts during the period of recruitment when school-girls realize through reading the literature and attending career nights that primary and secondary teaching are in one bracket and kindergarten teachers in a very different one. The girls themselves, their parents and their teachers comment on the difference in salaries, lack of superannuation, lack of a series of graded positions to move into, and some question the wisdom of working alone and of being employed by a committee of parents or lay people. *(APA 1970: 37)*

From the mid-1960s, the potential contribution of pre-school to the later educational development of the child was receiving unprecedented attention. In England, the Plowden Committee recommended a vast expansion of pre-school facilities (though not day care). This committee took the view that properly organised educational services could be a valuable supplement to the home. The committee also expressed the view that this type of service would be of particular benefit to children from 'deprived' or 'inadequate' backgrounds (Central Advisory Council for Education 1967: 19). In the United States also, economic and social factors as well as educational ones underpinned the establishment of large-scale schemes for pre-schooling. Project Head Start, established by the U.S. federal government in 1965 as part of a national campaign against poverty, drew on similar themes (Zigler and Valentine 1979).

Developments in educational theory, which argued the connection between early childhood and later educational achievement, fuelled the interest of a number of state education departments. Tasmania, in 1964, initiated an inquiry into education for children aged three to eight years, which resulted in pre-schools being incorporated into the state Education Department and provided as part of primary education (Committee on Pre-School and Kindergarten Education in Tasmania 1968). The Kindergarten Union in that state gradually became defunct as a result, and wound up its activities in the early 1970s. Similarly, in Western Australia a major inquiry into pre-school education, the *Nott Report*, led to the state government's establishing a Pre-School Board and taking over the running of pre-school services. In Queensland the state government took an increasing role in pre-school education; in 1972, the government committed itself to establishing pre-schools in conjunction with all primary schools (Brennan 1982: 100–4). No such enthusiasm was evident in New South Wales where Labor governments throughout the 1940s and 1950s – more strongly influenced by the Catholic church and traditional (male) trade union values – declined to take any responsibility for children below school age. The provision of pre-school services in both New South Wales and Victoria continued to be dominated by the voluntary agencies and, by the late 1960s, lagged well behind the states which had absorbed pre-school into the public education system.

During the 1960s, notions of compensatory education began to gain currency in Australia. The American Head Start program (which aimed to boost the school performance of children from poor families by compensating for what were believed to be the deficiencies of their homes) was widely discussed in Australia and attracted the attention of many educators in the early childhood field (de Lemos 1968).

Around this time, however, evidence began to emerge suggesting that children gaining access to pre-school education were from relatively privileged, middle-class families, rather than from poor families. In June 1968, the Australian Council for Education Research (ACER) devoted an entire issue of its *Quarterly Review of Australian Education* to the topic of pre-school. Dr Marion de Lemos identified four groups which, in her opinion, were disregarded by existing services: the 'economically disadvantaged' child, migrants, Aborigines and children needing full day care. In another article in the same issue of the journal, ACER's Chief Research Officer, R. T. Fitzgerald, commented that:

> The traditional philanthropic character of the kindergarten movement has steadily diminished ... Pre-schooling in Australia now tends to operate in such a way as to confer advantages on the child from the middle-class family rather than remedy the disadvantages of any impoverished social group.
> *(Fitzgerald 1968)*

Other local studies confirmed these findings. In Wollongong, a survey showed that the children most likely to attend pre-school were those whose parents were 'well-educated, upper-income Australians or British immigrants'; and conversely, that those least likely to have access were the children of 'less-educated, lower-income parents', especially if they were recent immigrants from mainland Europe (de Lacey and Fisher 1972). Even the Lady Gowrie centres seemed to lose their focus on needy, working-class children. Of the children attending the Hobart Lady Gowrie Centre in 1971, three-quarters were from families where the main breadwinner was a professional or a manager (Lady Gowrie Child Centre, Hobart 1971–72). Criticisms about the bias in pre-school provision towards the better-off drew a defensive response from the voluntary organisations. They pointed out that they did not determine the policies of state governments which led to middle-class groups being advantaged. They also argued that voluntary organisations could no longer keep pace with the rising salaries of pre-school teachers. In New South Wales, for example, pre-school teachers' salaries rose (from a pitifully low level) by more than 60 per cent between 1969 and 1973 (Spearritt 1974: 328). Existing methods of financing pre-schools (reliance on small state grants supplemented by the fund-raising activities of parent committees) meant that pre-schools were inexorably moving out of the reach of poorer families (Rudduck 1973: 22).

At the same time, some startling facts were beginning to emerge about inequalities in the provision of pre-school services *between* the various states and, more particularly, between the states and the Australian Capital Territory (Canberra). A survey published by the ACER showed that the proportions of eligible children attending pre-schools in 1970 ranged from an extraordinary 52 per cent in the ACT to a startlingly low 3 per cent in New South Wales. In Victoria, 29 per cent of eligible children attended pre-schools; in South Australia the number was 17 per cent; while in Queensland, Western Australia and Tasmania the corresponding number was 13 per cent (Fitzgerald and Crosher 1971: 18).

What were the attitudes of the major political parties to pre-school education and the role of the commonwealth government in supporting it? The 1950s and 1960s were times of intensive debate about the proper role of the commonwealth in education. Don Smart has described the pressures which led to the establishment of the federal Department of Education in 1966 and the attempts by the new bureaucracy and the new minister to find suitable areas into which the commonwealth could expand. Following the Senate election of 1967, the government introduced capital assistance for secondary school libraries and pre-school teachers' colleges. As Smart points out, capital assistance of this kind was far more attractive to the government than recurrent expenditure since the former 'provided Australian electors with highly visible evidence (buildings) of the Commonwealth's contribution to education [but] did not involve the Government in any long-term binding commitment to the area being assisted' (Smart 1977: 33).

Commonwealth initiatives in this period related solely to assistance for pre-school teacher training. A limited number of bursaries for students attending the colleges was introduced in 1966. In the 1968–71 triennium, capital funds amounting to $2.5 million were provided by the commonwealth to the private pre-school teachers' colleges on the mainland and to the Tasmanian Education Department. The purpose of the funds, which were provided under the *States Grants (Pre-School Teachers Colleges) Act*, was to assist these organisations to double their capacity. The money could be used to provide new facilities or to replace existing facilities which were inadequate or unsuitable (Department of Education and Science 1972).

The Child Care Needs of Working Mothers

Throughout the 1950s and 1960s the workforce participation rate of women, particularly married women, continued to grow. Whereas in 1947 only 8.6 per cent of married women worked outside the home, 18.7 per cent did so in 1961, and by the time of the 1971 census the proportion was 32.7 per cent (Richmond 1974: 269). Yet the issue of child care was barely raised in public debate.

The voluntary organisations, which might have brought the issue of child care to the attention of governments, continued to regard child care centres which made possible women's full-time employment with concern, if not hostility. Staff employed in the training colleges run by the various kindergarten unions regarded the work of John Bowlby (1951) on maternal deprivation as 'virtually gospel' and used it to oppose the establishment of child care centres (Gardiner 1982: 151). Bowlby, a British psychoanalyst, had conducted for the World Health Organisation a major study of children who had been institutionalised during the war. Most of these children were cared for in huge, impersonal, understaffed orphanages. Bowlby showed that these children were unable to develop emotionally because they were deprived of any meaningful, continuous relationships with adults. He argued that children, especially babies, needed to develop a primary attachment to one adult figure (generally the mother) and that this attachment was a necessary condition for the proper emotional, social and cognitive development of the child. Bowlby's work was mainly conducted with children who had been living in hospitals and residential institutions for months or even years on end. Children who attended day care centres were *never* the subject of his research although (ironically, as it turned out) he sometimes used them as a control group to demonstrate 'normal' development. In spite of this, Bowlby's findings were continually used to oppose the provision of day care services. For example, the New South Wales Department of Child Welfare, in justifying its decision to close down substandard child-minding centres in the 1950s, cited Bowlby's contention that 'children deprived of a normal life ... are a source of social infection as real and serious as the carriers of diptheria and typhoid' (Child Welfare Department of NSW 1955–56: 24).

Women employed outside the home were frequently chastised for neglecting their duties – a charge which is likely to have inhibited the expression of public demands for services which would facilitate their gainful employment. The Director of the Marriage Guidance Council of NSW, the Reverend W. G. Coughlan, claimed that 'the wife's gainful employment' was one of the most common causes of marital disharmony. According to Coughlan, although many wives claimed that they needed an outside occupation to make up for the boredom and neglect caused by their husbands' behaviour and also that they needed money as a protection against their husbands' unreliability as a provider, husbands regarded their working wives as 'escapists, money-grubbers, lacking in sense of duty to husband, home and children' (Coughlan 1957: 126).

Towards the end of the 1960s, partly spurred by concern about the damage which substandard childminding facilities were doing to the reputation of 'proper' pre-schools, the Australian Pre-School Association began to express concern about the lack of adequate child care services. The APA's concern, however, was always expressed in terms which suggested that the existence of child care was a necessary evil. There was certainly no suggestion that day care might be a positive alternative for some families.

Ethleen King, president of the Victorian Branch of the Australian Pre-School Association, was important in establishing APA's interest in child care. In 1957, following a visit to Canada and the United States of America, Mrs King told her branch: 'Whether we like it or not, the fact is undeniable that many married women with children now work outside the home ... Married women should have the freedom of choice to pursue this dual role, but it must not be done at the expense of the welfare of their family and children' (King 1957: 21).

In 1966, also at the instigation of Mrs King – but this time in her capacity as President of the National Council of Women (Victoria) – a Working Committee on Day Care was formed, consisting of representatives from the Australian Pre-School Association, the Victorian Association of Day Nurseries, the Victorian Council of Social Service, the Free Kindergarten Union of Victoria, the Playgrounds and Recreation Association of Victoria, the Association of Child Care Centres and the Victorian Society for Prevention of Cruelty to Children. This committee advocated an expansion of day care facilities but went out of its way to stress the general undesirability of children being in day care: 'This committee believes that young children need their own mothers to care for them, in their own homes and that the majority of mothers who want to work do so for socio-economic reasons' (National Council of Women, Victoria 1972: 3).

These attitudes were not confined to the pre-school educators within the early childhood field. Joan Fry, principal of the Nursery School Teachers College in Sydney, told the Victorian APA in 1969: 'We may not agree with the motives of mothers who work but we must accept their right to do so ... We must not allow our judgment of adults to prevent us from seeing our responsibility to children who are unable to defend their own rights for justice'. She went on to urge that the children of working mothers be given 'only the best type of care' and argued for reasonably sized groups, appropriate staff, and a requirement that staff have 'at least the same qualifications as those who work in other fields of early childhood education' (Fry 1969: 5).

The suggestion that there might be any mutual benefit for mother, baby and other family members in the provision of day care services appeared only rarely. One such rare occasion was an article by Dr F. W. Clements (previously the Chief Medical Adviser to the Lady Gowrie centres) who, in a review of the concept of 'maternal deprivation' published in the APA's journal, alluded to the fact that children in many other cultures learnt to relate to a number of people who could meet their needs. In urban cultures this happened occasionally, Clements commented, but not many mothers were emotionally mature enough or secure enough in their handling of their children to make this delegation (Clements 1966: 9).

In 1969 recommendations concerning the need for child care provision and the importance of gaining commonwealth support for it, were presented by the Victorian Branch to a national conference of the Australian Pre-School Association. Following some debate, these recommendations were adopted and the federal APA made a submission to the federal government calling for a national enquiry into day care. The submission pointed to the increase in the number of married women in the workforce, the fact that most existing child care centres were operated as commercial enterprises and the fact that not all states required child care centres to be licensed. The submission also pointed out that, while pre-schools were subsidised, government subsidies generally were not available to day care services. The APA directed its submission to the Department of Health – a logical decision given that this department administered the only other child care service with commonwealth sponsorship, the Lady Gowrie centres. However, the Director General of Health, Sir William Refshauge, informed the APA that he had passed their enquiry on to the Department of Education and Science as they, not the Department of Health, would be dealing with day care matters in future.

In 1964, a women's Section (the Women's Bureau) had been established in the Department of Labour and National Service – suggesting that official recognition was at last being given to the presence of women in the workforce. Given the general lack of interest (at times even hostility) displayed by the trade union movement towards issues of primary concern to women workers (such as child care, part-time work and maternity leave), the activities and publications of the Women's Bureau proved to be critical in stimulating interest and concern relating to issues such as child care and in providing information that could be used for lobbying (Prior 1982: 123–33).

In 1970, the Women's Bureau published a report on the number of registered child care centres throughout Australia and the number of children being cared for. This showed that there were 560 child care centres and 14,000 child care places. Almost all of these centres were run as private businesses and received no government subsidy. Only 40 centres received assistance from state or local authorities; each of these had been established to cater for 'needy' families. Most of these centres were operated by the Sydney Day Nursery Association and the Victorian Association of Day Nurseries. The approach of such centres made clear that they were providing a service for the deprived and under-privileged. The only children eligible for admission to centres run by the Sydney Day Nursery Association, for example, were children of sole parents, those whose parents were unable to care for them because of poor health, and those from homes deemed by the Day Nursery Association to be 'unsatisfactory or unhealthy'.

The Women's Bureau also pointed out that there was no commonwealth support for children's services (other than the Lady Gowrie child centres) and that two-thirds of the existing centres were located in Sydney or Melbourne. In short, there was a critical shortage of centres for the care of children. In the whole of Australia only two centres were operated by employers for the benefit of their staff; both of these were located in Melbourne (Department of Labour and National Service, Women's Bureau 1970).

In 1969, the Commonwealth Bureau of Census and Statistics conducted the first ever survey of the workforce participation of women with young children. This survey was a landmark in the politics of child care. It showed that 22 per cent of mothers of pre-school age children and 42 per cent of the mothers of primary school age children were at work (Bureau of Census and Statistics 1970). Further, the head of the Women's Bureau of the Department of Labour and National Service estimated that within a decade Australia would compare with the American pattern in which half the mothers of school age children and one-third of the mothers of pre-schoolers were at work (Cox 1971). The projection was not too far out; it took a little more than a decade for these proportions to be reached.

On the basis of the survey there were 102,800 women interested in returning to work if child care facilities were available; almost all of these (91,500) had at least one pre-school age child.

The late 1960s also witnessed the first stirrings of interest in child care by employers. The Victorian Employers Federation, for example, expressed concern that women, on the birth of their first child, would be lost to industry for at least five years and argued that industry, therefore, had a direct interest in helping to provide adequate day care facilities (*AFR* 14 October 1969). Underlying the employers' interest was the shortage of female labour which had developed. In 1971, a joint study by the Australian Clothing Manufacturers' Council and the Department of Labour and National Service concluded that women needed to be drawn into the workforce and recommended, among other things, the establishment of child care centres (Summers 1979: 190).

During the 1970 Senate election campaign (as a result of continuing pressure from the Department of Labour and National Service, the Australian Pre-Schools Association and employer groups), Prime Minister John Gorton outlined a plan to develop a network of child care centres which would 'contribute to employee morale, reduce absenteeism amongst female employees and indirectly help productivity' (Fitzgerald and Crosher 1971: 8). The predominant rationale for this scheme was the benefit it would provide to industry by making it easier for employers to attract and retain female labour. The plan was quickly dubbed the 'Gortongarten plan' – an indication, in part, of the press's limited understanding of the differences between kindergartens and child care centres.

While journalists may not have understood this distinction, the medical profession certainly did. In response to Gorton's announcement, psychiatrists at the Royal Alexandra Hospital for Children in Sydney issued a press statement criticising the proposal as being designed to encourage the mothers of young children to go out to work, thus jeopardising the mental health of their children. The press statement was expanded in a memorandum published in the *Medical Journal of Australia* a few months later, written by Dr Peter Cook, the director of the Department of Psychiatry and Child Guidance at the Children's Hospital, and endorsed by the Child Psychiatry Section of the Australian and New Zealand College of Psychiatrists. The memorandum strongly endorsed the view (ascribed to Bowlby) that the children of 'working mothers' were being 'denied the opportunity of those everyday mothering relationships which are generally required for healthy personality development'. It argued that mothers of young children should work part-time only – ideally not at all (Australian and

New Zealand College of Psychiatrists 1971). This was followed by the publication of a report by the New South Wales Association for Mental Health recommending that 'the Federal Government should seriously consider taking urgent action to encourage mothers to stay at home to look after their own pre-school children' and suggesting that a 'substantial' allowance be paid to such women until their children reached three years of age (NSW Association for Mental Health 1971).

The Labor Party's main response to Gorton's proposed network of child care centres was equally conservative. Clyde Cameron, Labor's spokesman on industrial relations, declared that the 'problem' of women working could be solved by a proper family wage system. This would do away with the necessity for women to work and have the additional advantage of making child care centres unnecessary. In May 1971 the debate died down as the government shelved its plans, ostensibly because of the need for economic restraint.

In 1970, the Victorian Council of Social Service (VCOSS) published a report entitled *Caring for the Children of One-Parent Families and Working Wives*. The committee which prepared this report was headed by VCOSS Chairman, Marie Coleman (later to become Director of the Office of Child Care established by the Fraser government). Although it was not publicly acknowledged, the Department of Labour and National Service subsidised the publication of this report in order to encourage public debate on the topic and increase pressure on the government to act. (The Director of the Women's Bureau within the Department, Lenore Cox, had persuaded her Minister, Bill Snedden, that this was an important policy area of which to gain control.) Cox, a personal friend of Marie Coleman's, acted as a consultant to the committee.

The VCOSS report canvassed a range of issues related to the needs of those who combined paid employment with responsibility for young children. These issues included after-school and vacation care services for school age children, tax deductibility for child care expenses, the particular problems of migrant families, part-time work and the encouragement of employer-provided child care. It also advocated 'a strong measure of community self-help and parent participation in the planning and administration of the services' and a strong role for local government. These issues had never before been canvassed in this way by a major community organisation. Reading the issues raised in this report is to read the agenda for the child care debate of the first half of the 1970s.

The most significant aspect of the VCOSS report was its clear statement that day care provision should be provided as a normal community service and not restricted to those deemed poor or underprivileged:

> ... one cannot regard the provision of day care facilities as a provision for family breakdown, although in some circumstances it may well be the provision of a service which will prevent family breakdown. In the great majority of cases ... adequate day care services should become a normal and proper community facility, every bit as much so as the provision of adequate hospitals and schools is a normal provision for its members. *(VCOSS 1970: 2)*

Another significant aspect of this report was the attention it gave to the needs of migrant families. The report published two submissions made to the VCOSS committee concerning the special child care needs of migrant families: one from the European Australian Christian Fellowship, the other from the Italian welfare organisation Comitato Assistenza Italiani (known as CoAsIt).

Around this time some critical comment was beginning to be heard concerning the quality of the service provided in child care – even in non-profit services run by professional early childhood educators. A paper presented to the eleventh biennial conference of the Australian Pre-School Association described the care provided by the Sydney Day Nursery Association as varying widely from one nursery to another and, within nurseries, between individual children. The emphasis in the centres, according to the author of this paper, D. F. W. Clements, was on routine which was often followed rigidly with little allowance made for individual variation, and a continued emphasis on haste: children 'must eat now', 'must go to sleep', 'must wait'. Dr Clements reported that, in his opinion, 'the general view seemed to be that it was undesirable to show affection to children', that the nurses adopted 'a "tough" disciplinary approach' and that 'a general air of depression ... prevails in most Day Nurseries and Nursery Schools in contrast to the exuberance of Kindergartens' (Clements 1967).

With the resurgence of the women's movement at the end of the 1960s, a new approach to the development of children's services began. Although child care was very much a minority interest among feminists (most of whom were childless), those who took an interest began to develop a position which had not been voiced before. They argued that services for children should not be regarded in a narrow way as either an educational service or a workplace facility. Rather, children's services were a fundamental social requirement for any serious challenge to be made to the sexual division of labour either in the workplace or in the home. Feminists insisted that the idealisation of intense and exclusive mother-child relationships oppressed not only women but children as well. They argued that child care could be undertaken outside the family and that it need not necessarily be done by other women; men could share this work whether inside the home or outside it.

One of the earliest statements of the feminist position on child care was made by community activist Winsome McCaughey (later to become the first woman Mayor of Melbourne):

> In our society, the nuclear family (read 'mother') has been held to be fully responsible for the development and socialization of the child under school age. Women's Liberation holds this to be an unreasonable and unsatisfactory method of childrearing. The recently formed Women's Liberation 'Community Controlled Child Care' action group ... denies the assumption that the ideal environment for the small child is home with mother, all day everyday ...
>
> Children are in a very real sense, the children of the whole community and [Community Controlled Child Care] believe it to be the responsibility of the government to make 'educational' facilities available to children under five years of age, in the form of good child care centres.
>
> *(McCaughey 1972: 3–6)*

Winsome McCaughey's involvement in child care had begun in New York in the late 1960s. Living in a Greenwich Village apartment with her husband and two small children, McCaughey had become involved in a co-operative child care arrangement with other local women. Apparently well-connected with radical political groups, they were initially given space in Congresswoman Bella Abzug's campaign headquarters in the building that housed the *Village Voice*. Later, they moved to the basement of a 'peace church' which was a centre for draft resisters, radical feminists and black activists. In McCaughey's words, '... we started off as a group of women minding each other's children; we ended up supporting one another's lives' (McGregor 1989: 3).

When she arrived back in Melbourne, McCaughey was approached by women who wanted to set up a similar service there. The group adopted the name Community Child Care and met informally, 'round the kitchen table', throughout 1972 to work out ideas and principles. The philosophy of the group was firmly grounded in a variant of feminism which placed a high value on self-help activities and opposed the 'professionalisation' of child care. As an early pamphlet explained: child care '[does] not have to mean simply handing your child over to professionals'. Notions of 'family' and 'community' played a significant part in the community child care ideal. These feminists were not out to 'smash the family'. Instead, they spoke of the role that child care might play in 're-surrounding families' and 're-creating communities' (McCaughey and Sebastian 1977). According to this ideal, women could develop child care services where they controlled what happened and were involved in choosing staff and planning the program. The skills and resources of residents of the local neighbourhood should be drawn upon wherever possible before recourse was taken to outside experts. It was a model in which, to use an expression of the times, professionals were 'on tap, not on top'. The integration of services for children of different age groups was another important feature. The division of children's services into pre-school for four-year-olds whose mothers stayed home, day nurseries for children whose mothers worked, and so on, was regarded as an arrangement based on the carving out of professional territory, rather than on the principle of providing services to families.

Community Child Care called for the provision of free child care centres, available to all parents, regardless of their reasons for use. However, they cautioned that child care services should not be provided simply to free women to work outside the home during the day at dreary, exhausting labour that left them with the housework to do at night. 'To only want day care on the ground that it will give us a chance to prove we are as good as men in a man's world is to entirely miss the point of the new feminism'. Rather, child care should be seen as part of a struggle towards less rigid sex role and generational stereotypes, and towards providing opportunities for individuals to maximise their choices concerning work, leisure and child rearing, depending upon individual temperament and ability.

Meanwhile, also in Victoria, another new source of pressure for child care was beginning to emerge. This group, known as Action For Adequate Child Care, was organised by women in the trade union movement. It, too, called for the establishment of government-funded, parent-controlled child care services. Its calls arose not from a sense of duty towards 'the needy' but from a positive notion of the rights of women and children. In 1970, this group, with assistance from VCOSS, the Union of Australian Women, the Inter-Church Trade and Industry Mission and several trade unions, organised a public meeting on child care at Richmond Town Hall. One of the guest speakers at this meeting was Bob Hawke, (then President of the ACTU, later to become Prime Minister). One result of this meeting was the publication of a Child Care Charter calling for after-school hours and holiday care services, as well as care for pre-school age children, to be established in all municipalities.

Child care re-emerged on the federal political agenda during the budget debates of 1972 when the Liberal-Country Party government, led by William McMahon, allocated $5 million for the construction of child care centres. In October of the same year, the Minister for Labour and National Service, Phillip Lynch, introduced the *Child Care Act* which enabled the commonwealth to make capital and recurrent grants to non-profit organisations.

The *Child Care Act* reflected the assumptions and general approach to day care adopted by the traditional voluntary agencies. The requirements concerning the employment of trained staff were almost identical with those which had been laid down in an Australian Pre-School Association document, *Day-Care Centres in Australia: Standards and General Principles* (1970). While the existence of the women's movement probably contributed to the pressures building up in the community for attention to be given to child care, feminists had no input into the legislation.

The *Child Care Act* enshrined the principle that the only services to receive federal funding would be those initiated by local groups. Money was to be disbursed solely on the basis of submissions; there would be no government planning for equitable provision. In addition, as Julie Rigg was quick to note, the act contained 'a number of features designed to discourage mothers of young children from working' (Rigg 1972). It defined 'children in special need' (those who were to have priority of access to government-subsidised centres) in such a way as to exclude almost all children from families where both parents had jobs. It called for research to be carried out into the reasons why women worked (a mystery, apparently, to the all-male government) and into ways of discouraging them. And it attached conditions to grants that obliged centre directors to provide 'family counselling ... where parents ... are seeking to place very young children in centres' (*CPD* HR, vol. 81: 2062; 2292).

The parliamentary debates which took place during the introduction of the legislation made it plain that the government had introduced the *Child Care Act* reluctantly and certainly did not intend it as a gesture towards women's rights. Indeed, as Tony Street, the Minister Assisting the Minister for Labour and National Service said, 'everybody would agree that the best place for a very young child is with its mother'. The legislation, said Street, was designed to assist those who were being denied 'the normal right of young children' (*CPD* HR, vol. 81: 3062). In the Senate, Margaret Guilfoyle (destined to become Minister Assisting the Prime Minister in Child Care Matters in the first Fraser ministry), added that she hoped 'parental responsibility' would stop parents using a centre for a child younger than three or four years unless it were the child of a single parent or a parent who was sick or incapacitated (*CPD* Senate vol. 54: 2196).

The Labor Party challenged various provisions of the legislation, particularly its reliance on the submission model of funding. Shadow Minister for Education, Kim Beazley (snr.), proposed a series of amendments including a recommendation that:

> the Commonwealth Government should take the initiative to establish Child Care Centres to meet the needs of working mothers, and should do this on a

basis of priorities ... rather than leave the provision of facilities to the chance interest of [sponsoring bodies] ... *(CPD* HR *vol. 81: 3048)*

The government, however, rejected the amendments. As Tony Street said: 'We aim to help those who are prepared to help themselves' (*CPD* HR vol. 81: 3048–50).

Before any funding under the *Child Care Act* had commenced the Coalition government was defeated at the polls and the first Labor administration for twenty-three years took office. The change in government, however, did not quickly produce any change in the act.

CHAPTER 4

Hitching Child Care to the Commonwealth Star

> Any function or activity which can be hitched to the star of the Commonwealth grows in quality and affluence. Any function or activity which is financially limited to the States will grow slowly or even decline. Further, a function will be fairly financed to the extent that the Commonwealth finds the money for it. A function will be unfairly and inadequately financed if the whole burden falls upon the States.
>
> E.G. Whitlam, *ALP Policy Speech*, 1972

The period of the Whitlam government, although brief, was a time of significant change in social policy. Although the economy was beginning to slow after the 'long boom' of the 1960s, Labor's mood was one of expansion and optimism. The new government regarded social welfare as a fundamental aspect of the wellbeing of all citizens. It placed considerable emphasis on the provision of services (such as health, child care and education) which benefitted a wide range of people. This contrasted with the approach of earlier postwar administrations which had generally adopted a much narrower definition of 'welfare' and which had focused on cash transfers (such as pensions and benefits) targetting the poor, rather than on the provision of universal services. These changes led to intense debate about the role of the commonwealth in the provision of social welfare, the legitimate targets of public expenditure (particularly the acceptability or otherwise of 'middle-class welfare') and the most appropriate means of delivering services.

The Whitlam years represented a high point of conflict between advocates of different forms of child care provision, as groups with different interests and values (early childhood educators, philanthropic organisations and feminists) sought to influence government policy and determine expenditure priorities. In many instances the conflicts played out around child care policy were a reflection of conflicts being played out more broadly within the social welfare arena; for example, the government's approach to child care funding, with its emphasis on 'community initiative' and 'self-help' projects and its challenge to the prerogatives of state governments and professional bodies, generated antagonisms similar to those which developed in relation to health policy. In other areas, the disputes were very specific to the field; for example, the question of whether the educational needs of three- and four-year olds should dominate the field or whether the government should also consider *women's* needs and provide a range of services which would enable them to move beyond the domestic sphere.

Conflicts between lobby groups were only one aspect of the disharmony which characterised the shaping of child care policy during these years. Within the Labor government itself there were sharp differences of opinion as ministers disagreed about the most desirable direction for child care policy and the most appropriate location for this new policy function. Bureaucratic clashes of interest also occurred as the Departments of Education, Social Security and others vied for control of the program.

The saga of the children's services program during the Whitlam years has been described by Sara Dowse (head of the Women's Affairs Unit under a subsequent administration) as 'a fascinating case study in government decision-making, an object lesson in what not to do when devising government policy' (Dowse 1988: 214). While the analysis of events presented here does not lead to such a dismal conclusion, it certainly points to the Whitlam era as a turning-point in the politics of child care and a period when crucial lessons about policy making, policy implementation and bureaucratic politics were learned (often at great personal cost) by Australian feminists. The period was also one of struggle and uncertainty for the women who dominated the traditional early childhood organisations and whose role as expert advisers to governments on pre-school and child care matters had previously been unchallenged. The hegemonic position of these groups was seriously undermined during the Whitlam years and has never been entirely recovered.

Political Context

At the time of its election, in December 1972, the Australian Labor Party, led by Gough Whitlam was committed to significant social reform. In the years leading up to the 1972 election, Labor party members and strategists had worked out detailed policy proposals in a number of areas – particularly in health, education and urban policy. Labor did not intend that these policy changes, however significant, should be the only distinguishing characteristics of its administration. Equally important in the thinking of key Labor figures was the ideal of establishing fundamental changes in the relations between citizens and government. Whitlam, in particular, stressed that under Labor governmental processes would become more open, ministers would be more responsive to ideas from outside the public service, policy making and implementation would be more democratic.

Throughout the 1960s, and especially during the 1972 campaign, Whitlam had developed the argument that the main causes of inequality in Australia were not those arising out of the ownership of wealth and property but regional disparities concerning the provision of urban and social services, particularly education, health and community facilities. An individual's standard of living, according to Whitlam, was determined 'not so much by income but by the availability and accessibility of the services which the community alone can provide and ensure' (quoted in Freudenberg 1986: 134).

Labor's electoral campaign had been especially directed at middle income families living in the suburbs of the major cities. To these voters Labor held out the promise that the commonwealth (with its superior financial powers and ability to take a national perspective) would adopt an active role in areas such as education, urban planning, health care and social services. This represented a distinct break with the philosophy of the previous government which had minimised the role of the commonwealth in relation to these areas, preferring to leave them to the state governments and to private enterprise. Nevertheless, Labor's prescription for reform was a modest one, aimed at redistributing resources through government activity rather than through any more profound challenge to the powers and prerogatives of capital. In the words of Peter Wilenski, the first Principal Private Secretary to Prime Minister Gough Whitlam, the Labor government 'had no quarrel with the prevailing socio-political structures, but ascribed inequality to the inactivity of the preceding 23 years of federal Liberal-Country Party Government and the ineptitude of various State governments' (Wilenski 1986: 117).

The establishment of statutory authorities and commissions outside the regular departmental structures was to become a feature of the new government. Labor set up a number of these bodies, some in areas where the commonwealth had not previously had a role and others where it was thought that policy advice and implementation had become 'tired and unimaginative' (Wilenski 1986: 125) : 'the "coming of the commissions" marked at least a temporary end to the dominance of the public service in policy-making and showed the readiness of the government, not simply to provide for known groups of "needy" citizens, but to seek out new groups and previously unrecognised needs' (Elliott and Graycar 1979: 95).

In addition to these new structures, there were significant changes in personnel. Many Labor ministers appointed advisers from outside the public service and these appointments were frequently controversial. The appointment to the Prime Minister's staff of a special adviser on women's affairs was particularly controversial. The media ruthlessly trivialised both the position and the appointee, Elizabeth Reid, an active member of the women's liberation movement who was a philosophy tutor with postgraduate qualifications from Oxford University.

Labor's desire to introduce a new philosophy and a new spirit into social policy was nowhere more evident than in the area of welfare and community services. Here the government's professed goal was to implement a new approach in which the citizen would no longer be a passive, grateful recipient of services but an active definer of local needs and a participant in developing strategies to meet them. ('Citizens' were either masculine or without gender in policy statements of the period. It was some time before the implications of these policies for women became apparent.)

According to the new Minister for Social Security, Bill Hayden, the government's aim in social welfare policy was to 'produce ... a social environment in which every individual has the opportunity to develop his [sic] unique potential, ... and in which various supports are offered to those individuals who need special assistance' (Hayden 1978: 123).

Changes in the content and delivery of social welfare programs and community services were important to the new government's agenda but policies to achieve these ends had not been worked out in any detail. One of the government's earliest actions was to establish a new policy-making body, the Social Welfare Commission, to provide advice in this area. Marie Coleman, formerly director of the Victorian Council of Social Service, was appointed chairman of the commission, thus becoming the first woman to be appointed to the first division of the commonwealth public service. The Social Welfare Commission did not directly fund or administer any programs; its role was to advise the government on the effectiveness of programs in the welfare field and to recommend appropriate initiatives. Both the government and the commission rejected the 'residualist' notion of social welfare which had characterised the period of conservative government and adopted a more 'universalist' approach, in keeping with the government's social democratic philosophy. Welfare, argued the commission, should be seen as 'a basic integrated institution within society, ensuring not only the provision of material needs, but also genuine opportunities for social and cultural satisfaction' (Social Welfare Commission 1975: 13). The Australian Assistance Plan (AAP) was the emblem of this approach. The AAP 'marked a widening of the target groups of social policy from disadvantaged individuals to whole communities, and a widening of the concepts of poverty and deprivation from purely monetary and physical factors to cultural ones' (Elliott and Graycar 1979: 95). The AAP aimed to provide opportunities for non-professionals to take part in 'planning, developing and controlling their own local community services' (Social Welfare Commission 1974: 7). The philosophy underlying the AAP was one in which classless and genderless 'communities' defined and articulated their own needs, with minimal assistance from professionally trained workers. This philosophy was extremely influential in determining the Labor government's approach to child care provision.

Resurgence of the women's movement

Labor's rise to power coincided with the surge of 'second-wave' feminism in Australia. The fact that the women's liberation movement was to confront a social democratic rather than a conservative government during these crucial years 'put a stamp on the nature of the involvement of feminists with and in government and indeed determined the parameters of the women's movement itself' (Dowse 1988: 208). The label 'the women's movement' implies a single organisation, united in its goals and purposes. In fact, far from being a single, united entity, this new social movement comprised a multitude of individuals and groups, often with varying analyses of society and conflicting ideas about how to address problems.

'Women's Liberation' was the name adopted by those who came together from the late 1960s onwards to analyse and to confront the sexism of Australian society. Many of these sought radical, indeed revolutionary, changes both in society and in personal relationships. The members of these early groups were usually women living outside conventional family structures; they tended to be young (in their twenties and thirties), childless and economically independent. Many were students or were employed in the arts or on the fringes of academe.

The Women's Electoral Lobby (WEL) emerged out of Women's Liberation. In the early months there was a considerable overlap in membership between the two groups but later WEL moved in a different direction and began to attract a quite different constituency –

women who lived in suburbia with husbands and children and who worked in conventional 'female' jobs. Modelled to a large extent on the National Organization of Women (NOW) which had been formed in the United States not long before, WEL, in the lead up to the 1972 election, adopted the strategy (also employed by NOW) of surveying all candidates and assessing their stance on issues of basic concern to women such as abortion, equal pay and child care. Its branches, in various states, also prepared a number of submissions to government on topics such as education and women's health. WEL, much more than Women's Liberation, was oriented to party politics. It was optimistic about the possibility of substantial reform through public policy measures. Its members were keen to be involved in the electoral and policy-making processes, even though few had had any experience in these areas. In the words of Lyndall Ryan, an academic historian and one of the early feminists to join the federal bureaucracy after the election of the Labor government: 'WEL saw itself as the pragmatic wing of Women's Liberation. It differed from its sister organization. Instead of eschewing the state and promoting revolutionary change, WEL demanded the right to participate in the decision-making processes of the state, and a share of the national cake' (Ryan 1990: 72).

Issues of state power and the relationship between the women's movement and the bureaucracy were vigorously debated amongst Australian feminists in the early 1970s. One of the most effective and well-publicised activities of the early Women's Liberation movement had been the establishment of services (particularly rape crisis centres and women's refuges) which operated without benefit of government funding. Usually, the women who worked in these services made decisions collectively and all received the same (derisory) level of pay. Opposition to hierarchical relationships was an important principle to many of these feminists and few of them, at least at that stage of their lives, would have countenanced employment in the public service with its sharply defined gradings, divisions and differences of status and pay. In the very early days there was no debate about whether or not to accept government funding for such services – none was available. Later, when it did become available, some groups refused to accept it because they saw it as making them beholden to the patriarchal state. To such women, the state and its structures were immutably patriarchal and the possibilities of reform through state action were therefore negligible.

Feminists whose background and political base were in the labour movement were less inclined to hold such views. Historically, the Australian labour movement has regarded the state as relatively benign, or at least neutral, and has looked to government to achieve reform.

However, women from the labour movement were not particularly conspicuous in social policy debates during the period of the Whitlam government; indeed they did not gain prominence until the Hawke era. Typically, the prominent feminists of the time were students, academics and professionals. There was both a class and an age dimension to this. Those who eschewed government funding and valorised the efforts of voluntary, self-help groups tended to be young, childless and not aligned with the labour movement.

As Elizabeth Reid was to comment, the direction taken by the early Women's Liberation movement in Australia was influenced profoundly by the number of historians amongst its members and the dearth of policy analysts:

> The historical approach, that of looking backwards to understand the present, and the associated stance of observing rather than changing, were to influence the ability of the women's movement to respond to the opportunities created by the Whitlam Government. The keen analytical powers of the early members of the women's movement had been used to understand the past and this understanding had, on the whole, taken place in an academic context. There was little experience in the women's movement in policy analysis or program formulation and implementation.
> *(Reid 1985: 3)*

The lack of experience of these women in dealing with governments and bureaucracies, their widespread suspicion of hierarchies, were to have an enormous bearing on the development of policies on children's services at the federal level.

Labor's Policies towards Women

Despite its general commitment to a fairer and more equitable society and its carefully worked out policies in a number of important areas, the Labor government came to office in 1972 without a program for women. It was only *after* the election that Peter Wilenski persuaded the Prime Minister that the demands of women needed to be taken seriously and that someone 'who could take up these demands and show their political and governmental relevance' should be appointed to the Prime Minister's personal staff (Reid 1986: 145). Nevertheless, even before such an appointment was made, the party's commitment to the expansion and redistribution of benefits, services and wages provided a basis for immediate action as well as for the formulation of a longer-term program. Within a few weeks of coming to office Labor had taken several steps to improve the position of women.

One of the government's earliest acts was to apply to the Arbitration Commission for the re-opening of an important hearing on equal pay. The intervention of the new government in the 1972 equal pay hearing was regarded by many women as an important symbol of Labor's commitment to women's independence and autonomy. Other initiatives taken by Labor in those early days gave further encouragement to the women's movement. Soon after coming to office the new government abolished the sales tax on oral contraceptives, introduced equal pay for men and women in the commonwealth public service and also announced its intention to introduce maternity leave for women employed in the commonwealth public service (Summers 1979).

Labor's Pre-School and Child Care Policies

Labor no more had a policy on child care when it came to office in 1972 than it had a policy on women. The party did, however, have a policy on pre-schools. Labor placed great weight on the potential of education to enhance equality. Pre-school education was seen as particularly important because of the way it might compensate for poor home backgrounds – thus giving all children an equal start, if not in life, at least in the education race. Ideas of compensatory education, such as those which underlay Project Head Start in the USA, had influenced a number of Labor politicians and during the election campaign Whitlam had promised to make pre-school available to every Australian child. It was, he said, 'the most important single weapon in promoting equality and in overcoming social, economic and language inequalities' (ALP 1972: 5).

Child care, too, was mentioned in the policy speech but it was not given nearly the significance accorded pre-schools. Most Labor politicians simply did not understand the differences between pre-school and child care services. In particular, they did not understand that sessional pre-school services catering only for three and four-year-old children were inadequate to meet the child care needs of working mothers. In short, Labor's policies on services for young children were an extension of its educational philosophy. The policies did not embody any of the concerns of the women's movement. The most significant outside influence on their formation had been the Australian Pre-School Association which had good contacts with Kim Beazley (snr.), the shadow minister for education. Beazley, a devout Christian, was personally very sympathetic to the pre-school lobby; he believed strongly in the notion of compensatory education and endorsed the traditional family values which the Association promoted.

Establishment of the Australian Pre-Schools Committee

Once in government, Labor moved responsibility for the administration of the *Child Care Act* away from the Department of Labour and National Service and placed it, along with the newly assumed responsibility for pre-schools, in the Department of Education. This was something which the Australian Pre-School Association had lobbied for in the lead-up to the 1972 election. The APA saw the move as signifying Labor's recognition that the care and education of young children were desirable ends in themselves; they were more than just a means of enabling women to enter the workforce. However, the shift also meant that the distinctions between child care and pre-school became blurred and that educationalists with very little knowledge about child care now had responsibility for implementing the government's policy in this area. Lenore Cox, who had battled strenuously for the commonwealth to become involved in child care precisely because of her awareness of the needs of women in employment, now had no involvement in the program.

The new Minister, Kim Beazley, moved quickly to implement the government's policy. In February 1973, just ten weeks after assuming office, he announced the establishment of a Child Care Standards Committee (to oversee grants under the *Child Care Act*), a Child Care Research Committee (to distribute research funds and advise on research priorities) and an interim Pre-Schools Committee. This last committee was required to advise the government on the measures which the commonwealth would need to adopt to ensure that throughout Australia, within a period of approximately six years, all children would be given an opportunity to undertake a year of pre-school education, and child care centres for children below school age would be established to meet the needs of children of working parents and underprivileged families.

The Australian Pre-Schools Committee (APC) was to be chaired by Joan Fry, former head of the Sydney Nursery School Teachers College. Fry and Beazley had a high regard for one another and shared similar views on moral and social issues. (Both were later to become founding members of a conservative lobby group known as the Australian Family Association.) Of the other eight members of the committee six were educationalists, one a psychologist and one a professor of child health. With the exception of the Australian Pre-Schools Association no community groups were represented. Thus, although the APC was to deal with both child care and pre-school matters, the committee had no representation from feminist groups such as WEL or Community Child Care.

The announcement of this committee, its terms of reference and its membership was greeted with hostility by feminist groups. The appointment of Joan Fry, as chairman, came in for particular criticism. Even though Fry's background was in the education of teachers for day nurseries (rather than pre-schools), feminists felt that the day nursery movement in general, and Fry in particular, regarded child care as an unfortunate necessity – certainly not as the right of all children and parents. (Ironically, Fry's appointment also drew the ire of the mainstream pre-school lobby; in their opinion Fry was allied with day care services.) Feminists also felt that the Labor government's child care policy should break away from the traditional philanthropic model of day nursery provision. They did not want large, institutional-type care in which parents handed their children over to professionals, but small, parent-run services in which professionals were available but not in control. Interestingly, although feminists were generally very keen to 'reclaim their history' and find their forgotten fore-mothers, they did not wish to claim the day nursery movement as part of their heritage. They showed little interest in, or sympathy for, the work that had been carried on by the Victorian Association of Day Nurseries or the Sydney Day Nursery and Nursery Schools Association – women's organisations which had struggled to provide day care for the children of impoverished working-class women for almost a century.

While the report of the Australian Pre-Schools Committee was in preparation the government came under increasing pressure from feminists, both inside and outside the bureaucracy, for the narrowness of its policy and for the restrictive terms of reference it had given the Committee. Elizabeth Reid, in the vanguard, sought immediately to have the terms of reference widened.

Feminist Pressure Groups

Of great significance to the development of child care policies under the Whitlam government was the fact that there was no *single* feminist group putting forward a coherent and widely agreed upon position and no *single* feminist vision of what a commonwealth child care policy might look like. Instead, there were a number of groups who frequently disagreed with each other and whose strategies were unco-ordinated. 'Free, 24 hour child care' was one of the earliest demands of the women's movement, but the fine detail of what might be involved in translating this slogan into a policy was something that very few feminists had thought about: 'Feminist demands are touchstones for feminism and provide focus for political campaigns. But demands reduce and compress complex issues into tidy packages ... The problem with the demand for child care is that the Australian women's movement took some time to undo the package again' (Franzway et al. 1989: 59).

The most sustained and influential lobbying by feminists on child care matters was done by women from the Australian Capital Territory, New South Wales and Victoria; the lobbying tended to be very much an 'eastern states' affair. The New South Wales and ACT branches of WEL were particularly active on child care issues. Women from New South Wales were also represented by the Media Women's Action Group and the state branch of the Labor Women's Committee. Community Child Care was the major voice of Victorian women. (There was no Community Child Care group in New South Wales until 1976.) Feminists from the other states were effectively absent from the debate at the federal level.

Media Women's Action Group

The Media Women's Action Group was a small organisation, but, on child care policy, it had a substantial impact on the views of influential figures (including Elizabeth Reid), particularly in the early months of the Whitlam government. The group had been formed following the hostile and largely frivolous reception given to Germaine Greer by journalists at the National Press Club when *The Female Eunuch* was launched in Australia in 1971. The purpose of the group was to encourage a more serious approach in the media treatment of issues of relevance to women. Its members included Julie Rigg, Susie Eisenhuth, Robyn Hughes, Pip Porter and Sandra Hall.

In mid-1972 this small band of women produced a pamphlet entitled *Child Care: A Community Responsibility*, which put forward the outline of a child care policy in the context of an explicitly feminist political analysis of the family. The document argued that the community as a whole should acknowledge its stake in the wellbeing of all young children. Its authors argued that the prevailing system, where the state intervened only to 'support' families in cases of neglect (through Child Welfare departments), or to provide minimal assistance to voluntary organisations offering pre-school services, was inadequate. A positive commitment to a total scheme of child care was essential. Child care, according to Media Women's Action Group should be regarded as a social responsibility like education or the care of the sick (Media Women's Action Group 1972: 2). Elizabeth Reid advised Whitlam that this was 'the best submission' she had seen on the subject of child care (Reid 1973).

Women's Electoral Lobby

The Women's Electoral Lobby, like the Labor government itself, took some time to develop a child care policy. As WEL had not long been in existence when Labor came to office there were many issues on which it did not have detailed policies. Child care was one of them. Many WEL supporters were prepared to endorse the demand for 'free 24-hour child care' but had no conception of what this might involve in terms of practical policies. Australian women's historical exclusion from political and bureaucratic power meant that there were very few who had any experience in negotiating with ministers or senior public servants, writing policies or monitoring their implementation. Elizabeth Reid, in her capacity as women's adviser to the Prime Minister, was thus obliged to take on the role of mediating the views of the numerous women's groups seeking to influence the government.

By the time of the 1974 election campaign, WEL had developed its child care policy and prepared a background paper on child care issues for distribution to all parliamentary candidates; this was largely due to the efforts of two Sydney women, Eva Cox and Carole Baker. In this paper, WEL advocated the provision of a range of child care services including day care centres and family day care. It also endorsed a number of policies which were later to become quite controversial amongst feminists and within the care movement. These policies included support for private centres (WEL recommended low interest loans for the upgrading of facilities and fee subsidies for children from needy families) and tax concessions for users of child care services.

WEL and other feminist organisations approached the development of child care policy as if there were only two major players on the field – themselves and the government. The antipathy of most feminists towards the large voluntary organisations such as the Australian Pre-School Association, the kindergarten unions and the training institutions, meant that they had no interest in consulting these groups or seeking any kind of mutual accommodation. The traditional pre-school groups were equally hostile to feminists.

United Women's Action Group

In May, due to the efforts of Elizabeth Reid, the Prime Minister met with a delegation of women to discuss child care matters. The women represented a dozen women's organisations and called themselves (in what proved to be a somewhat bitter irony) the United Women's Action Group. They also met with the Minister for Education, Kim Beazley, and with members of the Cabinet Committee on Social Welfare. The purpose of these meetings was to counter the influence of the traditional, conservative bodies in the early childhood field (particularly the APA) and to demonstrate to the government that a whole new approach to the question of child care was needed. The meeting with the Prime Minister was a political disaster. The women were totally unused to working at this level within the political system and did not have a well worked out strategy for their encounter. According to Anne Summers, (a senior Canberra political correspondent, later to occupy the position which evolved from Elizabeth Reid's): 'the women were ill-prepared, argued amongst themselves about exactly what was wanted, and, with their poor presentation, unfortunately reinforced the view that many Cabinet ministers held already, that this was an issue that they could afford to ignore' (Summers 1979: 194-45). On another occasion delegates from WEL gained an appointment with the Minister for Education, Kim Beazley. Unfortunately, they 'muffed the arrangements' by failing to remove Beazley's letter from a post office mail box on time. Apparently the mail was collected on a weekly basis! (WEL *Newsletter* May 1974: 7).

NSW Labor Women

In the early months of the Whitlam government, members of the New South Wales branch of the Labor Women's Committee worked tirelessly on child care issues. Their first goal was to change the policy of the ALP on pre-school and child care matters. A resolution to this effect was passed at the federal Labor Women's conference held in April 1973.

A few months later, at the Federal ALP annual conference, held in Surfers Paradise, a small group of New South Wales women succeeded in having the policy of the Labor Women's conference adopted by the party as a whole. This was a substantial achievement – especially given that there was not a single female delegate to the annual conference and that not even Elizabeth Reid had been permitted to attend. The New South Wales women (Ann Symonds, Jeannette McHugh and Anne Gorman) travelled to Surfers Paradise at their own expense. They approached their task in a systematic and professional manner. They provided each delegate with a document explaining the background to the resolutions which had been passed at the federal Labor Women's conference in April of that year and which they were seeking to have incorporated into party policy. (Child care was not the only issue on which these women had sought to amend ALP policy – equal pay, part-time employment and before- and after-school hours care had been in their sights as well.) Each resolution was set out in full and accompanied by explanatory text. In the case of the child care resolution, statistics concerning the number of pre-school children with mothers in paid employment were provided to demonstrate the need for services which offered more than sessional care. In addition, the women explained the limitations of existing Labor policy and expressed their criticism of the composition of the Australian Pre-Schools Committee and the Child Care Standards Committee. The narrow educational focus of these groups at the expense of 'professionals concerned with the emotional needs of the young child and its family' was also criticised. The women spoke personally to every delegate and explained why they saw the issue as important. The resolution stated that: 'a comprehensive child care service should be established throughout Australia on a priority needs basis. This service should be Government sponsored and community based. The aim of the service would be to provide community support for women to participate more fully in society' (ALP 1973: 17).

In addition to a change in policy, the New South Wales Labor women also sought to have responsibility for its implementation transferred from the Department of Education to the Department of Social Security. This, they claimed, would be an appropriate recognition of the wider goals that the new policy espoused. Despite the strong opposition of Education Minister Beazley, the resolution to change the government's policy (a resolution which had been moved and seconded by sympathetic male delegates) was passed. The attempt to have responsibility for the implementation of the new policy moved to the Department of Social Security was, however, defeated. In an 'emotional and dramatic' speech Beazley described the attempt to re-locate responsibility for child care as a 'gross indecency' perpetrated behind his back 'on the vague grounds that a lot of women want it' (*AFR* 11 July 1973).

Following the adoption of their resolutions as official Labor policy, several members of the New South Wales Labor Women's Committee formed a Child Care sub-committee. This small group continued tirelessly to lobby the government. They presented several submissions to federal Labor parliamentarians, pointing out that women were less likely than men to vote for the ALP and arguing that substantial initiatives in an area of great significance to women (such as child care) could well be the key to attracting votes and bridging the 'gender gap'.

Report of the Australian Pre-Schools Committee

By the time the report of the Australian Pre-Schools Committee, *Care and Education of Young Children* (also known as the Fry Report) was published, not only had Labor party policy changed radically but so had the whole debate about child care in Australia. The limitations of the traditional pre-school model had been extensively discussed in the media, the need for child care services to meet the needs of working mothers had been widely canvassed and there was a climate of opinion which favoured participatory, consumer-oriented services rather than those controlled by professionals and experts. The Fry Report, which had been developed in accordance with terms of reference which arose from Labor's (by then outdated) 1972 policy commitments, met a hostile reception.

One of the most controversial aspects of the report was the importance it placed on employing staff with special training in early childhood education. The authors wished 'to dispel the myth that the needs of ... children can be adequately met by merely warm-hearted people who are fond of children' (Australian Pre-Schools Committee 1974: 1). As an extension of this view they argued that trained professional staff would be needed to implement the program. Indeed it was because of this need that the 'preliminary' phase of the program would take twelve years to implement, instead of the six which had been requested in the terms of reference. By the time the program was fully implemented, the report argued, 'each group of children should be cared for by a professional and a trained support' (Australian Pre-Schools Committee 1974: 39).

In striking contrast to the elaborate provisions for four-year olds attending pre-school and for the tiny proportion of children attending day care centres, more than half of the children in the day care target group were to be catered for in family day care. This type of care had been advocated first in 1969, when the Victorian Council of Social Service established a standing committee to examine aspects of the care of children of single parents and working mothers. The committee contained representatives from commonwealth government departments and voluntary and community welfare organisations. Its report recommended a range of services, including the provision of 'day foster care', described as care 'where children from 0-6 years may be cared for in a home environment rather than in an institutional environment' (VCOSS 1970).

The Fry Report's recommendations on family day care involved untrained women caring for up to four pre-schoolers in their own homes with occasional visits from trained support staff. Yet these day care mothers would be precisely the kind of 'merely warm-hearted' people whom the report had declared unable to meet the needs of young children. It was difficult for critics to avoid the conclusion that the major reason for favouring family day care over centre-based day care was that this scheme could be run extremely cheaply, thus freeing the bulk of funds for pre-schools.

After the Fry Report had been received by the government, Elizabeth Reid immediately advised the Prime Minister that it was 'biased in its approach', 'insensitive in its analysis', and 'unimaginative in its solutions' (Reid 1973). Whitlam was convinced by her arguments: he later stated that the Fry Report was the worst report his government ever commissioned (interview with the author, May 1981). Reid suggested that the government table the report and invite wide public comment on its recommendations. This proposal was endorsed by the Cabinet and shortly afterwards Lionel Bowen (acting Minister for Education while Beazley was ill) presented the report to Parliament.

Most of the public reaction to the Fry Report, particularly from women's organisations, was hostile. Many people believed that the recommendations of the report reflected not the community's priorities but 'values and political interests of the Committee and the Department of Education' (Apps 1975: 77). The report came in for particular criticism because of the way it avoided addressing the problems of mothers in paid employment and insisted instead on an extension of traditional half-day pre-school programs. The touchstone of the report's insensitivity to the needs of working mothers lay in its proposal that day care be provided for only 10 per cent of children by 1985. As the Committee itself acknowledged, the 1969 *Child Care Survey* had revealed that 19 per cent of children below school age were the responsibility of people in the workforce, and a further 9 per cent were the responsibility of persons who would work if suitable care were available (APC 1974: 53). Given that the committee's estimates were for 1985 (16 years after the survey) and given the strong trend for more women to enter the workforce, their projection was extraordinarily low. Neither was it the case that the terms of reference tied the committee's hands, for they themselves acknowledged in the report that 'the terms of reference do not indicate the level at which full-day early childhood education and care services might be provided'(APC 1974: 54). Not even all the pre-school lobbies supported the report. The Victorian branch of the Australian Pre-School Association resolved that 'the lines of expansion suggested in the report cut across the accepted procedures in Victoria and ... Victoria preferred the retention of State prerogatives' (Free Kindergarten Union 1974: 6).

Essentially, however, the objections to the Fry Report were far broader than a dispute about day care versus pre-school. The report was antithetical to prevailing government philosophy and out of touch with community attitudes. It ignored Labor's thrust towards regional planning and administration, suggesting arrangements which simply bolstered existing state government structures. Similarly, in spite of the growing interest in parent involvement, it gave no serious attention to this issue. In these and other ways, the report seemed oblivious to major social developments. As the Women's Electoral Lobby commented in its formal response to the Fry Report: 'The Committee has totally failed to recognise that ... nearly all families with young children now require some form of early childhood service – these services can no longer be neatly pigeon-holed into day care for the poor and pre-school education for all the rest' (WEL 1974: 2)

Not all the critical comments emanated from feminist organisations. Patricia Apps, an economist based at the University of Sydney, produced a detailed and thoughtful analysis of the Fry Report which demonstrated that children who attended sessional services were to be more heavily subsidised than those in full day care. Thus, a child whose parents were both employed, whether from choice or necessity, would be penalised. Apps concluded: '... the evidence would suggest that the allocation of limited funds to the different services is based not on careful consideration of the community's need priorities, or demand for care services, but on the values and political interests of the Committee and the Department of Education' (Apps 1975: 77).

The Social Welfare Commission and Priorities Review Staff Reports

As a result of the Labor Party's revised policy on child care and the outcry which greeted the Fry Report, the government requested the Social Welfare Commission (SWC) to prepare a new set of proposals 'consistent with the Government's policy commitments and the ALP Party Platform on pre-school opportunities and day care' (*Australian* 19 February 1974). This report, commissioned in February, was to be ready for consideration by cabinet in the budget session. Meanwhile, the Labor government's policy think tank, the Priorities Review Staff, was also requested to develop proposals in regard to early childhood services.

The project team appointed by the Social Welfare Commission 'had, on the whole, little involvement with pre-school education, a commitment to community based action oriented programs and a sympathy for feminist values' (Burns 1976: 80). The team was headed by Lenore Cox, former head of the Women's Bureau in the Department of Labour and National Service, who had persistently lobbied the former Coalition government on women's issues, particularly child care. Four members of the project team were active in the Melbourne-based group Community Child Care. The skills and interests of psychologists, statisticians, economists and trade unionists were also represented on the team.

The report of the Social Welfare Commission, presented in July 1974, challenged a number of the fundamental assumptions of the Fry

Report – assumptions which had also informed previous ALP policy. The Social Welfare Commission report, *Project Care*, argued that disadvantaged groups did not simply need 'larger doses of the same service that is available to non-disadvantaged groups' (i.e. pre-schools) but that an entirely different range of services could be more appropriate. Importantly, *Project Care* also stressed that 'all children in poor families require support from society, not only children of working parents' (SWC 1974: 37).

Unlike the Fry Report which had specified pre-school for 70 per cent of 4-year olds and day care for 10 per cent of children aged 0-5 , *Project Care* recommended that the Australian government sponsor a range of early childhood services including pre-school, day care, family day care, play groups and toddler groups, baby sitting clubs and support services for private minders. The mix of services in a particular neighbourhood would be decided by local residents assisted by a community worker or 'catalyst'. These community workers would be required to be thoroughly versed in the Australian government's policy and have a considerable knowledge of the local area. They would be required to publicise the policy through local media, public meetings and small groups and to explain to people how they could use the program.

In the area of staffing, the Social Welfare Commission rejected the approach of the Australian Pre-Schools Committee which, it claimed, was unrealistic; failed to recognise the major social changes occurring at the time; and was 'conservatively conceived', with its strong emphasis on pre-school teachers as the major professional input. The commission suggested that a far wider range of professional skills be integrated into the program. For example, people qualified in planning, research, teacher education and administration would be needed as would social workers, paediatricians, physiotherapists and speech therapists (SWC 1974: 131).

Parental participation in services was to be a high priority and *Project Care* suggested many ways of involving both employed and non-employed parents. Women at home with their children could perhaps give half a day's work in exchange for several half-days' care. The report recognised that parents who worked full time would have little time or energy to put into a centre. Nevertheless, various measures 'to encourage the overlap between home and centre life' were suggested; for example, the provision by the centre of a communal meal once a week, laundromats, sewing rooms and workshops (SWC 1974: 77).

A key aspect of the Social Welfare Commission report was the mechanism it proposed for allocating funds according to local government areas. The commission suggested a way of ranking local government areas on the basis of: the occupational status of the residents (both men and women); the proportion of residents with secondary and tertiary educational attainments; the level of unemployment, the proportion of migrants (with particular attention given to those from non-English-speaking backgrounds); and certain other characteristics such as the proportion of public housing and the proportion of dwellings occupied by single family units. Local government was given a crucial role in implementing the proposed scheme. While a notional allocation of funds would be worked out for each local government area, the grants would only be made to local governments which demonstrated that they had consulted with their residents. Local governments were expected to 'initiate community planning, make the final decisions as to which groups [would] be funded, disburse funds and co-ordinate the programmes in each area' (SWC 1974: 66).

The Social Welfare Commission report took a more cautious approach to family day care than did the Fry Report, noting that its merits relative to other forms of care and its effects on child development had received no systematic study in Australia. It also suggested, if only implicitly, that parental preferences would be constrained if family day care were to be the only setting that provided individualised, personal and intimate care. *Project Care* suggested that an effort be made to develop these features in centre-based services as well.

In broad outline the recommendations of the Social Welfare Commission were endorsed by the Priorities Review Staff (PRS) report which suggested that the government adopt the SWC's report in principle. However, it suggested two changes. Firstly, that grants be allocated to local government *areas* rather than local government *authorities*, since 'the ability of local government to play a role in administering [such a program] varies from place to place and arrangements must recognise these variations'. Secondly, sensitive to the bitter disputes between Beazley and the women's movement (the report had largely been written by Lyndall Ryan who had strong feminist sympathies), the PRS suggested that administration of the program be re-assigned 'to a Minister without vested interests in any specialized aspect of the program' (PRS 1974: 2).

Well before it was presented to Parliament, the Prime Minister used the recommendations of the Social Welfare Commission report. In his election campaign speech, given at the Lane Cove Town Hall, in the heart of Sydney's middle-class suburbia, Whitlam promised a child care program the key features of which were free pre-school education, subsidised child care with parents contributing according to their means, and the encouragement of child care centres and holiday programs sponsored by industry. The proposed program, Whitlam claimed, would break down the rigid distinction between child care and education. Referring to the needs for care and education, Whitlam stated, 'Our program – a program of vision and imagination based on a compassionate understanding of the needs of the child, the parent and the community – is designed to meet those needs and to meet them immediately. Such a program will cost $130m in a full year. We proudly accept this commitment' (Whitlam 1974a: 4).

Child care had come right into the centre of the political arena. No doubt there remained within the Labor Party a residue of the Catholic church's opposition to such services, but other members of the Party had come to regard the child care policy as central to its chances of attracting women's votes and bridging the gap between male and female support for the party (NSW Labor Women's Committee 1974). After the election, Whitlam himself was to announce that he had 'no doubt that this commitment had much to do with our return to power' (Whitlam 1974b: 2).

In the 1973–74 budget $8 million had been allocated to existing programs under the *Child Care Act*, enabling them to continue until they could be incorporated into the new program. A further $10 million had been allocated as an interim measure for pre-school education. In January 1974, the Prime Minister advised the premiers that although the government intended to proceed with the pre-school program it had decided to look again at priorities between pre-school education and child care and would be considering diverting more of the available resources to child care services. The premiers were invited to make submissions for funds. Most of these were prepared by state Departments of Education and represented a continuation of programs which did not reflect Labor's policies. Most states proposed sessional pre-school projects and nothing else. State committees were generally dominated by Department of Education officials who in turn chose the community representatives (Pincus and Shipley 1976: 4). Under these arrangements, capital funds went towards building new pre-schools and paying off the mortgages on existing ones. In at least one state, Victoria, the Prime Minister's emphasis on new priorities and the subsequent decision that the pre-school allocation could be used for child care projects not eligible under the *Child Care Act* (namely family day care) were not passed on from the state Department of Education to the state authority responsible for child care (PRS 1974: 10).

In an interview on the ABC radio program *A.M.*, three days before the 1974 election, Elizabeth Reid was questioned about the government's commitment to the child care program. She observed: 'Words are alright but the sad thing is when politicians learn the jargon, exploit it for political ends and then forget to put their money where their mouths are'. On 23 July 1974 (just seven weeks after Whitlam's Lane

Cove speech) the Treasurer, Frank Crean, announced (in a minibudget which included the announcement that the government had decided to defer commencement of the full-scale child care program until 1975), that for 1974–1975 expenditure on the child care program was to be reduced from $130 million to $34 million.

It would be difficult to exaggerate the bitterness that this announcement aroused within the women's movement, the pre-school lobby and within other sections of the community. From all accounts it appeared that no-one within the government had fought to save the program. As Yvonne Preston commented, it seemed that the Labor Cabinet 'fielded not one battler in the cause of disadvantaged small children' (*National Times* 29 July–3 August 1974). The intense lobbying which the decision provoked culminated in a noisy and colourful children's party organised by the Women's Electoral Lobby and conducted on the lawns in front of Parliament House. Over the next few months child care funds were 'deflated and re-flated like the proverbial balloon' (Spearritt 1977: 207). The federal budget, announced in August, finally allocated $75 million.

In September 1974 Lionel Bowen, Special Minister of State and Minister Assisting the Prime Minister in matters relating to the Public Service, announced Labor's proposal to establish a Children's Commission. This was to be an independent body, outside the control of any government department, and it would become the central policy-making, funding and administrative body concerned with children's services. Mr Bowen stated: 'As a government we are breaking new ground. Never before has such a wide scale attempt been made to assist local communities in the initiation, planning and implementation of services of such crucial importance to themselves and ultimately to this country as a whole' (Bowen 1974a: 1).

Central to the new program was the idea that services should be flexible, community-based and integrated. No rigid distinction was to be made between educating children and caring for them. By 1980 'all children in Australia [would] have access to services designed to take care of their physical, social and recreational needs'. This historic announcement committed the federal government to the universal provision of children's services. As Peter Manning noted in the *Bulletin*, the government was moving into an area 'that could prove heavily controversial'. Under the proposed program grants were to be made to a wide variety of groups 'on a scale as yet unseen in Australia' (26 October 1974: 19).

Under its terms of reference the Interim Committee for the Children's Commission (ICCC) was charged with sponsoring and promoting 'the rapid development of a comprehensive range of diversified and integrated children's services'. These were to include early childhood education, full day care, family day care, play groups, occasional care, out-of-school-hours care, emergency care and 'any other service ... deemed necessary or desirable'. In addition, the committee was to examine the relative needs of communities throughout Australia and to devise a rating system which would facilitate the disbursement of funds according to need. It was to recommend the financial principles on which services were to operate, to suggest appropriate standards for services funded under the program, to initiate (and where necessary conduct) training courses and to arrange the drafting of legislation for the Children's Commission. Upon its establishment the ICCC also became responsible for the administration of all national commitments in the area of pre-schools.

The membership of the Interim Committee was announced in October 1974. The chairman, Tony Ayers, was a senior public servant from the Australian Department of Environment and Conservation. The other full-time members were Tricia Kavanagh, a welfare officer from the Australian Workers Union in Sydney and member of the NSW Labor Women's Committee and Barbara Spalding, co-ordinator of a family day care scheme organised by the Brotherhood of St Laurence in Victoria. In addition, there were seven part-time members. The members, according to Bowen, were 'selected not on sectional or geographic grounds, but as individuals, having in mind their personal talents and achievements and potential to contribute to the exciting task ahead' (Bowen 1974b).

In theory, the ICCC was an independent body. It was responsible to the Special Minister of State, who was regarded as 'neutral' in that he did not have a vested interest in the question of whether children's services should be primarily educational or serve some other end. In reality there were many constraints and the independence of the ICCC was largely illusory. By the time it commenced its activities, bitter conflict had developed between the Australian Labor government and the non-Labor state governments over sponsorship of various health, welfare and urban programs. These states were resolutely opposed to the central government funding local government or community organisations directly, fearing that this approach (which was also being attempted in other areas of welfare provision) would undermine state authority. The establishment by the commonwealth of state-level committees was, therefore, an attempt to save the program. Resistance to the program by conservative states was formidable: several threatened to challenge the Children's Commission in the High Court; amendments to the legislation, which would have completely destroyed its purpose, were moved in the Senate; the 'needs priority' of the policy was rejected out of hand by several states which refused to have 'needs' criteria applied to their own submissions for pre-schools (Centre for Urban Studies n.d.: 29).

The 'Community' Model

At the heart of Labor's new policy was a conviction that child care services should reflect the aspirations of local groups and not result from a bureaucratic 'top-down' strategy. Further, they should be controlled by users and local residents (generally referred to as 'the community'), not by professionals. This philosophy was very similar to that which underpinned the Australian Assistance Plan; Marie Coleman, director of the Social Welfare Commission, had played a significant role in devising both. It was also, in part, a reaction against the professionalism espoused by the Fry Report and was very much in keeping with the approach of feminist lobby groups. The twin approaches of community initiation of projects (generally referred to as the 'submission model of funding') and community management of services were central to the new policy. However, both ideals rested on a notion of 'community' which was highly problematic. Not the least of its problems were the implications of 'community' for women. As the journalist Yvonne Preston perceptively commented:

> Community groups may be favoured Canberra terminology but community groups expressing priority needs do not readily spring up like mushrooms in outer suburbs ... Are we entering an era of tremendous exploitation of a handful of women who must now add another job, that of 'community representative' to those of wife, mother and employee ... Surely no other government program, expending such sums of money to do such an important job, would be operated in such a way. *(1973)*

While publicity documents blandly invited 'communities' to apply for money to establish child care services, the realities of funding were rather more complex. The commonwealth did not disburse funds to 'communities' but to 'approved organisations' and these, it transpired, were required to be legally incorporated, non-profit bodies, or organisations with the formal backing of the local council; many 'community groups' spent months – in some cases years – battling through the legal maze of incorporation (Community Child Care NSW 1981). The kindergarten unions and day nursery associations had a head start in the submissions race: they were already incorporated as charities or non-profit companies; they were familiar with the ways of bureaucracy; they had been writing submissions for years and they had numerous sympathetic contacts. In any case, becoming incorporated was only the first step. In order to attract funds, groups had to write successful submissions. These were, essentially, pleas for funding. The ICCC was very 'flexible' about what constituted a submission; but what this meant, in effect, was that there were few guidelines to assist those who were unfamiliar with the process. Submissions had to demonstrate a need for some type of service, suggest a way of meeting this need and show that there was a group of individuals who were willing to take on responsibility for establishing the service, administering the grant and overseeing all aspects of the program. Within a short time, the process became highly competitive. It was not uncommon for submissions to include an architect's sketch plans, colour photographs of the proposed site and detailed statistical evidence of 'need'. Very often, groups had to engage in considerable fund-raising in order to prepare their submissions! This was particularly likely if there were few professional resources in their area. While parent committees in middle-class areas might well include an architect, an accountant or a lawyer (perhaps all three), groups whose members did not have these professional skills had to purchase them – or go without.

It is not clear how (or even if) the ICCC attempted to measure relative need amongst the applications it received. In any event, the Social Welfare Commission's detailed recommendations concerning the allocation of funds on the basis of objectively determined 'need' was not put into practice: the most needy areas were the least likely to develop submissions. Some attempt was made to overcome this by employing community workers or 'catalysts' to assist local groups articulate their needs and develop proposals for their area. This scheme, however, did not do much to help the most disadvantaged groups (Centre for Urban Studies n.d.: 190).

Another problem for the committee was, ironically, the hefty size of its budget. The enlarged budget of $75 million for which women's groups had battled so vigorously, turned out to be a major stumbling block for the wider policy goals of the program. Pre-school organisations and state Education Departments had enormous advantages over the rest of the community given their knowledge of bureaucracies, their access to (even representation on) state-level committees and the ease and confidence with which they could develop submissions. As a result, 'while the new parent groups were assiduously doing their groundwork, very substantial allocations were approved for formal State government sponsored kindergarten building programs and ... their staffing' (Centre for Urban Studies n.d.: 54).

Another policy which drained significant amounts of funds away from informal, community-based services was the generous funding made available by the federal government for salaries in pre-schools.

This policy had a major impact on the distribution of funds throughout Australia, particularly in Victoria where a relatively high number of pre-schools already existed. In Victoria, about 80 per cent of the federal allocation went directly to the state government, and of that amount some 90 per cent was expended on pre-schools (CCC 1975). In theory, the federal subsidy was to be given only if a pre-school integrated a range of programs into its core service; for example, a centre might extend its hours, provide a meeting place for parents, run play groups or offer occasional care. In practice, this policy was virtually impossible to monitor. In many cases 'integration of services' merely involved the padding of one or two unrelated activities around an existing sessional pre-school program, for no other purpose than to become eligible for the federal subsidy.

Pre-school organisations often strongly resisted the government's policies regarding the extension and integration of services. Often they expressed deep resentment and fear of the commonwealth's intervention into 'their' arena. They were particularly hostile to the program of change being put forward by feminists. These attitudes were dramatically expressed in the 1974 annual report of the Free Kindergarten Union of Victoria:

> ... suddenly during this last year or so the pre-school movement as it is accepted in our community and as we know it through kindergartens and kindred groups, became attractive first to the Education Department, then to the Social Planners, to political extremists and feminist movements. Each has wanted to bend the Kindergarten to a shape fitting its own hobby horse [sic]. Extremely strong political pressures have been exerted. Moneys dispensed from the Commonwealth level for pre-school services have strings attaching which if accepted would change the whole object of kindergartens as we have advocated them. This could change the role of the family in relation to child rearing, undermine optimum child growth to the detriment of society and even interfere with our democratic freedom. *(FKU 1974: 6)*

The following year the Free Kindergarten Union again expressed its strong disapproval of government policy: 'We believe that there is no better place for infants and young children to begin life than in happy homes with their own parents.' The Union needed to assert this principle, said the Director, Miss Heather Lyon, because 'extremists appear to have been making such a strong bid to urge women away from family commitments and into the work force'. The provision of more child care services 'for mothers who are not obliged to work', warned Miss Lyon, was likely to result in 'generations of emotionally rejected children' (FKU 1974: 7).

Despite the strong disapproval of groups such as this, the legislation to establish the Children's Commission was introduced into the Parliament in April 1974. Various attempts were made by the Opposition in the Senate to weaken or destroy the bill by amendment, but it was finally passed and received royal assent on 11 June 1975. The act, however, was never proclaimed. This was chiefly because no decision on the membership of the commission had been announced before the dismissal of the Labor government in November of that year.

The rather naive enthusiasm of some members of the Labor administration for schemes employing 'community development' and 'power to the people' strategies led the government to adopt a policy framework for child care which greatly disadvantaged those who lacked the skills to write submissions and the resources to strenuously pursue their own interests. In the short run, this resulted in well organised pre-school groups siphoning off most of the funds; groups seeking services such as long day care fared very poorly in comparison with the pre-school lobby despite the intentions of policy makers within the Labor government. In the medium term, the 'community initiative' approach also resulted (inadvertently) in middle-class areas benefitting disproportionately in terms of access to child care generally. The aspirations of working-class women to have services located near to their places of employment received virtually no attention; the systematic evidence of the surveys was taken up by some of the protagonists but largely ignored by the policy makers.

In spite of these failings, the Whitlam government made some significant advances in the child care field. It introduced, for the first time in Australia's history, the idea that the federal government could become involved in a national program of child care provision and it tried (albeit unsuccessfully) to develop ways of administering the program so that the destructive power of some of the bureaucrats, conservative groups and state governments would be minimised.

Significantly, however, throughout these years child care was conceptualised as a discrete area of social policy. Once the 'educational' focus of the program had been scuttled, neither the government nor any of the major lobby groups sought to integrate child care priorities with other government objectives. The link between child care provision and women's right to employment was not a major theme during these years. The emphasis was much more on self-help and community activities as ends in themselves.

CHAPTER 5

Playing Beneath the Sword of Damocles

> At a time when economic restraint and cuts in government spending are widely canvassed, it is little wonder that the forthcoming budget is viewed [by child care groups] in much the same way as Damocles eyed off his sword.
> *Marie Coleman, Director of the Office of Child Care, 1981*

From late 1975 until early 1983 Australia was governed by a coalition of the Liberal Party and National-Country Party, headed by Prime Minister Malcolm Fraser. The political and economic climate which prevailed in Australia during these years was completely different from that of the Whitlam period and, as a result, there were major transformations in the relationship between feminist organisations and the state. The means by which the Whitlam government had been ousted by the conservatives had caused deep divisions in Australian society. Most radical and reformist groups regarded the incoming government with profound hostility and distrust – as much for the way in which it had achieved office as for its policies. The new government came to power promising significant reductions in public expenditure, particularly in areas such as social welfare. For both economic and ideological reasons it was committed to promoting the role of the family rather than expanding state-provided services to care for children and other dependents. Furthermore, the new administration was intent on bringing to an end what it saw as the 'excesses' of open government as practised by Labor. Procedures such as seeking advice from outside the public service, establishing independent policy-making bodies, publishing reports for public discussion and giving citizens relatively easy access to ministers were destined to come to an end.

In the lead-up to the 1975 election, Fraser had argued that much of the increased commonwealth government expenditure under Labor had been wasteful and extravagant. The role of government should not be to provide services but to create an environment in which the market could flourish and individuals could find their own solutions to 'private' problems such as child care. Fraser saw the aim of a coalition government as being the promotion of 'the maximum degree of personal freedom, decision-making and independence', and claimed that these qualities were threatened by 'big-government'. He also criticised the provision of 'universal services administered by a centralised government monopoly' on the grounds that these 'in the end, make everyone dependent on what the government chooses to provide'. In order to achieve the objectives of his party outlined above, Fraser declared they would cut government expenditure and introduce significant incentives for private enterprise (Elliott 1982: 123–24).

The Labor government, by contrast, had accorded a major role to the commonwealth in funding a variety of social welfare programs, including child care. This approach sprang from the belief that only the commonwealth, with its major financial powers and ability to plan programs at a national level, could ensure some degree of equality of provision throughout the nation. It was also an acknowledgment that some kinds of social goods were not likely to be produced at an affordable level by 'the market' and would never be provided by state governments.

'Responsible economic management' was another of the Liberal Party's key themes during the December 1975 election period. Fraser had campaigned strongly on the basis that the Liberals would be superior economic managers. He cited high inflation, increased unemployment and the rapid growth in commonwealth outlays as evidence of the inability of the Labor government to manage the economy. (In fact, inflation in Australia peaked at 17.5 per cent in March 1975 compared with a peak of 27 per cent in the UK, 26 per cent in Japan and 24 per cent in Italy. During the seven years of the Fraser government inflation in Australia was consistently higher than that of its trading partners. Unemployment in Australia moved at an average rate comparable with its four major trading partners during 1974–75, but rose to a much higher level under Fraser.) Reducing government expenditure was promoted as the key to bringing down inflation and ending the 'crowding out' of the private sector which was said to have occurred under Labor. In addition to its significance as an economic tool, the aim of reducing the role and responsibilities of the commonwealth accorded well with the Liberals' traditional belief in small government and individual self-reliance.

The Whitlam government had frequently been accused of centralism – an accusation that was made most often by the conservative governments of Queensland and Victoria. One of the grounds for this claim was that under Labor the proportion of all monies that went to the states as tied grants rather than as general revenue assistance had increased markedly. Another reason for discontent was that the Labor government had devised a number of strategies for by-passing the states and giving grants directly to community groups and local authorities. This was particularly so in health and social welfare – areas which had traditionally been seen as state responsibilities. Under the rubric of 'new federalism' the Fraser government committed itself to reducing the use of tied grants to the states and increasing their general revenue assistance. It also promised to guarantee the states a fixed proportion of income tax and to empower them to levy their own income taxes (Groenewegen 1979). The aim of the 'new federalism' was said to be the clarification of the respective roles of the commonwealth and state governments and the elimination of areas of conflict and overlap. It also functioned as part of the Fraser government's attempt to reduce the size of the public sector and was interpreted by some as 'a reaction to the reform policies of the Whitlam Government' (Groenewegen 1979: 69). The goals of the new federalism were largely to be achieved by commonwealth withdrawal from the social welfare and urban planning initiatives of the Whitlam government.

From the point of view of child care groups and others seeking consolidation of the policy gains for women achieved under the previous government, the difficulties created by the conservative parties' contractionary social policy stance were further compounded by the fact that there were few links between feminists and members of the incoming government. According to journalist and political commentator Anne Summers, the new government had 'virtually no commitment to women's issues as they were defined by the women's movement' (Summers 1979: 199). The social democratic, reform-oriented approach of the Whitlam government had enabled feminists to build a number of alliances with members of the previous government, including some ministers. There were also key points of access to the government which could be used to channel claims and to pursue women's policy interests, such as the Women's Adviser to the Prime Minister (the position held by Elizabeth Reid until October 1975) and various Caucus committees. Those feminists who were members of the Labor Party had additional avenues such as Labor Women's Committees and the ALP national conference through which they could attempt to influence government policy. Each of these strategic points had been important in the struggle to get the Labor government to arrive at its eventual commitment to universal child care provision. A commonwealth government committed to re-establishing traditional family values, reducing commonwealth expenditure and returning power to the states presented a different and, at first glance, more difficult set of constraints.

Given this climate, one might have predicted under Fraser the dismantling of commonwealth-funded child care services, or, at the very least, a major transfer of responsibilities to the states or to private enterprise. In fact, while each of these possible courses of action was canvassed at one time or another within the Coalition government, none was fully embraced. During the Fraser years, expenditure on children's services was severely curtailed. Seven budgets were introduced by the Fraser government and in each except the last expenditure on children's services was reduced in real terms. By 1981–82 there had been a real reduction of 30 per cent from the Whitlam government's peak allocation for 1975–76. The Fraser government's final budget gave a slight boost to children's services but even so the level of expenditure in 1982–83 was 22.4 per cent below the level it had been in Labor's last year of office (Brennan and O'Donnell 1986: 40). Importantly, however, most of the program's key features remained intact. This outcome was the result of several factors. Women in the bureaucracy played a crucial role in maintaining and defending the child care program during the years of the Fraser government, as did women within the Liberal Party. In addition, the activities of state-based child care lobby groups became far more co-ordinated and a national organisation was formed. The role of each of these factors is explored in this chapter; the industrial dimension of child care – including both the wages and conditions of child care workers and the need for employed parents to have access to child care services – is the focus of the following chapter.

Early Moves to Restructure Commonwealth Child Care and Pre-school Policies

Within a few months of coming to office, Prime Minister Fraser announced that his government would not proceed with Labor's proposed Children's Commission. Instead, an Office of Child Care was to be established within the Department of Social Security. This decision heralded a distinct ideological and political change from the previous government's approach. One of the objectives of establishing an independent Children's Commission had been to move child care away from the control of established federal bureaucracies. It could then be seen not as an extension of the education system nor as an aspect of welfare provision but as a community service in its own right. An independent commission would also have been likely to enhance the status of child care and to lift its profile as a public issue. The Coalition's decision not to proceed with the proposed commission indicated its rejection of these goals. Clearly, the Fraser government did not wish child care to remain a high profile policy issue. Nor did it wish to see an independent commission given responsibility for functions which it regarded as being within the province of the social security portfolio.

Marie Coleman (who had headed the former government's Social Welfare Commission and who had chaired the committee which produced *Project Care*) was appointed director of the new Office of Child Care. Coleman was an experienced and skilful bureaucrat; at that time she was the only woman ever to have held first division status in the commonwealth public service (Sawer 1989: 433). In addition she was a committed feminist and had a long history of involvement in children's services. Hers was to prove an extremely important appointment.

Establishment of the Office of Child Care

The new government was quick to make clear its dissatisfaction with the pattern of expenditure which had developed under Labor, particularly the priority given to pre-schools. The Coalition's concern that social welfare programs be restricted as far as possible to 'the needy' was clearly at odds with Labor's universalist philosophy. As applied to child care it was also a rejection of the feminist position that children's services should be available to all families in recognition of the responsibility of the community as a whole. Nevertheless, few feminists disagreed with the Coalition's contention that pre-schools were accessible mainly to those families who could afford to have one parent remain out of the workforce and that they were of little assistance to single parent or two-earner households. (Indeed this was precisely the argument which had been mounted by Labor Women and others in their efforts to change Labor's original policy.)

Prime Minister Fraser, announcing the establishment of the Office of Child Care in June 1976, framed this argument within the philosophy and rhetoric of the conservative Coalition:

> Over the past three years pre-school education has had a considerable boost through the provision of substantial Commonwealth funds. Approximately 75 per cent of Commonwealth expenditure on children's services has gone to pre-schools in the States.
>
> Many children from needy families, however, have been not only without the advantage of pre-school education but too often without the benefits of

basic adequate care. It is essential to concentrate the Government's resources in areas of greatest need, and the Commonwealth wishes to give greater emphasis to child care for children of needy families in the development of the Children's Services Program. *(Coleman 1978a: 4)*

Withdrawal of commonwealth funding for pre-schools

For the conservative early childhood organisations (such as the Australian Pre-School Association and the various kindergarten unions) this statement came as a blow. These groups had high hopes of continued commonwealth support for pre-schools, particularly as they saw this service as more in keeping with the pro-family beliefs of the Coalition than the child care services demanded by feminists. Such hopes were further dashed in November 1976 when the commonwealth announced its intention to contribute to pre-schools by way of a fixed annual block grant to each of the states. This meant that the commonwealth would no longer fund individual pre-schools directly; instead it would provide each state with a lump sum to distribute to pre-schools. These block grants were not to be indexed and would thus lose their value over time. This announcement effectively signalled the end of active commonwealth involvement in pre-school funding and policy making. It re-established (and indeed cemented) the division between 'education' and 'care' services for children below school age. Labor's attempt to end the distinction between these two types of activity and to adopt a more integrated approach to the needs of pre-school children had failed.

The changes in pre-school funding were in keeping with the government's 'new federalism' policies. The commonwealth did not wish to continue to fund pre-schools because pre-schools were deemed to be educational and education was the responsibility of the states. What this line of reasoning failed to address was the fact that the commonwealth had become involved in pre-schooling precisely because a number of states were *not* prepared to put money into this area, thus creating vast discrepancies across Australia in access to pre-schools. It is possible that if pre-schools had been more prepared to open their doors to a range of age groups and to provide a greater variety of services they could have maintained commonwealth funding. It would have been economically rational for the commonwealth to keep pre-schools within a broad system of children's services, if only because they represented a vastly under-utilised capital resource. There were many country towns, for example, in which a fully equipped pre-school (built with commonwealth funds) was open for only a few half-day sessions per week. The rest of the time these buildings were closed even though families in the district needed a variety of child care services. The determined refusal of many pre-school committees to expand their services and to cater to the children of mothers in employment eventually cost them commonwealth funding (DSS 1984).

Primarily as a result of the shift to funding pre-schools by way of an unindexed block grant, there was a significant increase in the proportion of all commonwealth children's services expenditure which went to other types of services, reversing the pattern of expenditure which had emerged under Whitlam (see Table 2, p. 130). As Eva Cox, a prominent feminist and analyst of social policy, pointed out: 'This shift under a conservative government was actually closer to women's needs than the unclear priorities of the previous reformist government' (Cox 1988: 203). Significantly, however, *within* the child care category, expenditure on centre-based services declined in relation to expenditure on home-based family day care schemes throughout the years of Coalition government. Whereas in 1975–76 child care centres had received 87 per cent of these funds, by 1981–82 their share was down to 45 per cent (Brennan and O'Donnell 1986: 44–5). By 1980 child care money was being spent on general family support, youth and child life protection services, welfare rights officers, training programs and community information centres. As one writer commented, the Children's Services Program had become a 'general welfare slush fund' (Nicholls 1982: 52).

Further, government subsidies to children's services were not adjusted to keep pace with inflation. Funding for family day care schemes, for example, was not increased at all between 1976 and 1981. Centre-based services also suffered from the failure to adjust subsidies. These funding cutbacks had multiple consequences. Users of services faced sharp increases in fees, management committees were obliged to undertake endless fund-raising and sponsoring bodies were forced to increase their contributions (even though many had entered into the area with the explicit understanding that their role would be an administrative rather than a financial one).

The first real moves towards an alliance between the traditional early childhood organisations and feminist supporters of child care took place towards the end of the 1970s. These moves were partly motivated by the recognition that conflicts between supporters of different types of services deflected energy from broader campaigns against reductions in government expenditure. Changed attitudes on the part of some of the key players (both individual and organisational) also had an effect on bringing the camps closer together. In 1979 the Australian Pre-School Association changed its name to the Australian Early Childhood

Association in an effort to broaden its image and to signal that its concern was for the wellbeing of children in general, not merely for the promotion of one type of service. A year later, Carole Deagan, one of the leading feminists actively lobbying for increased child care provision, made a plea for an end to the bickering between advocates of different types of services which had characterised the 1970s: 'The crucial question is *not* "Why is a disproportionately high percentage of the resources in the field allocated to 'educating' some children and a disproportionately low proportion to 'caring' for the rest?" The more important question to be asking is "Why are so few resources allocated to services for children under five?" ' (Deagan 1980b: 53).

These developments did not signal an end to all disputes in the area of children's services; traces of the deep hostility generated by past battles, particularly those of the Whitlam years, remained into the 1990s. Moreover, new issues have arisen on which there are strong divisions within the field; for example, work-related child care, subsidies to users of commercial centres and tax deductions for child care expenses. However, from the late 1970s onwards a general determination to present a united front to government emerged amongst the major lobby groups representing community-based (that is, non-commercial) services for children. One symbol of this was the increasing use of the term 'children's services' in preference to 'child care'. This was intended to symbolise unity between advocates of various service types.

The Gathering Momentum of 'Pro-Family' Rhetoric and Policies

An essential element of the context of child care policies under Fraser from the late 1970s onwards was the emergence of an explicit debate in the political arena concerning 'the family' and the need for 'family policies'. The material context in which these ideas emerged and gathered strength was one of increasing unemployment combined with significant cutbacks in commonwealth expenditure on a range of welfare and community services (Cass, Keens and Moller 1981). Unemployment had been rising since 1974 and the increase in commonwealth expenditure on unemployment benefits was one of the major reasons why commonwealth expenditures were not falling as quickly as the Coalition had hoped. In addition, outlays on other payments such as supporting parent's benefit and invalid pension were also rising in response to the increased incidence of joblessness. However, although the government was not able to limit its spending on these transfer payments as much as it desired, it *was* able to cut back in many other areas of the social wage. From 1976 onwards there were significant reductions in expenditure on health, education, urban services and housing (Scotton 1980).

Underpinning both the pro-family rhetoric and the cutbacks in social wage programs was the desire to enforce a return to traditional notions of the family and to re-assert the 'proper' roles of men and women. The pro-family sentiments expressed during this period frequently constituted a direct attack on the workforce participation of married women (especially mothers) and were intended to counter feminist demands for state provision of services such as child care. In the words of Bettina Cass:

> In many ways, the emphasis on 'family policies' in the latter half of the 1970s can be understood as an attempt to 'domesticate' the demands made by organised women's groups in the late 1960s and early 1970s: demands for equality in the labour-market and the work-place; for the right to control fertility and to share domestic responsibility and domestic labour with men.
> *(1982: 19)*

Family policy was specifically placed on the Australian political agenda following a meeting of social welfare ministers held in 1977. At this meeting it was resolved that regular conferences should be held on 'family and community service policy' and the first such conference (entitled 'Towards a National Family Policy') was held in 1980. The same year an organisation known as the Australian Family Association (AFA) was formed 'to provide a forum and a vehicle for those individuals and organisations in the community concerned with strengthening and support of the traditional family' (AFA 1980: iv). The AFA aimed to ensure that 'the family' rather than the state took responsibility for such matters as care of children and care of the elderly. The rhetoric of its supporters combined two of the major preoccupations of contemporary conservatism: reduced public expenditure and a return to 'traditional' roles for women: '... in recent times the cry has been for more and more government bureaucratic action in areas where The Family not only has rights and responsibilities, but can and should act; because it will be more effective, more efficient and certainly less costly' (Callinan 1980: 4).

The key activists and patrons of the Australian Family Association were conservative politicians and academics, many of whom were known for their anti-feminist views. They included Lachlan Chipman, Professor of Philosophy at Wollongong University and Jerzy Zubrzycki, Professor of Sociology at the Australian National University. Kim Beazley (snr.) (who had been Minister for Education in the Whitlam government and who had frequently clashed with feminists over child care policy) was one of the founding patrons of the organisation. Another was Dr Clare Isbister, a prominent Sydney pediatrician, who had once characterised women who used child care services as 'the equivalent of Harlow's monkeys' (Isbister 1973: 6). Dr Isbister's attacks were directed not simply at the existence of child care services but at the women who used them. A paper which she delivered to a meeting of the Australian Family Association included a vitriolic attack on working mothers: 'the mother who hands her small infant into a substitute care situation can no longer be said to be a functioning mother' (Isbister 1982: 22).

The objects of the AFA were to 'strengthen and support the institutions of Marriage and Family ... to examine laws and ... policies for their effect on the well-being of The Family and to formulate and promote policies in these areas as it deems necessary' (AFA 1980: iv). The views of the AFA's supporters in relation to the respective roles of the family and government in the provision of welfare services are encapsulated in the following extract from the keynote speech at the 1981 conference:

> Increasingly it is argued that the care of small children, the chronically ill, and the aged are public responsibilities to be carried on in publicly funded institutions outside the home – child care centres, hospitals, twilight homes...
> It is imperative that such views be resisted. Instead of removing such dependents from family care and attention, we should be making it easier for them to receive it, by removing the disincentives to provide home care for the very young, the very sick, and the very old. It is not just that it is cheaper for such support to be given ... in the home ... from relatives; far more important is that the underlying principle governing care and attention is mutual affection, and not that of paid employment ... It should be part of a national family policy to identify, and where practicable, remove those factors which genuinely prevent the provision of care and attention for the needy in the home by other members of the family.   *(Chipman 1981: 10)*

Chipman's call for 'the family' to take up its proper responsibilities was, in effect, a call for women to withdraw from the labour market and resume their roles as unpaid carers. Many other, less veiled, attacks on married women's employment, were made during the period under discussion. B.A. Santamaria, a founder of the National Civic Council, claimed that 'the withdrawal of 40 per cent of married women from the home into the workforce' was in itself 'a fundamental cause of family breakdown'. According to Santamaria, the public hospital system was overloaded with thousands of old people who could be cared for at home if only women had not abandoned them. The cost of family breakdown (apparently regarded by Santamaria as synonymous with women's workforce participation) was 'inflation and bureaucracy'. And, he added: 'What was once a task carried out by the family [sic] for nothing simply passes into public expenditure ... You cannot cut the costs of the welfare state without restoring the family' (Santamaria 1976: 9).

The call for 'market roles for men, motherhood roles for women' (Poole 1983) thus represented an attack on one of the most fundamental principles of feminism – women's economic independence. To what extent were the views of conservatives such as Chipman and Santamaria shared by members of the government? During the years of the Coalition government, the general view on the left was that the Fraser government was like the Thatcher and Reagan administrations: a government of the 'new right', committed to drastic cuts in public expenditure, undermining the welfare state, breaking the power of unions and so on. This, however, was too simple a view. Certainly on such matters as women's employment and the funding of child care there was no more a single view within the Coalition than there was in the Labor Party.

Conservative pressures notwithstanding, there was some expansion in the provision of some kinds of child care services between 1976 and 1980 – although total expenditure on children's services fell. This expansion was due in large measure to the efforts of the minister in charge of the program, Senator Margaret Guilfoyle. As minister, Guilfoyle showed considerable interest in child care and was prepared to argue in Cabinet for the continuation of the program (which became known as the Children's Services Program after 1976). Sustained advocacy from the Office of Women's Affairs (a small policy unit which was originally located within the Department of Prime Minister and Cabinet but which was moved to the Department of Home Affairs after the 1977 election) was also important. The office developed economic arguments to support continued funding of child care – pointing particularly to its importance in enabling supporting parent beneficiaries to enter employment, thus reducing welfare expenditure.

Throughout the Fraser years the growth in the number and proportion of single-parent families became an increasing focus of public concern. Between 1974 and 1982 the number of single parents increased by 68 per cent (from 182,500 to 306,400). Furthermore, in the context of economic recession and declining job opportunities, such families were increasingly likely to depend on the government for pensions or benefits. In 1982, 82 per cent of female and 20 per cent of male-headed sole-parent families were in receipt of pensions or benefits compared with 65 per cent and 10 per cent in 1974 (Cass 1985). The labour market participation rate of single parents was markedly below that of their married counterparts.

Lack of access to affordable child care was increasingly being revealed as an important factor contributing to both unemployment and underemployment amongst parents. In one large-scale study almost 30 per cent of single parents said they had been prevented from using child care because of the lengthy waiting lists, high fees or the inaccessibility of services (English et al. 1978: 45). The poverty experienced by many parents due to their lack of employment opportunities, was thus being directly linked to the problems of child care.

Post-1980 Developments

Although Fraser was portrayed by his left-wing critics as a member of the 'new right', indeed, as the Australian equivalent of Thatcher and Reagan, within his own party he came in for considerable criticism for his liberal tendencies. The economic rationalists within the Coalition castigated him as weak, particularly because of his inability to significantly cut social welfare expenditure. According to one such critic, 'Fraser was really a bit of a bleeding heart' (Henderson 1983: 36).

Following the 1980 election, the economic rationalists, or 'dries', within the Coalition began to press their demands for reduced public expenditure with increasing vigour. Although the Coalition had scored its third successive victory, the election had been hard fought and the government's majority in parliament had been substantially reduced. Within the Liberal Party there was considerable discontent about the failure of the government to effect its promised reductions in commonwealth outlays, to reduce inflation and to bring the economy out of recession. Within this new context the government's approach to expenditure on social programs began to harden further. In a post-election Cabinet re-shuffle Senator Fred Chaney was allocated the Social Security portfolio. Though known to many of his colleagues as 'Red Fred', the new minister was firmly of the opinion that government policy should be aimed at 'strengthening the family' rather than supporting publicly-funded, community-based services. His view of the appropriate role for government in children's services – a particularly narrow one – caused considerable alarm amongst advocates of publicly-funded child care: 'I think most Australians would accept that the primary obligation for the care of children rests with parents and that the role of government is to intervene and to assist in those cases where, for a variety of reasons, the parents themselves may not be able to meet their obligations' (quoted in Jones 1983: 16).

However, it was not simply the personal views of the minister that caused concern. Early in 1981 a Review of Commonwealth Government Functions was set up to investigate ways of reducing public sector expenditure. The committee appointed to review government programs (a committee which became known as the 'razor gang') was intended to effect 'a quick and ruthless pruning of programs' (Weller 1989: 245).

Within a few weeks of the announcement of this review it was widely rumoured that the commonwealth's involvement in children's services was to be substantially reduced and that the government might be considering withdrawing from the field altogether and handing its functions to the states. These rumours galvanised supporters of publicly-funded child care into action. A campaign was hastily mounted by child care activists (mainly based in Sydney and Melbourne), who contacted every member of the government urging that the commonwealth retain primary responsibility for children's services. Attention was also drawn to the government's failure to index its subsidies and the fact that this had brought many services to the brink of collapse. Demonstrations were held in the major capital cities and a fair degree of media attention was gained. This campaign was the first major mobilisation for child care since the Whitlam years.

Interestingly, this new drive was not led by broad-based feminist organisations, such as WEL, but by much more narrowly focused child care lobby groups, such as Children's Services Action in Sydney and the Child Care Federal Funding Campaign in Melbourne. These groups had emerged from the community child care movement in their own states but were not explicitly linked with any feminist organisations. Further, although many of the individual members were politically active in child care precisely because of their commitment to feminism, this was by no means true of all. Child care was becoming a major industry and many of the new activists in political campaigns were child care workers. Users and would-be users of child care services were another important group. Finally, many 'newcomers' were becoming involved in child care campaigns: these included college and university lecturers, children's services development officers and public servants working on the implementation of the child care policies.

According to political journalist Anne Summers, the campaign mounted in 1981 was 'instantly successful' and the government's intention of disengaging from the area was 'quietly dropped'. Summers was extravagant in her praise of the action, claiming that 'for weeks afterwards ministers spoke almost in awe, of the extraordinarily well-organised campaign' (*Sun-Herald* 18 October 1981). Behind the scenes, however, much unseen effort had been put into preserving the child care program by Liberal women MPs and by the National Women's Advisory Council (NWAC). The federal government had established the NWAC in 1978 to provide 'a channel of communication and a public vote for women at federal level' (Sawer 1989: 431). The formation of the NWAC had been a controversial step. To both its critics and its supporters it represented a public acknowledgement that the issues which the women's movement had placed on the political agenda had real legitimacy. Although it appears the government may have originally intended the council to be mainly symbolic and to promote its own policies amongst women in the community, this was not how things turned out. Largely due to the commitment and skills of its convenor, Beryl Beaurepaire, the council adopted an independent stance, frequently (and effectively) opposing the direction of government policies and advocating alternative positions. Beaurepaire had considerable personal influence with the Prime Minister. She was a member of one of Melbourne's leading families and a senior member of the Liberal Party – throughout the period that she convened the NWAC (1978–1982) she also served as vice-president of the party's Victorian branch.

Beryl Beaurepaire was very important in convincing the government not to transfer responsibility for child care to the states. She openly opposed Chaney's 'minimalist' approach to government involvement in service provision and, in a gesture of defiance, declared child care to be the major research priority of the NWAC for the coming year.

The Spender Report

The Review of Commonwealth Government Functions did not make any recommendations concerning children's services. However, one offshoot of the review process was the establishment of a committee, chaired by Liberal backbencher John Spender, to review the whole program. The brief given to this committee was to examine the policies and administration of the Children's Services Program and to make recommendations with a view to achieving greater consistency between these aspects of the program and the principles of family responsibility, restriction of government subsidies to the needy, avoidance of overlap with the state governments or the private sector and containment of government expenditure (Spender 1981: Annexure 1).

In keeping with the style of the Fraser government, the establishment of the Spender committee was never publicly announced, nor was its report ever published. However, the committee's existence became widely known among children's services groups as a result of judicious leaking of information by women in the federal bureaucracy. Some groups and individuals even made submissions to the committee.

In the light of the guidelines which had been given to the committee, the major recommendation of the Spender Report (as the committee's report came to be known) – that the commonwealth should retain responsibility for the Children's Services Program and that 'no attempt should be made at this stage to devolve it to the States' (Spender 1981: 38) – was something of a surprise. The general thrust of the Spender Report was towards strengthening commonwealth control over various aspects of the program; for example, bringing back to direct funding those components which were funded via the states, such as out-of-school-hours and vacation care and child care in women's refuges. The report urged that 75 per cent of funds within the Children's Services Program should be reserved for 'mainstream' projects, defined as centre-based and family day care services, out-of-school-hours care and vacation programs. These recommendations were of course very well received by community-based child care groups.

Other recommendations of the Spender Report, however, were much less acceptable. For example, in a discussion of services funded under the *Child Care Act*, the report expressed concern about having the commonwealth's subsidies linked to award wages (described as 'an open-ended' funding arrangement) and implied that it would be better to link them to the enrolment of children in need (Spender 1981: 14). Spender also suggested that any future expansion in the Children's Services Program should give priority to family day care which he described as 'the most cost effective area' (Spender 1981: 39).

Another bitterly contested recommendation was that 'parents, according to their means, should make a significant contribution towards the cost of the services provided' (Spender 1981: Annexure 7). Many parents were already experiencing difficulties in paying for child care and, in addition, most services had to undertake regular fund-raising activities in order to meet their normal running expenses. The possibility of even higher fees was thus regarded with genuine anxiety. Yet subsequently Senator Chaney went even further than Spender, arguing that 'parents able to pay the full cost of day care should do so' (Chaney 1981a). This threat to increase the already high fees of child care services once again led to an upsurge in political activity amongst children's services advocacy groups.

The other recommendation of the Spender Report which aroused considerable opposition was the proposal to subsidise users of commercial child care centres. Private child care operators regarded subsidised services as 'unfair competition' and had claimed in a submission to the government that, since the introduction of government-funded services, 'there [had] been considerable erosion of the market available to the independent area'. As the private operators themselves acknowledged, across Australia there was a 30 per cent vacancy level in private child care centres (Australian Federation of Child Care Associations 1981: 25).

In New South Wales, the Association of Child Care Centres, a lobby group for profit-making child care, had stated that 'extending government subsidies to needy parents whose children were enrolled in commercial centres would allow the government to make full use of existing services, before having to provide expensive capital and recurrent funding. It would stop discrimination against Private Centres and therefore may encourage expansion of private capital into this field ... (Association of Child Care Centres of NSW 1981: 5). A similar claim was made at the national level. In a submission to Senator Chaney in February 1981, the Australian Federation of Child Care Associations argued that the government could save money on recurrent expenditure by 'redirecting' its needs subsidies to users in the commercial sector.

Opposition to the commercial child care proposal from community-based groups was intense. As a basic principle, advocates of parent-managed, non-profit services regarded the profit motive as incompatible with the provision of a high quality service to children. They also claimed that standards of care were lower in for–profit services, despite the fact that these were subject to the same state government licensing requirements as community-based services. Some of the practices of the commercial operators suggested that they were keen to avoid certain relatively costly measures (such as employing trained staff) even when the importance of these was widely recognised. In New South Wales, for example, where state regulations required trained staff to be employed only if thirty or more children were being cared for, a large number of commercial centres had taken licences for precisely twenty-nine children (NSW Department of Youth and Community Services 1980). Another criticism of commercial centres was their lack of commitment to parent involvement. Whereas all community-based services receiving federal funding were required to provide opportunities for parents to become involved in the management of the services, commercial centres did not operate under any such strictures. Parents who had had experience of commercial child care frequently complained about this. Not only did commercial centres fail to provide avenues through which parents could influence the management of services, but quite often parents were not allowed to accompany their children inside the centre or to visit them during the day. Such practices obviously conflicted with the most fundamental principles of the community child care movement. In addition, opponents of the Spender proposal pointed out that private centres tended to be located in relatively affluent areas and that subsidising users in these areas would do very little to help the government's target of 'the truly needy'.

Political activity around the child care issue became more vigorous than ever during this period and support for publicly-funded services came from some unexpected quarters. Liberal Party feminists publicly warned the government that it was likely to lose votes at the next election if it went ahead with proposals to subsidise private centres. Eve Mahlab, founder of the Victorian Liberal Feminist Network and the *Bulletin*'s 1981 Businesswoman of the Year, claimed that while Liberal feminists supported private enterprise in general they believed that high quality child care could best be provided by non-profit, community-based care. Mahlab argued that subsidising enterprises which were not viable would only make them more inefficient (*Bulletin* 1 December 1981).

Outside the parties, too, there was considerable lobbying. By late 1982 a new national organisation had been formed to promote the interests of non-profit making children's services. This organisation, the National Association of Community Based Children's Services (NACBCS) was backed up by state-based groups such as Children's Services Action in New South Wales and the Child Care Federal Funding Campaign in Victoria.

In spite of the lobbying which followed the leaking of the Spender Report, statements made by Senator Chaney at the time of the 1981–82 budget made it clear both that the government was determined to introduce income testing and that it would proceed with a pilot study of the proposed subsidy scheme for users of commercial child care centres. Senator Chaney announced that the year would be one of 'consolidation and review' of children's services and indicated that the funds allocated would almost all be needed to maintain the existing program; there would be virtually no expansion of services that year (Chaney 1981a). A few weeks later the sponsors of some 500 proposed child care projects were notified that their submissions had been rejected.

In August 1982 Marie Coleman was removed from her position as director of the Office of Child Care – a position she had held since the office had been established in 1976. Coleman's relegation to a position as 'special adviser' to the Social Welfare Policy Secretariat was greeted with considerable anger by child care groups around the country, as well as by a number of high ranking Liberals (*SMH* 9 August 1982). Coleman's removal provided a rallying point for child care activists. She had gained the trust and respect of numerous child care groups. The National Association of Community Based Child Care expressed 'anger and disgust' at the move and WEL called for the Office of Child Care to be moved away from the Department of Social Security 'which clearly has no interest in child care' (*National Times* 15–21 August 1982). Dame Beryl Beaurepaire, who had encouraged the NWAC to make child care its first priority in 1982, was said to be appalled; so, apparently, was Dame Margaret Guilfoyle.

Restricting child care to 'the needy'

Central to the stated child care policy of the Fraser government was the idea that services should be directed to children 'in need'. In practice, however, 'need' appears to have been only vaguely conceptualised. The usual way in which the government (through the Office of Child Care) addressed this issue was by publishing lists of the various groups it regarded as 'needy'. These lists varied from time to time but usually included: children from low income families, children from single parent families, children from families with both parents working, migrant children, children with sick or incapacitated parents, isolated children, Aboriginal children, handicapped children and children at risk of maltreatment. No statement as to which of these groups should receive the highest priority was ever given, nor was any rationale for selecting these groups ever provided (Jones 1983: 15). Since most children in Australia would have fitted within at least one of the government's categories of 'need' and since the actual level of provision of child care services was far below what would have been required to accommodate even one or two of these groups, service providers were left to decide for themselves how to implement the government guidelines.

The constant assertion that 'the needy' were the intended beneficiaries of the Children's Services Program fitted well with the Coalition's overall philosophy of welfare which regarded the family and the market as the primary mechanisms for distributing welfare, with government providing a 'residual' service for those unable to call upon family networks or to avail themselves of market-based solutions. In this way, publicly-funded child care was constituted as a 'welfare' service rather than a basic community provision. At the same time, the restriction of the definition of the 'needy' legitimated real reductions in expenditure which in turn affected the likelihood that those designated as 'needy' would gain access to the services.

It is important to note, however, that even the Fraser government had come to accept that the commonwealth needed to retain at least a minimal level of responsibility for children's services. Within the government, Tasmanian Liberal Senator Shirley Walters was one of those least sympathetic to publicly-funded child care. In 1981 she made a scathing attack on the notion that child care should be regarded as a community service, claimed that it was an 'appalling suggestion' and that 'every mother worth her salt would shrink from [it]' (*CPD*, Senate, vol. 89: 1457).

Yet even Senator Walters was prepared to concede that subsidised child care should be provided for 'the mother in real need who has to go out to work to support her family, the single mother or the mother whose husband is unemployed or who has a very low income'. The woman who 'just wants to go out to work and whose husband is well able to support the family comfortably' was the real object of her (and the government's) attack.

Several aspects of the government's policy conflicted in practice with its rhetorical emphasis on need. The policy of continually reducing allocations to the children's services area was the most obvious of these. Cutbacks in funding affected all users and potential users of child care services but had their most severe impact on groups such as single parent families, migrant families, those on low incomes and those with sick or handicapped members. Cutbacks prevented the development of new services, thus limiting everyone's chances of finding the services they required; and, because government subsidies to centres were not adjusted to take account of the effects of inflation, rising costs forced centres to reject children whose parents could not afford to pay full fees.

During the late 1970s the funding crisis in children's services became so grave that many centres were obliged to allocate places in such a way as to make their own financial commitments a first priority; the question of meeting users' needs had to take second place. Equipment purchases were limited, hours of opening reduced and highly trained staff replaced by those less qualified. Many centres had to 'freeze out those families most in need of care' so as to remain financially viable; other centres took the course of increasing fees across the board (Childhood Services Council of SA 1980: 121).

The fees charged by government-subsidised child care services became a big issue during this period. A survey conducted by Community Child Care in New South Wales found that in many centres child care fees were higher per week than those charged by elite private schools (Community Child Care NSW 1983: 12–13). In introducing the *Child Care Act* in 1972, Phillip Lynch, the Minister for Labour and National Service, had specifically noted the importance of government subsidies in enabling low and middle income users to gain access to services of reasonable quality. Reviewing the circumstances which had led to the introduction of the bill, he said:

> existing child care facilities were inadequate, qualitatively and quantitatively, for the growing numbers of young children needing them. Not only were there too few centres but in many cases the provision was only for child minding and not for the quality of child care appropriate to the educational, emotional and developmental needs of the young children involved ... child care which was beneficial to the child's overall development was prohibitively costly for the large body of parents, and ... the child-minding arrangements

which most parents could afford fell far short of the quality that was required in the interests of child welfare. (CPD, HR, *vol. 81: 2289*)

In contrast to this, the view which developed in the Fraser government was that most parents should pay the full cost of care. The Spender Report had recommended that families whose combined income was above average male weekly earnings should not receive the benefit of any government subsidy. Approximately three-quarters of all two-parent families in which there was at least one pre-school aged child and in which both parents worked had incomes above this level. What would have been the implications of full cost recovery for such families? The Family and Children's Services Agency (FACSA), a small unit which had been established by the Wran Labor government of New South Wales in 1976, attempted to answer this question by estimating the minimum weekly expenditure required to meet the needs of a family with two adults and two children and an income equivalent to male average weekly earnings. Their conclusion was that, after having met all essential expenses, such a family would have *no* income at all to pay for child care (nor for that matter would they have any spare cash for recreation, holidays, household maintenance or savings) (1981: 14).

Opposition to the submission model of funding

Another aspect of federal government policy which undermined its credibility as a champion of 'the needy' was its continued reliance on the submission model of funding. As already noted, the use of submissions had been a device much favoured by the Whitlam government and had been promoted as a way of enabling 'ordinary people' to have their say in the allocation of services, rather than allowing bureaucrats to make all the decisions. By the late 1970s, however, a better understanding of the ramifications of this funding model was beginning to emerge. It was a system which benefited those with the most time, resources, and knowledge of lobbying and submission-writing techniques, while it systematically disadvantaged those who were less well-off.

The pressure to abandon the submission approach to funding children's services came most strongly from New South Wales. Women in this state had never embraced the community development philosophy which underpinned the submission model and which was much more a feature of the Victorian Community Child Care movement. Unlike their Victorian counterparts, New South Wales women did not see child care as being about 're-surrounding families' or 're-creating communities' (two slogans used by the Victorian movement). They were far more inclined to see child care as being about enabling women to enter the workforce. They therefore took a more businesslike approach to setting up services.

The first salvo against the submission model was fired by Carole Deagan at the National Child Care Conference held in Adelaide in 1980. She described the community submissions approach as 'fundamentally anti-planning' and argued that the most needy groups in the community were also the most unlikely to write submissions.

Subsequently, the NSW Council of Social Service published *Scarce for Kids: Which New South Wales Children can Find the Services they Need?* This report, co-authored by Eva Cox, who was then Director of the Council, provided detailed information on the availability of child care in each local government area in the state. It showed the number of children aged 0–4, the number and type of licensed child care places, the proportion that were government-funded and the number of children per place. This study provided the basis for a rigorous critique of the submissions approach to child care funding. It showed that there was an almost directly inverse relationship between the availability of children's services and the needs characteristics of a particular area; municipalities with high concentrations of single parents, low income families, migrants and working mothers were the most poorly served in terms of government-subsidised child care. Only 28 of the 196 local government areas within the state provided *any* centre-based care for 0–2-year olds. Only one of these (the City of Sydney) had a realistic ratio of places to resident children in the age group. In the entire state, at a time when 15,000 children under two years of age had mothers in the workforce, a mere 403 child care places existed – a situation described by the authors of the report as 'scandalously and criminally inadequate' (Robertson and Cox 1982: 7).

The NCOSS study also showed the way in which patterns of service provision continued to buttress and promote 'traditional' conceptions of women's role. Whereas nearly every local government area in the state had some provision for mothers who stayed at home, or who were employed only within the very limited hours covered by pre-school sessions, more than half provided no services at all for those who needed more than six hours of care per day for their children.

Another New South Wales report, this one published by a government agency on child care needs in western Sydney, also came down strongly against any continuation of the submission approach. It argued that 'if the present system of distributing funds ... is continued, Western Sydney in particular and the urban fringe areas in general, will fall further behind relative to other areas' (FACSA 1979: 3). Aside from inequities in the distribution of services there were other problems caused by this funding model. The time taken to establish services was excessively long (many services had taken four or five years to become operative) and the construction costs of individual services were far higher than they would have been if some kind of standardised, streamlined process had been in operation.

The Victorian group, Community Child Care, did not support New South Wales' opposition to the submission model. In the words of Winsome McCaughey: 'a basic principle of Community Child Care is that you never set up something for somebody else. You help them to do it themselves' (McGregor 1989: 3). Another reason why the Victorians may not have opposed the submission model is that they were not disadvantaged by it in the same way as groups in New South Wales. An analysis of the pattern of funding during the first three fiscal years of the Fraser government showed that, although 34 per cent of all Australian children resided in New South Wales, it had received only 27 per cent of the funds; by comparison, Victoria with 27 per cent of the nation's children, had received 29 per cent of the funds (FACSA 1979). This outcome reflected Victoria's relatively strong tradition of local initiative, plus the vast effort which Community Child Care itself had put into promoting community-based child care projects and encouraging the employment of local children's services development officers.

The key issues – reductions in the real value of subsidies, high fees, the inadequacy and maldistribution of services and whether or not to implement some kind of planning approach for the development of new services – were widely debated within the children's services field. However, there was little dialogue between the government itself and interested groups. The Fraser government did not establish any structures to facilitate community participation in policy making and a general atmosphere of hostility and confrontation developed between the government, the child care movement and a number of other organisations committed to the extension of the commonwealth's role in social welfare and community service provision.

The most important achievements of child care groups during the Fraser period were defensive ones. The sustained resistance of these groups to changes mooted by the government (especially in the Spender Report) contributed to ensuring that the Children's Services Program was *not* handed over to the states; that full cost recovery was *not* introduced; and that the pilot scheme for subsidising users of commercial centres did *not* go ahead. The unsung work of Liberal Party women, the delicate manoeuvring of feminist bureaucrats and the rallies and other public activities of child care groups, all played a role in this.

The other important area of achievement during the period under consideration related to the forging of new alliances. Firstly, the Fraser years had witnessed the beginnings of an alliance between the older, traditional early childhood organisations and the more recently formed, feminist-inspired lobby groups. Secondly, workers employed in child care were becoming involved in advocacy for an expansion in the number of services and for increases in the level of government funding of existing services.

Notwithstanding these advances, by the end of the Fraser government's period in office morale within the children's services field had reached a low point. Despite the partially successful resistance and the formation of strategic alliances, funding had been significantly reduced, submissions for hundreds of new child care projects had been rejected and existing services were struggling to remain viable. The Fraser government had set a new agenda for the commonwealth in child care, firmly indicating its view that this service should not be seen as a mainstream social provision but should be restricted to those who could prove their 'need' in accordance with government guidelines. In keeping with this philosophy, the criteria for eligibility for subsidies made it almost impossible for families with two incomes to benefit. Yet fees remained comparable to those charged by elite private schools. Finally, in spite of overwhelming evidence that the submission model of funding created inequities in service provision and was contrary to the government's own policies of 'concentrating assistance and resources on the most needy', the government refused to take any responsibility for planning the location of new services.

CHAPTER 6

For Love and *Money*

> The development of a strong industrial consciousness amongst child care workers is important not only to ensure that they receive the pay and conditions commensurate with their responsibility for the physical, emotional and intellectual development of young children, but also to ensure that a significant group of women gain recognition of themselves as 'workers'. Such a development will make a major contribution to ensuring that good quality, government funded child care services become a widespread and ongoing feature of our society.
> *Brenda Forbath, ACTU Child Care Co-ordinator, 1984*

Until the mid-1970s, the groups which dominated the child care debate were concerned mainly with claims upon the state regarding the provision of services – in particular with the availability, type, cost and location of services. From about this time, however, industrial aspects of child care provision became an additional focus of attention and trade unions began to emerge as important participants in child care debates and campaigns. In the period from 1973 to 1983, the relationship between the trade union movement and child care providers and lobbyists was transformed. The level of unionisation and political activity amongst workers in pre-schools and child care centres steadily increased, necessitating the negotiation of some formidable obstacles – from the deeply ingrained attitudes of service and voluntarism held by most early childhood workers, to structural impediments such as the isolation of workers in small centres and the fragmentation of union coverage. Similar developments occurred, although on a smaller scale, amongst the home-based caregivers employed in family day care schemes. From the early 1980s onwards, trade unionists and child care lobbyists made explicit links in their campaigning between the amount of government funding for children's services, the wage levels and working conditions of the staff and the quality of service provided to children and their families. In this way, political and industrial issues became meshed and areas of potential conflict between parents and staff were minimised. Child care workers' wages and employment conditions were the subject of an important test case brought before the Industrial Relations Commission by the Australian Council of Trade Unions in 1992. This resulted in substantial gains for some workers. Nevertheless, burnout and high turnover of staff remain major problems for the child care industry.

The Industrial Status of Early Childhood Workers Before 1972

Caring for young children is the epitome of 'women's work'. It is a low-paid, low-status occupation, often perceived as unskilled. The American *Dictionary of Occupational Titles*, a volume which ranks some 30,000 jobs, ostensibly in terms of the complexity and level of skill required for each, claims that the job of child care worker requires less skill than a parking lot attendant and that of nursery school teacher requires less skill than that of trainer of marine mammals (Kapp Howe 1977: 239). These features of child care work, combined with the fact that collective forms of provision emerged from a tradition of charitable and voluntaristic endeavour, have hampered the development of industrial consciousness amongst workers in the area and encouraged their acceptance of low pay and poor working conditions.

The voluntary organisations which established children's services in Australia saw their work as having a distinct educational as well as a philanthropic dimension. Despite hostility and even ridicule from some quarters they consistently emphasised the importance of employing qualified staff and vehemently rejected suggestions that the work could be done instinctively by 'nice ladies who love children' (Stonehouse 1988). Alongside the earliest services, they set up private training colleges for teachers. Not surprisingly, the young women who attended these colleges were drawn almost exclusively from the private girls schools in the major capital cities. Their family backgrounds were comfortable: 'not necessarily, or even usually, wealthy ... but of such an economic position as to be able to afford first, the independent school and then college fees ... ' (Gardiner 1982: 58; also Spearritt 1974). Kindergarten teaching was thus regarded as 'a genteel occupation for upper-middle class girls whose families were in a position to support them ... It was a respectable "fill-in" activity for a girl between leaving school and settling into married life' (Commonwealth Department of Education 1981: 168). On completion of their training, graduates received rates of pay which were well below the basic wage. Indeed, according to Gladys Pendred, the Federal Officer of the Australian Pre-School Association, salaries prior to 1940 were so low that the work of kindergarten teachers was virtually honorary (Pendred 1964: 391).

The early records of the kindergarten unions reflect their profound ambivalence on the question of teachers' remuneration. Whilst acknowledging the fact that the low salaries resulted in a shortage of teachers, they also believed that those who chose to work with the children of the poor should somehow be above base considerations such as money: 'One dislikes very much to talk of salaries and grumble about their smallness in connection with work such as this, which really cannot be measured by gold or silver' (Kindergarten Union of NSW 1919: 9).

From the establishment of the earliest services, kindergarten teachers were keen to present themselves as professional educators and to persuade the community of the importance of employing trained staff. They did not, however, form unions or become involved in political or industrial campaigns to improve their wages or working conditions. The idea of doing so would have been anathema to many of these women whose professional identities were founded in notions of dedication and service to others. A tradition of pride in their ability to 'make-do' in difficult circumstances would have contributed to this attitude.

There is a wider context to be considered as well. Until the 1960s trade unionism in Australia was overwhelmingly the preserve of working-class males. In 1920, 48 per cent of male employees but only 21 per cent of female employees were unionised; in 1969, according to the ABS, the figures were 56 per cent and 35 per cent; and in 1981, 60 per cent and 48 per cent respectively (Rawson 1986: 25). Although some groups of women workers (such as the tailoresses) had developed traditions of unionism and militancy, kindergarten teachers were unlikely to have felt any affinity with them. Both class position and gender militated against the likelihood of industrial organisation amongst kindergarten teachers.

The ethos of the training institutions which prepared these women for employment did not encourage students to develop an active interest in industrial issues. Each of the five colleges (located in Sydney, Melbourne, Adelaide, Brisbane and Perth) had developed under the auspices of the local kindergarten union; the Nursery School Teachers College had been formed to supply teachers for the Sydney Day Nursery and Nursery Schools' Association. Staff at these colleges were acutely aware of the difficulties experienced by committees in raising the money to pay teachers' salaries. Whilst they might have been sympathetic about the low wage rates their students would attract after completing their training (their own salaries were far lower than those of their colleagues who taught in other teacher training programs), they are unlikely to have encouraged them to press for higher rates of pay. According to Ruth Harrison (principal of Sydney Kindergarten Teachers' College from 1967 to 1981), the attitude which the College encouraged amongst students was that the monthly pay cheque 'should be received with a sense of surprise and appreciation' (Harrison 1985: 354).

Before the 1970s, most kindergarten (or pre-school) teachers worked for non-profit organisations such as kindergarten unions, church-based committees or independent parent groups. Even if these bodies were in receipt of state government assistance (and not all of them were) this contributed only a small proportion of the total costs of running each kindergarten; the remainder had to be funded through a combination of fees and fund-raising. Demands for higher wages on the part of pre-school teachers would simply have resulted in higher fees and increased fund-raising by the voluntary committees. Consequently, many put up with wages and working conditions which would not have been tolerated in other parts of the workforce. Aside from their direct involvement with children, many were required to do cleaning, cooking and administrative tasks. Some pre-school committees 'dismissed' their workers during vacations and re-instated them after the break so as to avoid the cost of holiday pay (Edney 1983: 29).

It should be noted, too, that the underpaid workers in early childhood services were supported by large numbers of unpaid volunteers. Mothers were (and in some centres still are) regularly required to perform such tasks as preparing morning and afternoon teas, setting up equipment and assisting teachers with group activities. Working bees at which essential maintenance and major cleaning tasks are carried out were (and still are) a regular part of the pre-school scene. An ethos of voluntarism and self-help has pervaded the early childhood field since its inception.

The broadening base of pre-school teacher education and improvements to industrial conditions

From 1966 onwards, students undertaking pre-school training became eligible for commonwealth teacher training scholarships. This led to a slight broadening in the range of backgrounds from which new recruits to the profession were drawn. In 1968 the commonwealth extended its involvement by providing capital funds to the pre-school training colleges in order to help them expand their capacity. Under Whitlam the commonwealth assumed complete financial responsibility for tertiary education; university and college fees were abolished; and a system of student living allowances was introduced. As a result, all kindergarten colleges became colleges of advanced education – a change in structure which required the sponsoring organisations to relinquish control (Australian Commission on Advanced Education 1973). Following their integration into the general system of advanced education, the colleges were at last on a secure financial footing. Academic staff began to receive the same salaries as their colleagues in other colleges and students became eligible for the same benefits as their peers in other university and college courses.

At the same time as changes in the organisation and funding of teacher education were taking place, some improvement in the salaries of pre-school teachers was also beginning to occur. The sheer growth in the number of pre-school services during the 1960s was an important factor here, but of particular importance was the increase in the number of pre-schools which were operated in conjunction with primary schools. Historically, the salaries of pre-school teachers had been much lower than those of primary school teachers – despite the fact that pre-school teachers undertook a longer period of pre-service training (Fitzgerald and Crosher 1971: 13–15). This anomalous situation could only be sustained while the two types of service were separately operated. Such a situation prevailed until the late 1960s when a number of schools (both government and private) established pre-school education as a downward extension of their primary programs. In Tasmania, pre-school education was provided by the state, from the late 1960s onwards, as an adjunct to primary schools and all teachers were employed under the same conditions. In 1970 the Assistant Masters and Mistresses Association of New South Wales gained an award which introduced a common wage scale for pre-school and primary teachers employed in non-government schools. In Victoria, parity between pre-school and primary teachers was achieved in 1971.

Pre-school teachers welcomed the boost to their professional standing (and their pay packets) which resulted from their wages and industrial conditions being tied to those of primary teachers. However, these gains did little to improve the position of other staff employed in pre-schools, such as untrained assistants. Nor did they benefit staff employed in child care centres.

New Services, New Courses, New Workers

The entry of the commonwealth government into the field of children's services quickened the pace of industrial change and conditions of employment. The *Child Care Act* of 1972 had stipulated that services would only receive Commonwealth funding (set at 75 per cent of award wages) if they employed qualified teachers and nurses. This represented a considerable victory for the Australian Pre-School Association. The major affiliates of the association, the kindergarten unions, had lobbied for decades for the introduction by state governments of regulations requiring the employment of trained teachers in pre-schools. Their progress in this endeavour had been slow and uneven. Yet here was the commonwealth government not only prepared to insist that child care centres (traditionally regarded as custodial rather than educational services) employ trained teachers, but prepared to contribute 75 per cent of the salaries. The balance of the salaries, plus any additional funds required (for support staff, equipment and so on), had to be raised through the traditional avenues – fees and fund-raising.

In 1974, when the Whitlam government brought pre-schools within the commonwealth's orbit, the subsidies allocated for teachers were even more generous. In keeping with its view that free pre-school education should be made available to all children the government provided the total cost of the teachers' salaries. This dual system of funding continued until 1977. In that year the Fraser government ceased providing assistance to individual pre-schools and instead allocated a block grant to each of the states. Although the value of the block grant was less than the combined value of the previous individual grants, pre-school teachers themselves were not disadvantaged by this as state governments proved willing to step into the breach. Pre-school teachers remain the most privileged group of workers in children's services, enjoying not only higher salaries but considerably better working conditions than other staff.

The position of workers employed in services other than pre-schools was (and remains) more problematic. Although the *Child Care Act* continued to be the legislative basis for funding children's services, its provisions appeared increasingly anachronistic. For example, during the Whitlam period it became clear that many of the new groups involved in children's services did not share the Australian Pre-School Association's view that pre-school teachers should be employed in child care services. Feminist policy makers and community development advocates were particularly opposed to this idea. They saw the provisions of the *Child Care Act* regarding the employment of teachers in child care centres not as the laudable achievement of a group of underpaid and undervalued women workers, but as the self-serving accomplishment of a conservative professional body. They regarded pre-school teachers as ill-equipped to work in the more informal services (such as family day care, neighbourhood centres and parent run co-operatives) which were being developed. The part played by individual pre-school teachers and the Australian Pre-School Association in campaigning against the establishment of child care centres was fundamental to these attitudes. In the view of many influential feminists, pre-school teachers were narrow-minded, elitist and unconcerned with the needs of working mothers. The bitter struggle between feminists and the pre-school lobby over the direction of government policy under Whitlam did more to harden opinions than to produce any accommodation between the two sides.

In any case, regardless of the views of policy makers about the desirability of people with particular kinds of training being employed in early childhood services, there was little to attract pre-school teachers to the new types of services which began to emerge after 1974. Compared with employment in a pre-school (which involved relatively few hours of face-to-face teaching, ten weeks annual leave and time off to prepare lessons) the conditions in other services were markedly worse. Due to the longer opening hours of child care centres and the range of needs they served, staff usually worked shifts, were involved in face-to-face teaching all day long, received only four weeks annual leave and did not get any preparation time for classes. In addition, the emphasis during the Fraser years on giving priority of access to children with particular needs, meant that a high proportion of the children in day care came from families suffering stress of one kind or another.

From the point of view of policy makers there was yet another problem: even if pre-school teachers had been the most appropriate people to staff the new services and had been prepared to work in them, there simply were not enough of them. Even before commonwealth funding produced an explosion in the number of services, there had been a shortage of pre-school teachers (APC 1974: 7; Derody and Sheehan 1978). From the mid-1970s, many new training programs were initiated. The most significant of these was a two-year course known as the Child Care Certificate. This qualification, offered by Technical and Further Education (TAFE) colleges, was originally intended as a qualification for teachers' assistants, particularly in day care. The 'triple C' proved to be very popular and its graduates were generally well regarded. The course was designed around children in the whole 0–5-year-old age range and specifically took into account the needs of children in day care. Further, because of its base in the TAFE system, and the fact that its educational pre-requisites were lower than those required for teacher training, the 'triple C' attracted students from working-class as well as middle-class homes. This was seen as a particular bonus by those concerned about the narrow social base from which teachers were drawn. In 1982 the Australian Pre-School Association (which still had the power under the *Child Care Act* to accredit teachers) reluctantly declared that Child Care Certificate graduates could be regarded as teachers. This decision, understandable as it was in the context, sharpened one of the crucial distinctions between pre-school education and child care. The APA decision only applied to commonwealth-funded child care centres. It did not have any effect on pre-schools which, by this time, were largely state-funded. The APA would never have agreed that certificate holders should be regarded as equivalent to teachers if they were employed in pre-schools. The message thus transmitted to the community (and the profession) was that a three-year program of study at a tertiary institution was required for pre-school teaching while a two-year certificate from a technical college would be adequate preparation to work in child care.

From 1974 onwards, the number of children's services increased rapidly and, in the space of a few years, thousands of new workers were drawn into this area of employment. A number of developments in the early childhood arena were leading to an environment more conducive than ever before to the development of industrial consciousness amongst these workers. Pre-school and child care workers were being drawn from a greater range of social and economic backgrounds than before; they were being trained in large, state-funded institutions rather than in small, private colleges; and trade unions were beginning to show an interest in gaining award coverage for them. Further, the considerable debate at the time about the low level of wages in female occupations generally, might have been expected to generate debate in the early childhood arena as well.

Impediments to the Industrial Organisation of Child Care Workers

All these developments notwithstanding, concern about the pay and industrial conditions of child care workers did not become a significant issue during the period of the Whitlam government. The strong historical legacy whereby this type of work was done 'for love not money' no doubt played a large part in this. In addition, most jobs in children's services (other than teaching in traditional pre-schools) were relatively new and the workers had yet to develop a strong sense of their own identity. The fact that most of the feminist organisations in the area were preoccupied with getting services established and gave almost no attention to industrial issues is also likely to have played a part.

One of the most important factors holding back the development of industrial consciousness amongst child care workers in non-profit services was the system of funding and management under which these services were operated. Although the commonwealth provided funding for these services it did not operate them directly. Instead, it provided funds to sponsoring bodies, usually local councils or incorporated community groups, which then assumed total responsibility for the running of the service. This system, known as 'community management', was, in philosophy and practice, the corollary of the submission model of funding. Its purpose was to minimise government involvement in day-to-day administrative tasks and to allow local groups to manage their own services. Community management meant that a vast amount of work (from overseeing the construction of centres through to advertising the service, hiring staff, administering the commonwealth grant and liasing with state agencies) was performed by unpaid 'volunteers'.

Many management committees were totally unprepared for the amount of work they were required to do. Further, they were given no training and very little support (Alexander et al. 1980). Typically, the management committee was a very small group of local mothers who had come together because of a need to have some kind of child care service for their own children. The long delay experienced by most groups between applying for funds and receiving grants meant that by the time a grant was received there had often been considerable turnover in membership. Many groups were overwhelmed by the responsibilities attached to receipt of the grant – responsibilities which amounted to conducting a small business. It was not unknown for groups to actually return their grants (Deagan 1979). Of those who persevered, most had no conception of themselves as employers and no idea of their obligations to their employees.

The chronic underfunding of services (which, as we have seen, became even more severe during the years of the Fraser government) created additional problems. Government subsidies never entirely covered the wages of child care workers – each committee had to raise the balance from a combination of fund-raising and parent fees; they still do. Consequently, during times of economic stringency workers were sometimes asked to accept under-award wages and to forgo other entitlements in order to 'help out'. The ideology of community management – an ideology which conveys the message 'we're all in this together' – made it extremely difficult for staff to assert their rights. The close relationships often forged between staff members, the children they cared for and their parents (who usually formed the management committee) further complicated the picture. Most child care workers would have found it almost impossible to insist on their industrial rights knowing that this would result in all parents paying higher fees and some parents withdrawing their children for financial reasons. Management committees faced parallel problems. The difficulties of acting as an employer, whilst being deeply sympathetic to the claims of child care workers for better wages and conditions, were clearly expressed by the Secretary of the Neighbourhood Children's Centres Association of Victoria, Margot Beever:

> There is no doubt that salaries are insufficient and conditions intolerable, except to the very dedicated band of people who work in the centres. The issue is how to go about improving them. How does an organisation like a neighbourhood children's centre ... fit itself into a structure of employer-employee relationships in which conflict of interest is assumed? We have had to decide which side we are on in a battle we don't want to fight.
>
> *(CCC 1981: 12)*

Yet another difficulty confronting workers in children's services was the sheer number of unions involved in this area. A survey by the ACTU in 1983 showed that there were twenty-two unions covering child care workers and at least thirty-eight awards and determinations governing their employment (Forbath 1983: 40). Thus, in a small centre it was quite possible for each employee to be covered by a different union. This fragmentation led to two kinds of difficulties. Firstly, it impeded the work of union organisers since child care workers are thinly spread and represent only a very small proportion of the membership of the unions which cover them (which tend to be big unions, such as the Miscellaneous Workers Union and the Municipal Employees Union). It is extremely costly for unions to enrol them as members and not many unions have the resources to try. It is also difficult to build solidarity and a collective consciousness amongst workers who are so isolated from each other. The second kind of difficulty caused by the fragmentation of union coverage relates to the varied entitlements contained in awards. For example, staff working side by side in a centre might have sick leave entitlements (depending on which award they are covered by) ranging from ten to thirty-three days per year. An emphasis by staff members on adherence to award conditions and entitlements could thus be seen as divisive. Consequently, some child care staff become hostile to unions and industrial activity generally because they see them as undermining the friendly and informal character of their workplace.

Despite these difficulties, union coverage of child care workers grew throughout the 1970s and such workers began to become active in campaigns around child care funding. The reductions in government subsidies to child care services which occurred throughout the Fraser years stimulated many child care workers to become politically active. 'Funding cuts' were not merely an abstract injustice to these workers. They were a daily reality which meant a deterioration in the service offered to children and constant reductions in the working conditions of staff.

Convergence of Political and Industrial Campaigns

In 1978 the Neighbourhood Children's Centres Association of Victoria and the Hospital Employees Federation (the union which covers the majority of child care workers in Victoria) formed a working group aimed at three things: encouraging union membership amongst child care workers, informing parents about the costs associated with good quality child care and generating community debate on the links between low wages for child care workers and the status of women in society. This was one of the first attempts to come to grips with the industrial implications of funding reductions in child care. In 1980 the Neighbourhood Children's Centres Association set up its own committee on industrial issues. The responsibilities of this committee included running workshops to raise the awareness of management committee members about their responsibilities as employers. At about the same time similar developments were occurring in New South Wales under the auspices of Community Child Care.

Uncertainty about the future of commonwealth funding for children's services, generated by the Spender Report, spurred many child care workers to become involved in political campaigns. Two recommendations in particular caused concern. The first was the suggestion that the commonwealth cease linking its subsidies to the award wages of child care workers. The second was the recommendation that the commonwealth give priority to the establishment of family day care schemes rather than centre-based services on the grounds that the former were more 'cost effective'.

As previously noted (Chapter 5), lobby groups were formed in Melbourne and Sydney to oppose both the funding reductions under the Fraser government and the recommendations of the Spender Report. Both the Child Care Federal Funding Campaign (in Melbourne) and Children's Services Action (in Sydney) recognised the potential divisiveness of the funding cuts. They wished to diminish the possibility that parents concerned about rising fees and workers concerned to maintain (and preferably improve) their own wages would clash. To this end they disseminated pamphlets and information kits aimed at both staff and parents. These were intended to persuade both groups that the problems they faced (poor wages, inadequate subsidies, high fees) were political problems, not problems of individual service management. They urged parents and staff to take action such as writing to the press or to their local member, taking part in demonstrations and raising the issue of child care funding within their own unions (White 1983: 26).

Table 2 *Expenditure trend in Children's Services Program, 1973–74 to 1982–83*

Year	Expenditure on pre-schools $m	Expenditure on other services $m	Total expenditure $m	% Pre-school	% Other services
1973–74	6 479	2 495	8 974	72	28
1974–75	37 077	8 153	45 230	82	18
1975–76	47 029	16 941	63 970	74	26
1976–77	49 018	18 068	67 086	73	27
1977–78	45 994	25 203	71 197	65	35
1978–79	32 750	31 086	63 836	51	49
1979–80	33 090	36 136	69 226	48	52
1980–81	31 183	42 851	74 034	42	58
1981–82	33 005	47 355	80 360	41	59
1982–83	33 090	64 954	98 044	34	66

Source: Department of Social Security (1983), *Annual Report.*

The Determinants of 'Quality' Child Care

The dissemination of the findings of several major United States studies into the determinants of 'quality' child care and the links between the industrial conditions of staff and the service provided to the children, proved to be very important in maintaining the momentum of political and industrial campaigns amongst child care workers. The most important of these studies, a four-year project initiated by the US Department of Health, Education and Welfare, was designed to investigate whether and to what extent the experiences of children in day care were affected by features of the centres which could be controlled by government regulation; for example, staff-child ratios, group size and the education, experience and training of staff (Ruopp, Travers et al. 1979). The resulting report, *Children at the Center*, gave strong support to the employment of qualified staff by showing that there were significant benefits for children in being cared for by staff with specific training in child care and development: qualified staff were shown to spend more time with children, to demonstrate more affection towards them and to encourage more social interaction. Children in the care of qualified staff were more co-operative, more likely to persist at tasks and made greater cognitive gains.

Other research published around the same time showed that the working conditions of staff had direct consequences for the quality of service they were able to provide. Workers who were stressed because of under-staffing, because they did not receive adequate holidays or because they were unable to take time off were more likely to become ill and less able to give their best to the children in their care. As one

Canadian study concluded: 'unsatisfactory working conditions result in situations where workers can do no more than just cope. They can provide a safe environment, but they are unable to create the enriched experiences that they are trained to provide. Work that should be challenging and stimulating is instead frustrating and tiring (Judge 1978: 135).

A United States study of the relationship of the working conditions of child care workers to the high turnover rate of staff in the industry framed its conclusion in similar terms: 'Burnout ... is not just an inconvenience – it results in a lack of trained, experienced workers and creates morale problems for those left behind. Most importantly, continual changes in staffing limit efforts to build consistent, creative and responsive environments for children and their families' (Whitebrook 1982: 213).

Information of this type, enabling child care workers to make links between their pay and conditions and the quality or standard of service received by the children in their care, encouraged workers to participate in campaigns around funding levels and industrial conditions. It was as if staff needed reassurance that their actions were not simply self-seeking but could be justified as being in the interests of the children and families as well.

Family Day Care

Each of the features which makes it difficult for the workers in long day care to develop strong industrial traditions – the fact that most child care workers are employed in small centres which operate under a system of community management, the fact that close relationships often exist between the workers and the families of children they care for and the widespread perception that no specific training or skills are required in order to carry out this job – is very much magnified in family day care. Further, the fact that family day care is undertaken in the homes of the caregivers makes it even more difficult for them to see themselves (and be seen by others) as part of the workforce.

Family day care is a modern, professionalised version of the oldest and most widespread form of child care – private childminding. (In Charles Dickens' novel, *Our Mutual Friend*, the laundress takes in her neighbour's children to be minded, explaining: 'I love children, and Four-pence a week is Four-pence!') In Australia, the first attempts to regulate private minding were made in the late 1960s in Western Australia. Given the almost total absence of formal, licensed child care services in that state at the time, the large numbers of women who were drawn into the labour market were forced to make whatever arrangements they could for the care of their children. At the 1966 Census, 24.3 per cent of married women in Western Australia between the ages of 20 and 34 were in the labour force, together with 52.1 per cent of separated, divorced and widowed women in the same age range. At the time there were 15 child care centres in the whole of the state, only one of which received a government subsidy (Department of Labour and National Service 1970). For the majority, this meant relying on private child minders who were not covered by state licensing requirements. During the 1960s increasing concern was expressed over the standard of care offered by private minders – claims were made of overcrowding, poor nutrition, inadequate or inappropriate play equipment and even physical abuse of children. Accordingly, the Western Australian government introduced a system of registering private minders. This was intended to provide a minimal guarantee to prospective users of the service that the person doing the work was a fit and proper person and that the premises were suitable.

In the early 1970s, following a study of the needs of families in Fitzroy which showed day care for the children of working mothers to be the top priority in the area, the Brotherhood of St Laurence in Melbourne established the first formal family day care scheme. The Housing Commission at that time was moving families into the area at the rate of two hundred per week and existing services were severely overloaded. The Brotherhood employed Barbara Spalding (later a member of the Interim Committee for the Children's Commission) to examine the whole issue of child care provision in Fitzroy. Spalding advised that it would not be appropriate to attempt to meet the need for child care by building an additional child care centre since 'this would have resulted in the establishment of yet one more independent, isolated day nursery, built at great cost with all the same financial problems confronting the other day nurseries' (Brotherhood of St Laurence 1972a: 1). Instead, she suggested a more informal, community-based solution: a family day care scheme which would link up those women who wanted to go out to work and who needed child care with those who wanted to stay at home and who needed extra income. The scheme was regarded as a pilot study and was intensively evaluated (Brotherhood of St Laurence 1972a, 1972b, 1973).

In comparison with the family day care schemes which have since been established, the Brotherhood's pilot scheme was very well staffed and resourced. In addition to Barbara Spalding, an experienced social worker, it employed a full-time pre-school teacher and a part-time administrative assistant. The Brotherhood regarded this high level of support as very important for the proper running of the service, arguing that any future service would need to be 'well staffed, tightly controlled and generously financed if it is to develop into the sort of service that can be justified in child care terms' (Brotherhood of St Laurence 1972a: 4).

In its final evaluation report, published towards the end of 1973, the Brotherhood gave cautious endorsement to this form of care but advocated that it should only be established as an *extension* of a centre-based child care program, not as an *alternative* to it. The Brotherhood also warned against regarding family day care as the answer to the nation's child care problems, noting that '... it would appear to greatly oversimplify the issues to imagine family-based care on a grand scale providing the answer to the shortage of out-of-home day care places currently being felt in many Australian communities' (Brotherhood of St Laurence 1972b: iv).

Official perceptions of the caregivers in home-based day care: 'real workers' or community service volunteers?

Just one month after publication of this final report, the Australian Pre-Schools Committee presented its blueprint for the development of early childhood services. The Fry Report recommended that more than half of the children in day care should be accommodated in family day care schemes rather than centres. The report, however, made only passing reference to the issue of remuneration for caregivers. It commented that the money paid to them should be enough 'to meet the cost of food, insurance and "consumable" play material as well as to serve as an inducement to the mother to contribute to the needs of children and the community ... ' (Australian Pre-Schools Committee 1974: 100). Thus, implicitly, the caregivers were not to be regarded as employees in the conventional sense, but as providers of a community service who did not receive a wage but merely an 'inducement'. The notion of community service was also implicit in a statement made by the Minister for Education, Kim Beazley (snr.), that family day care would provide children from industrial suburbs with 'a home that has a very nice garden and very nice facilities [and] a lady who is not going out to work' (Beazley 1973).

The report of the Social Welfare Commission, *Project Care*, gave slightly more attention to this issue. It discussed two alternative approaches to the employment of family day care mothers. In the first, the woman 'incorporates an extra child or children into her household' but remains 'principally a housewife and mother'. In the second, the woman was regarded as a worker: 'providing child care is her principal function or occupation'. As the Social Welfare Commission's report noted, the choice between these alternatives was a significant one for decisions about payment, since 'if they are conducting a child care centre in their own home on behalf of an agency ... their remuneration should be commensurate with out-of-home employment ... On the other hand, if they are providing family care ... payment should be based on a rate for each child for whom they are providing care' (SWC 1974: 43).

The commission advocated that it would be more in keeping with the spirit of family day care for the caregivers to be regarded as housewives carrying out additional duties, rather than as workers. Accordingly it argued that the caregivers need not be paid at a rate commensurate with out-of-home employment, but merely an amount for each child minded, which would not relate to any award level of pay.

Interest in home-based child care grew during the early 1970s and the Whitlam government funded other research and demonstration projects into its feasibility (Burns et al. 1975; Tinney 1975). None of these examined the question of the industrial conditions of the caregivers, even though the high turnover rate amongst caregivers (and the consequent instability of many of the children's placements) was frequently noted.

The women's movement was divided in its attitude to family day care. As shown in Chapter 4, the New South Wales Labor Women's Committee had lobbied strongly during the Whitlam years in support of family day care and had endorsed the reservations expressed by the Australian and New Zealand College of Psychiatrists concerning young children in group care. Other feminists actively involved in child care politics at this time supported family day care for different reasons. Elizabeth Reid, for example, regarded it as a desirable way of rapidly increasing the supply of child care places. She was attracted by the fact that family day care did not require significant capital outlays (and thus fitted well with the government's 'people before bricks and mortar' approach) and also the fact that it did not require the employment of expensive, professional staff. At a time when well organised pre-school lobby groups were attracting the bulk of government funds into sessional services for three and four-year-old children, Reid, together with feminists in the bureaucracy, saw family day care as a way of providing desperately needed care for the children of working mothers.

In view of the criticisms which were later levelled at family day care, it is important to note that in the early days some feminists supported it precisely because of its potential to provide employment opportunities for women with few marketable skills other than their ability to care for children. While early childhood teaching was regarded as almost exclusively the preserve of young middle-class women, family day care was seen as a system which could recognise and reward the skills of a far less privileged group of women. From this perspective, the fact that it enabled women to receive some (albeit very low) level of payment for carrying out traditional 'women's work' was regarded as very positive.

Other feminists expressed serious reservations about family day care from the start. For them it embodied values and practices fundamentally at odds with the goals of feminism. Eva Cox and Carole Baker, for example, warned that family day care could lead to a situation where 'some women gain their freedom at the expense of their sisters'. They argued:

> at one level we complain about women being cooped up with small children on their own, and here they are with up to five. We talk about low pay and yet countenance women being paid maybe $60 a week [to care] for three children other than their own for up to 12 hours a day, with no holidays, sick pay, lunchbreaks or any of the minimal workplace requirements. (*1975: 38*).

They urged feminists to 'have very serious debate' about family day care 'as in its present form it can provide the basis for exploitation and isolation of a group of women workers'. As the expansion of family day care proceeded apace under the Fraser government, other feminists attacked it as 'part of the state's attempt to revive the stereotype of women as wives and mothers whose place is in the home' (Simpson 1980: 45).

The views of the majority of feminists, particularly those with young children of their own, were probably located somewhere between these positions. Very few voices were to be heard in support of centre-based care as positively desirable, particularly for infants and toddlers. For many, ideological conviction and their own private feelings did not match. While most women actively involved in feminist politics were prepared, out of principle, to support centres as a necessity, not many used them for their own children. One important reason for this, of course, was that there were very few child care centres in existence during the 1970s, and hardly any that accepted children below the age of two years. Aside from this, however, the image of the child care centre as an austere, regimented environment and the continuing community prejudice against women who 'dumped' their children in centres, encouraged many to turn to family day care.

Caregivers' perceptions of their industrial conditions

Family day care expanded rapidly under the Whitlam government and even more so under Fraser, becoming a significant source of employment for women as well as a major form of child care provision. Within a decade, some 6,000 home-based minders were caring for 18,000 children throughout Australia under the auspices of family day care schemes (Department of Social Security 1980: 3–4). Yet, despite repeated expressions of concern by child care groups about the pay and conditions of employment of the caregivers, policy makers gave very little attention to these issues. During the 1970s even trade unions evinced little interest in these home-based workers.

In 1980 the Family and Children's Services Agency sponsored an evaluation of family day care which was carried out under the auspices of the New South Wales Council of Social Service. The subsequent report, *'She's the Perfect Substitute Mother'*, became a major source for those lobbying to improve the working conditions for the caregivers. The authors of the report were highly critical of employment conditions in family day care. They reported that in many schemes a caregiver would:

> ... work up to twelve hours a day, five days a week, year round, with no sick or holiday pay. She normally has no organised relief from the arduous and constant job of taking care of small children, for as little as $25 per week. She is expected to be 'warm and friendly' and yet to be able to assert herself sufficiently to ensure that the child's parent pays her on time, and picks up the children [on time] ... She often has limited mobility and this may become isolation as the number of charges increases since travelling on public transport becomes proportionately more difficult, and suitable activities for three or four pre-schoolers hard to find. Finally, she may be expected to cope with sick or disturbed children with limited assistance from scheme staff. *(NCOSS 1980: 70–71)*

The findings of the study regarding the qualities which co-ordinators looked for in recruiting minders were of particular interest to those concerned with industrial issues. The desired qualities were overwhelmingly drawn from traditional stereotypes of femininity and motherhood: caregivers were expected to be 'warm, sensitive, loving women', 'adaptable', 'motherly' and 'aware of the needs of others' (Brotherhood of St Laurence 1977: 43). Moreover, the study found that prospective carers who showed concern about 'adequate remuneration or satisfactory conditions of work' were often excluded on the basis that such interest suggested they did not have the right attitude. As the authors commented:

> Day care mothers are selected on criteria relating to their personalities in terms of their acceptance of the 'non-paid work' nature of their tasks rather than their skills in caring for children. This would explain their reluctance to protest poor working conditions. While it is regarded as normal for applicants to enquire into pay and working conditions for other jobs, this appears to be a major and unjust disqualification for selection as a day care mother. *(NCOSS 1980: 82)*

Not surprisingly, given the criteria for recruitment, most of these carers identified themselves primarily as wives and mothers; they were uneasy with any suggestion that they were 'workers'. Committed to traditional notions of femininity, these women were frequently judgemental about the 'working mothers' whose children they cared for. Several offered the view that they (the caregivers) were the only 'real' mothers these children had. Group discussions with carers, organised as part of the research project, 'frequently centred around what were seen as exploitative parents insensitive to the needs of their children or of the carers' (NCOSS 1980: 40).

In some respects, however, the family day care mothers *were* conscious of themselves as workers and wished to mark out a part of their lives which was private and could not be intruded upon by the demands of the scheme. Many expressed resentment at what they saw as a frequently made assumption that their domestic routines could always be re-organised to accommodate the needs of others. Some reported that they were asked to provide services such as early morning care, late evening care, overnight care, and care for sick children – often without notice and always without additional remuneration. In one extraordinary incident, parents left their children with the caregiver for the whole weekend without prior arrangement (Denshire interview 1985). In summary, one of the much vaunted characteristics of family day care, its flexibility, was shown to be achieved only at considerable cost to the providers of the service.

Unions and family day care

Meanwhile, concern about the pay and working conditions of family day care providers was beginning to register within the trade union movement. The steering committee which oversaw the conduct of the Family and Children's Services Agency project included a representative from the New South Wales Labor Council – one of the first indications of dawning union interest in the area. In the same year, the Working Women's Centre in Melbourne took up the cause of family day care workers in a publication entitled *Child Care – an Industrial Issue* which was circulated widely within the Victorian labour movement (Working Women's Information Service 1980).

At the beginning of the 1980s caregivers in various states began meeting to discuss industrial issues. Initially, these moves were hampered by the structure of family day care, particularly the distinction between the 'professional staff' (co-ordinators, child development officers, social workers) and the 'caregivers'. In several states this distinction had been institutionalised with the formation of family day care associations which did not permit caregivers to join. The fact that caregivers were reliant on co-ordinators to put them in touch with each other sometimes caused problems. Not all co-ordinators were willing to do this, especially if they knew that the purpose of a proposed meeting between caregivers was to discuss their industrial conditions. Some were suspicious of discussions about the industrial rights and employment conditions of caregivers, fearing that interest in such matters had been generated by feminists whose real goal was to undermine family day care by making it prohibitively expensive (Denshire interview 1982).

Although some caregivers were beginning to take tentative steps towards improving their industrial position, there was little interest in forming a union or gaining an award (NSW Labor Council 1983). The majority of caregivers were opposed to this idea. Most, however, were prepared to support changes which gave them some protection from unreasonable demands and which clarified what was expected of them in the normal course of their duties. This view became even stronger as opportunities arose for family day care providers to compare pay and conditions across different schemes. Although family day care was a commonwealth government-sponsored form of care, the isolation of the individual schemes resulted in vastly different conditions applying across schemes. Co-ordinators who gave a high priority to the employment conditions of the caregivers had been able to gain agreement from the federal funding body, the Office of Child Care, to provide levels of pay and special benefits which did not apply elsewhere. In some schemes caregivers were paid extra money if they took children before a certain time in the morning or had charge of them beyond a certain time in the evening. Some schemes paid overtime rates if care was provided for more than eight hours per day, others paid an allowance if children had to be regularly taken to special appointments. Rates of pay tended to reflect the general affluence of the area. Caregivers who became aware of these disparities usually agreed that it was unfair for people doing the same work to be treated differently. However, for many, the establishment of rules, the codification of duties, the introduction of time-sheets and so on represented a threat to the nature of the service. These steps – rules, codes, time sheets and the like – were difficult in personal and emotional terms. They involved re-conceptualising as *paid work* activities which previously had been regarded simply as 'kindness' or 'helping out'. As a result, not all caregivers welcomed these moves. Some saw them as bureaucratic intrusions into what was essentially an informal exchange.

Nevertheless, despite reservations, there was a gradual growth in industrial consciousness amongst home-based child care providers. As with centre-based child care workers, the recommendations of the

Spender Report in 1981 galvanised a number of family day care staff into political action. This report was published at a time when government subsidies for family day care had not been increased for four years although costs had escalated considerably. The suggestion in the Spender Report that government policy should emphasise the expansion of family day care as the most 'cost-effective' form of provision, thus provoked considerable anger. In Victoria, a working group including both caregivers and co-ordinators made a submission to the federal government opposing the Spender Report's recommendation on family day care. The group argued that family day care was only 'cost-effective' because it was inadequately funded: not only were the pay and conditions of the caregivers inadequate but so were support services, equipment grants and special needs subsidies.

At the national child care conference held in Sydney in 1983 a spokesperson for this group put forward a proposal that payment for caregivers should be based on the untrained child care workers' award, with loadings for holiday and sick pay. This was the first time that an attempt had been made to establish a link between the payment for family day care workers and an award wage. As one delegate pointed out to the conference, it had been difficult for many of the caregivers to get to the point where they could publicly claim a right to adequate wages and conditions: 'it is hard to talk in monetary terms when the prevailing ideology claims that the special and unique characteristic of these women is that they care for children primarily because they enjoy it. To demand a proper wage is to somehow bring into question their commitment and integrity' (Wyse 1983: 35).

One of the major impediments facing family day care workers seeking to gain some of the entitlements of the rest of the workforce (such as sick pay and worker's compensation) was the commonwealth's contention that the caregivers were self-employed and therefore could not justly claim to be treated as 'employees'. This issue was resolved in 1989 following a case brought by the Municipal Employees Union on behalf of the Victorian Home Based Caregivers Association and Tasmanian Caregivers. The Industrial Commission found that the caregivers were not self-employed but were employees of the various sponsoring bodies. Consequently, the commission found that the Municipal Employees Union could legitimately seek an award to cover these workers.

In 1983, not long after the election of the federal Labor government, ACTU President Cliff Dolan presented the keynote address to a national conference on child care organised by NACBCS. In his speech he argued that 'by taking up child care as an industrial issue, trade unions were becoming involved in a wide range of issues which would affect the lives and living standards of their members both as parents and as workers in child care'. He went on to argue that in doing this unions were making a number of clear assertions:

> They are recognising the right of women to participate in the paid workforce on an equal basis with men.
>
> They are accepting that society has a collective responsibility for the care of young children and thereby working towards the establishment of universal access to publicly funded child care services for all families wishing to use them.
>
> They are recognising that both parents should be able to share the experience of child rearing *(Forbath and Dolan 1983: 12)*

The trade union movement had moved a considerable distance in a few short years.

CHAPTER 7

Child Care – an Industrial Issue

> Of all the issues which constantly recurred in discussion [with factory women], one alone stood as the most tremendous, gut-tearing, and paralysing enigma, to which there was no adequate solution – the problem of what to do about the responsibility they felt for their children. It far surpassed every other problem in the degree of anxiety it produced.
>
> *Helen Hurwitz (1977: 226)*

Historically, trade unions in Australia have concentrated on improving the pay and conditions of male workers and have disregarded, or even been hostile to, the interests of women. The resistance of male unionists to the long campaign waged by women for equal pay has been a principal source of conflict. Until as late as 1977, the ACTU supported the notion of a 'family wage' and sought to discourage the necessity for families to have two incomes. In keeping with this, the ACTU's child care policy called for child care services to support the needs of 'women who under present economic circumstances have to work' (Hargreaves 1982: 31). During the late 1960s and early 1970s, however, a number of changes occurred which affected the way both men and women perceived the relationship of women to trade unions. Throughout these years married women entered the labour market in increasing numbers, and, as women's participation in the labour force increased, so did their participation in unions.

The 1970s was a period of 'vigorous and often successful organisation among women in trade unions' (O'Donnell and Hall 1988: 11). In 1970 a Women's Action Committee was formed by women unionists to promote issues such as equal pay, part-time work, maternity leave and child care. The following year women picketed the ACTU Congress, demanding support for equal pay, child care, abortion, contraception and maternity leave. An Alternative Trade Union Women's Conference in 1973 called on the ACTU to draw up a charter for women. (The ACTU responded with a document which omitted a number of the women's claims and demanded an allowance for mothers to stay at home!)

The influence of independent women's organisations on union matters was strengthened in 1974 when several groups (the Women's Electoral Lobby, the Union of Australian Women and the National Council of Women) made their own submissions to the National Wage Case. Women were signalling to the union movement that it was no longer acceptable to them to have their interests represented by men.

The election of the Labor government in 1972 and the designation of 1975 as International Women's Year gave further impetus to women's groups within the union movement. (By this time, women represented 40 per cent of the workforce.) The Working Women's Centre in Melbourne was established in 1975, funded by a grant from the commonwealth government to the Australian Council of Salaried and Professional Associations (ACSPA), the peak council of white collar unions, plus contributions from a number of individual unions. The same year, the Women's Trade Union Commission (WTUC) was established in Sydney also with a grant from International Women's Year funds together with union contributions. Both groups acted as 'focal points for research, publicity and consciousness-raising around the issues of women in the workforce and unions' (Hargreaves 1982: 42). The Sydney-based group was to become particularly significant in promoting work-related child care facilities.

Meanwhile, women in unions were continuing to campaign for the adoption of a charter which would cover such issues as the right to work, one rate for the job, equal employment and education opportunity, child care, maternity leave, birth control, abortion and flexible working hours. Women aimed to have the charter adopted by the ACTU and as many individual unions as possible. Strategies were to be developed to implement its various demands. Feminists working in the various areas worked together with women unionists to develop the charter.

The ACTU adopted the Working Women's Charter in 1977, the same year that it finally abandoned support for the family wage. The charter provided the ACTU with 'a comprehensive and coherent set of policies on promoting the interests of working women through trade union action' (O'Donnell and Hall 1988 :12). It included the following statement on child care: 'the Trade Union movement must campaign for acceptable child care facilities and for support by government and local government bodies. Trade Unions should participate in the establishment of such centres which should be at low cost to the parent' (ACTU 1981).

Child care – an industrial issue?

Among the first unions to commence negotiations with employers over child care were the Clothing Trades, Food Preservers, Metal Workers and the Vehicle Builders. In 1976, in response to an attempt by the Vehicle Builders' Union to include child care in a log of claims, the Australian Conciliation and Arbitration Commission declared that child care was not an industrial issue within the meaning of the *Conciliation and Arbitration Act*. This led Linda Rubinstein, the coordinator of the Working Women's Centre, to comment: 'it is, however, an industrial issue where it counts most, in the factories, the shops, the offices and in the homes of the many thousands of women who would take paid employment if they could make arrangements for their children' (1978: 33).

Certainly a number of research studies were lending weight to the suggestion that child care was a critical issue for working women. Amongst migrant families in particular, where the rates of female workforce participation were far higher than in established Anglo-Australian families, child care was seen as vital. Migrant groups responded with particular enthusiasm to the idea of work-based child care. In a study of migrant women workers in Sydney conducted by Cox, Martin and Jobson (1976) for the Royal Commission into Human Relationships, child care was the issue most frequently nominated by respondents as their most significant problem in working or looking for work: 86 per cent of those with pre-school aged children saw child care as a problem. A further study of women employed in factories, this time conducted by the Centre for Urban Research and Action in Melbourne, also pinpointed child care as a major concern of migrant women:

> We talked with women who left small children (under 3) alone at home ... Other women told us that they and their husbands worked alternate shifts ... and that this was causing a multitude of social and family problems. Others ... had to pay someone they did not know to look after their children, and that this caused problems. Many related stories of young mothers becoming so worried that they had accidents or became psychologically or physically upset. *(Storer et al. 1976: 37)*

Three-quarters of the mothers surveyed in this study favoured the idea of a child care centre located at or near their place of work.

The Galbally Report, *Migrant Services and Programs*, gave further impetus to the notion of work-based child care. A number of submissions received by the Galbally committee pressed the desire of migrant women to have child care located at or near their place of employment. The Galbally Report advocated the establishment of work-based services, the funding of services run by specific ethnic groups and the employment of staff to work with ethnic communities to help them assess their child care needs (Galbally 1978: 24).

A number of studies conducted at about this time showed that children whose parents did not speak English were noticeably under-represented in community-based children's services. The reason for this was *not* that these families preferred to rely on their extended family and friends, but that they felt excluded by services which denied or failed to respect cultural differences. One survey conducted in Newtown and Surry Hills (two inner Sydney suburbs with high migrant populations) found that 'Ethnic families would use centre-based services if [there were] bilingual staff and greater cultural and religious considerations were practised by services' (Ethnic Child Care Development Unit 1982). Another Sydney study, this time conducted in Rockdale, found that although 30 per cent of children in the area were born in a non-English-speaking country or had at least one parent born in a non-English-speaking country, only three of the twenty-two children's services in the locality had a staff member who spoke a language other than English (Ethnic Child Care Development Unit 1983).

In 1976, a number of ethnic community organisations had received funds from the Office of Child Care to set up long day care centres. These organisations were to act as sponsors, in the same way as churches, local government and other community organisations. The services would be open to all – not restricted to use by particular ethnic groups. Nevertheless, there was considerable misunderstanding about these centres, with many people assuming that the services would restrict access to certain ethnic groups. In order to counter this misconception, and also to assist the sponsoring organisations to negotiate the bureaucratic maze that surrounded children's services, an Ethnic Child Care Development Unit was opened in Sydney in 1979. The following year, a similar organisation, the Victorian Co-operative on Children's Services for Ethnic Groups (VICSEG) opened in Melbourne. These organisations, as well as working to make children's services more sensitive to the needs of children from a range of ethnic and cultural backgrounds, have since become important focus points for campaigns in support of work-based child care.

In the mid-1970s, a number of spokespersons for ethnic communities began to criticise the funding model used by the Office of Child Care and its reliance on the community child care philosophy. Barbara Gayler, a worker with a Greek welfare organisation, pointed out that the only 'communities' which seemed to gain recognition were geographic ones. She argued that other groups, such as ethnic groups, should also be recognised as 'communities'. (Later still, trade unionists would call for the recognition that the workplace was a significant community for many people.) Gayler was critical of the 'idealistic and utopian' community child care philosophy, especially its assumption that all could participate equally in the running of services when in fact 'it is well nigh inevitable that the values of the confident, articulate, middle-class, white anglo-saxons will prevail' (Gayler 1976: 4).

A similar point was made by another ethnic community worker, Janet Elefsiniotis, who called for a re-assessment of the stress being placed on parent involvement by the community child care movement. The idea that all child care services should be managed and controlled by the parent users could be oppressive, she argued (Elefsiniotis 1981: 32).

The Ethnic Communities Council called for an expansion of services, an end to the submission model of funding and the development of policies for work-related care and ethnic-specific services. The council also called on training institutions to ensure that their students were equipped with the appropriate skills and insights to work in a multicultural society (Ethnic Communities Council of NSW 1984). The arguments in favour of work-related services and services with a specific ethnic focus centred on the needs of children as well as adults:

> Imagine the early childhood educator arguing the benefit of placing a young child in an environment that speaks a different language, serves strange food, has conflicting child rearing practices and often a very different concept of childhood. Yet this is what we have been doing to migrant children for decades. These children need an environment which reinforces and extends the development of their self-concept. There is a need to lessen the gap between home and centre so that there is little conflict for the child.
> (Levy 1980:14)

Work-based vs community-based services

Within the union movement, however, and also within sections of the community child care movement, there was considerable uncertainty about the desirability of work-based child care. Before any services had actually been developed, this notion was usually thought to imply a service located within a particular workplace, owned or managed by the employer and used exclusively by employees of that company. All kinds of objections were raised against this type of service. The most fundamental objection was that such services would be highly unlikely to embody the ideals of user participation and user control – ideals which were basic to publicly-funded, community-based centres. Another fear was that such services might not be subject to state regulation; in a situation of scarce public provision of child care, services run by employers could be used to depress wages or in other ways control the workforce. Yet another set of concerns related to children. The Victorian-based Community Child Care organisation was adamant that children should be cared for in their local neighbourhood, not at their parents' workplaces (CCC 1978).

The type of work-based child care which actually developed in Australia turned out to be very different from that which many had feared. Although there has been no single model, most work-based child care centres have a number of common features: they have generally not been run on a commercial basis, but instead have received funding from the commonwealth government; as a condition of such funding, services have had to be controlled by parents and staff – not by management. Further, all publicly-funded services have had to be open to residents of the local community; there have been no work-based services restricted to the children of particular employees. Work-related child care in this country has thus reflected the strong tendency of both the labour movement and the women's movement to look to the state to contribute to the solution of social problems. In effect, work-related child care in Australia has been simply community-based child care in a different location.

The first such centre to be established was Eden Park Child Care Centre in the Sydney suburb of Ryde. This was also the first child care centre in Australia to be built as part of an industrial estate. The developer, Tim Copes, built the centre as an integral feature of the estate at the suggestion of his wife (*Australian Women's Weekly*, 21 December 1977). He did not, however, wish to manage the centre himself. A newspaper article alerted the WTUC to the existence of the centre and the fact that the developer was seeking someone to manage it. The WTUC was chosen from among a number of individuals and organisations who applied to run the centre. The developer leased the centre to the WTUC for a peppercorn rental.

Members of the WTUC had a strong commitment to providing a service which would offer a low cost, high quality service to working women. Hence, they applied to the Office of Child Care for recurrent funding. After an extensive campaign, funding was received and the centre opened in March 1978. Its management structure reflected the commitment to parent involvement which had become such a strong feature of other publicly funded services. The management committee consisted of five parents, one representative of the Women's Trade Union Commission and one representative of the developer.

CHILD CARE – AN INDUSTRIAL ISSUE 147

Another of the early work-related child care centres was sponsored directly by the union movement. The Working Women's Centre in Melbourne, like the WTUC, regarded child care as one of its priority issues. From 1977 onwards it employed a research worker specifically to examine the issue and to encourage interest in child care amongst unions. In 1979 the ACSPA (the union under whose auspices the Working Women's Centre had been established) proposed to the ACTU that the two organisations jointly sponsor a model work-related child care centre. (In 1980 the two peak councils, the ACSPA and the ACTU, amalgamated. The Working Women's Centre then changed its name to the ACTU Working Women's Centre.) It was intended that this centre would provide the trade union movement with first-hand information on the issues, problems and costs associated with the provision of child care.

The location chosen for this venture was in Moorabbin, an outer suburb of Melbourne. This area had a high need for child care, yet (according to advice received from the Office of Child Care) no applications had been received from within the area. The area presented an opportunity to involve a large number of unions in the project; in 1977 there were 1,157 factories and forty warehouses in Moorabbin and 12,000 women employed (Cropley and Chadwick 1981). The ACSPA approached thirteen unions which had members working in the area, and received many positive responses to the idea of setting up a union-sponsored child care centre. In 1978 a submission for funding was made to the Office of Child Care and a favourable response was received. Between the time that the ACSPA was informed of the success of its application and the opening of the centre in January 1981, various activities were undertaken in Moorabbin in order to create 'a more receptive and sympathetic climate in the community, both for the centre and the trade union involvement' (Panckhurst 1984: 102). These activities included surveying the child care needs of employees in 31 workplaces in Moorabbin, establishing a group of local residents who were prepared to contribute to the management of the centre and preparing a directory of local services for children and families. The centre adopted a two-tiered management structure. A company known as ACTU–ACSPA Child Care Centre Pty Ltd assumed legal and financial responsibility for the centre and a management committee (comprising four parents, four trade union representatives, a staff representative, a local alderman, an ACTU representative and an employers' representative) oversaw issues of staffing and general policy which affected the day-to-day operations of the centre.

In the late 1970s and early 1980s, the issue of child care provision was taken up by all the peak organisations of the trade union movement as well as by a number of individual unions – for example, the Council of Australian Government Employee Organisations, the Australian Council of Salaried and Professional Associations, the Australian Insurance Employees' Union and the Victorian Secondary Teachers' Association. This was, at least in part, because from the mid–1970s onwards women had become the main source of growth within the trade union movement. In the eight years to December 1983, women made up 73 per cent of the total increase in union membership. In the same period, women's rate of unionisation rose by 16 per cent, compared with an increase of 3 per cent in male union membership (George 1985). These trends gradually pushed the union movement into taking greater account of issues such as child care. However, there was also a growing realisation that child care could not be regarded simply as 'a women's issue' but was in fact a matter of concern to a large proportion of the workforce, male and female. By the late 1970s the two-income family was becoming established as the norm in Australia, and women's wages were increasingly acknowledged as a basic element in the standard of living of many households. Affordable child care made it possible for both parents of young children to have jobs, thus clearly providing benefits to both men as well as women.

The Labor government and work-based child care

Although, as discussed in the next chapter, the Labor government which came into office in 1983 was committed to further expansion of the public child care system, it faced considerable pressures to reduce costs. One way of doing this was to develop cost-sharing arrangements which enabled employers to contribute to community-based services for the benefit of their employees. Such arrangements were consistent with the ACTU's advocacy of non-profit child care services based on parent involvement. Commonwealth guidelines to assist employers to become involved in this way were first announced in 1986. Under these guidelines, private sector employers were permitted to contribute to the building costs of these centres and they were effectively able to purchase up to 30 per cent of the places in a community-based child care centre and reserve these places, over an agreed period, for their employees. In order to allay community fears, the guidelines stipulated that centres were to be managed by a non-profit organisation which would include representatives of parent users and the local community. Further, an employee who left his or her employer (for whatever reason) would be assured of continued access to a child care place until a community place became available at the same centre. The government promoted the idea of work-related child care to employers by arguing that such facilities would improve employee recruitment, retention, performance and satisfaction (Department of Community Services and Health 1986).

The first company to take advantage of these new guidelines was IBM – one of thirty companies which had participated in a pilot affirmative action program conducted by the commonwealth government in advance of the introduction of affirmative action legislation. The impetus for IBM to become involved in child care came from management. The provision of child care was seen as an opportunity to boost the company's image in the community as well as an extension of its involvement in the affirmative action program (*AFR* 10 October 1986). Under an agreement entered into with Baulkham Hills Shire Council in New South Wales, IBM paid a sum of money equivalent to the capital construction costs of a new child care centre and, in return, was able to reserve ten of the forty places in the centre for its employees. Because the centre received Children's Services Program funding, all places (including those reserved for IBM employees) had to be filled according to the government guidelines. This meant that first priority had to be given to low-income families. Users were entitled to fee relief on the same basis as other users of commonwealth-funded child care services.

A few other companies entered into similar cost-sharing arrangements with community-based child care services. Generally, however, the response of employers to the government's initiative was poor. A 1987 survey by WEL of employer-sponsored child care showed that companies which had participated in the affirmative action pilot program were far more likely to have positive attitudes towards employer involvement in child care than those which had not. Almost all of the companies which had participated in the pilot program had considered providing work-based child care, had formally discussed the idea at senior management level and had developed a specific proposal; just under half were willing to make a financial contribution to the running of a service and had made an approach to a government body. By contrast, only one in ten of non-participating companies had discussed the idea of establishing a work-based child care centre and none of those surveyed was willing to contribute financially.

Despite their initial interest, however, most companies did not go ahead with their plans to establish child care. The main reasons for this (according to the WEL survey) were cost, the complexity of the state and local government regulations governing child care centres, the requirement that services receiving commonwealth funding be open to the general public, the difficulty of locating suitable sites – particularly in inner-city areas – the failure of funding bodies to respond to enquiries and general concerns about running a child care service.

Labor's 'industry initiative'

In 1988, the commonwealth government made another attempt to encourage employer contributions to child care provision when it announced that an 'industry initiative' would be established as part of the National Child Care Strategy (Department of Community Services and Health 1988). Under this initiative, 1,000 of the 4,000 centre-based day care places to be built as part of the National Strategy were to be set aside for employer-sponsored, work-based care. The government sought expressions of interest from employers, and stated that the annual cost of running the centres would be shared between users, the commonwealth and the employer. The commonwealth would provide fee relief of up to $70 a week per child (compared with $90 in other services) but no operational assistance. It was expected that parents would pay fees comparable to those charged by community-based services. In order to keep fees at this level employers would be expected to provide the equivalent of the commonwealth's operational assistance grant and top up the level of fee relief. Services were to be run on a non-profit basis with parents and centre staff having the opportunity to participate in planning and management. Children of employees who left their jobs could retain their place for up to three months – a provision intended to allow them time to arrange other care. Employers would be obliged to implement the government's guidelines on priority of access. They would, however be permitted to reserve *all* places for their employees.

To further encourage employers to take advantage of the scheme, the government announced that it would fund resource staff to assist companies to set up centres. If an individual company did not have sufficient demand to support a centre it could enter into a joint venture with other companies. Contributions made by employers would be tax deductible and employers providing child care on their premises would be exempt from fringe benefits tax. Employers in the textile, footwear and manufacturing industries and others with a large female workforce were the specific targets of this government initiative. Public sector employers and tertiary education institutions were excluded from participation.

The Office of the Status of Women (which had been noticeably silent in the public debates over community-based child care) and the Minister Assisting the Prime Minister in Women's Affairs, Senator Margaret Reynolds, gave strong support to this initiative. It commissioned research into the costs and benefits of employer-provided child care and distributed a package of materials to enable employers to assess the likely costs and benefits of providing child care (Office of the Status of Women 1989).

Corporate child care

Until the 1980s large corporations in Australia showed almost no interest in the family responsibilities of their workers. This has slowly begun to change. In 1987 the *Australian Financial Review* (31 March 1987) published a six-page feature article entitled: 'The new corporate dilemma: who's looking after the kids?' (A decade before it would have been almost unthinkable for Australia's leading business newspaper to publish an article of this length on child care.) The article claimed that a small but growing number of executives, both male and female, were beginning to make decisions (such as refusing promotions and transfers) based on their family's interests rather than on their own personal interests. This was forcing some companies to begin to think about the family responsibilities of their employees. Further, with women now occupying a greater number of management and executive positions than ever before, some companies were finding that the lack of child care was causing them to lose some of their most valuable employees. In response to concerns such as these, a few companies had decided to establish centres which were totally independent of government funding. Such services were, of course, usually for the benefit of senior, well-paid employees and were unlikely to benefit women in low-level, poorly paid jobs. This new approach to child care provision has generally become known as 'corporate child care'.

Undoubtedly the most publicised private sector initiative of this type has been the joint venture between Esso Australia and Lend Lease Corporation which led to the establishment in 1987 of 'Messenger's Cottage', a long day care centre in Sydney's Rocks area, catering for fifteen children from birth to age three. According to the Chairman of Esso Australia, the company decided to take this step when it introduced its own system of equal opportunity monitoring in the late 1970s and discovered that its ability to attract and retain women employees was 'clearly unsatisfactory'. Esso believed that the Australian government would sooner or later introduce some kind of mandatory equal employment opportunity requirements and, accordingly, decided 'to get ahead of the game' by introducing measures to encourage the employment and retention of skilled women. The success of these measures, together with the introduction of maternity leave in 1979, resulted in an increasing number of women expecting to return to work after the birth of their babies:

> Unfortunately, the shortage of long day care centres ... was resulting in a large number of these women leaving our workforce after taking maternity leave, and that was a real cost to us. Our figures indicated that it was costing

us about $100,000 to train a professional person up to the skill required to move on in the company over about seven years. That also seemed to be about the time that we were losing many of the professional women after they had taken maternity leave. *(Schubert 1989: 4–5)*

Lend Lease had made a similar discovery about its loss of highly skilled professional women. Accordingly, the two companies (whose head offices were located near one another) decided to set up a private service to act as 'a hook to attract and retain valued staff' (*AFR*, 31 March 1987). The decision to establish a private centre, rather than to proceed under the commonwealth's 'industry initiative' was taken so that the companies could determine access without being bound by the commonwealth's guidelines concerning priority groups. The process of establishing the service and ensuring compliance with state regulations was a lengthy one. Five years elapsed between the decision to proceed and the opening of the centre. Whilst it would be unreasonable to attribute this entirely to bureaucratic delays, Esso's Chairman, John Schubert, noted that 'the time and effort expended in arranging inspections and licences [was] quite unbelievable'. Schubert told a 'corporate child care' conference in Sydney in 1989 that establishing the child care centre took about as long as bringing a remote oil field into operation and was much more difficult.

Despite their initial difficulties, both Esso and Lend Lease contend that they have derived significant benefits from the existence of Messenger's Cottage. An evaluation published jointly by the two companies in 1989 claimed that, because of the centre, they were experiencing lower turnover rates, increased productivity, improved morale, reduced absenteeism and lateness and the earlier return to work of staff who had taken maternity leave. (An impressive list given that the centre accomodates only fifteen children!) What the companies have undoubtedly gained is an extraordinary amount of favourable publicity for a relatively small outlay. To renovate and equip the centre each company paid $30,000. Maintenance and rental costs have been shared between them. The fees paid by parents completely cover all other operating costs. By 1989 Messenger's Cottage had been featured in over twenty newspaper and magazine articles, five television news programs and a radio program (Esso and Lend Lease 1989).

Community-based child care groups such as the National Association of Community Based Children's Services and Community Child Care have expressed ambivalence about the development of corporate child care. However, such centres have not attracted the same kind of criticism from community-based groups as commercial centres because, to date, all centres established by large corporations have been non-profit-making and have provided services of a high quality. The major reservation expressed by child care lobby groups concerns the cost of the services. Centres which receive no government subsidy need to charge very high fees in order to cover their costs *and* maintain a high standard of care. Hence, although in theory these centres may be open to all company employees and are said to contribute to equal employment opportunities for women, in practice they often exclude all but the very highly paid. Another problem with corporate child care, from the point of view of community advocates, is the lack of parental involvement.

One Sydney-based group which is part of the community child care movement but which has taken a very positive attitude towards corporate child care is Child Care at Work (CCAW). This organisation grew out of the Women's Trade Union Commission and, for several years, received funding from the commonwealth government to assist with the establishment of non-profit-making, work-based child care. (The existence of CCAW is one of the main reasons why work-based child care has developed in Sydney at a far more rapid rate than elsewhere in Australia. The other reason is the very active support for work-based care given by the Labour Council of New South Wales.) The staff of CCAW spend a good deal of their time assisting companies to assess their child care needs and to develop appropriate services. They have supported corporate child care because of its potential to relieve some of the pressure on community-based services by catering to families who can afford to pay the full cost of care. They also take the view that since private companies benefit from the labour of men and women who have young children, those companies *should* be contributing to the cost of services which care for those children. CCAW encourages companies to include parents in the management of services (although it has not always been successful in this), it opposes 'for profit' child care, and regards its role as being, in part, to educate employers about the importance of providing high quality services which offer parents more than just a place to 'park' their children while they are at work.

Child care for public sector employees

While the establishment of child care in private companies has usually been motivated by management's desire to retain highly qualified staff or to overcome labour shortages in particular areas, within the public sector pressure has tended to come from trade unions and employee groups with quite different interests. In a sense there has been a mismatch between the attitudes of employers, the enthusiasm of workers and the preparedness of the government to assist in establishing work-based child care in each of the two sectors. Thus, the attempts by the Hawke government in the 1980s to encourage private employers to set up child care services met with only limited success. At the same time, there was little sign of private sector *employees* putting pressure on companies to persuade them to take up the government's initiative. In contrast, unions and workers in public employment have become increasingly vocal and well-organised in support of child care despite the fact that the special provisions designed to encourage work-based child care specifically excluded the public sector.

What accounts for this difference between public and private sector employees? In 1985 the Australian Institute of Family Studies conducted a nationwide study of the take-up of maternity leave entitlements. (Maternity leave has been widely available to Australian women since 1979. Approximately 94 per cent of women are covered by awards which contain maternity leave provisions. In order to be eligible, employees must have completed twelve months continuous service with their employer at the time they intend to commence their leave. They must also be employed on either a full-time or part-time basis – casual and seasonal workers are not covered.) The purpose of the study was to obtain a broad overview of the operation of maternity leave from both employee and employer perspectives. As part of this study, all women who had given birth in a particular week in 1984 were contacted approximately eighteen months after their babies had been born. The response rate to the survey was 50 per cent and analysis of the sample showed it to be broadly representative of the total population of women who had given birth in that week, although non-English-speaking women were slightly underrepresented.

One of the most striking findings was that women employed in the public sector were far more likely to take maternity leave than those in the private sector. Indeed, the discrepancy was so marked that the author of the report, Helen Glezer, stated unequivocally: 'the taking of maternity leave is a public sector phenomenon' (1988: 41). Glezer found a number of important differences between the two groups which helped account for the different take-up rates. Women employed in the public sector came from households with higher incomes (42 per cent had household incomes of $38,000 or more compared with 15 per cent in the private sector); a higher proportion of them than their private sector sisters had managerial or professional occupations (42 per cent compared with 11 per cent); they were more highly educated (47 per cent compared with 15 per cent had some kind of tertiary qualification); and they were far more likely to belong to a union (70 per cent compared with 30 per cent). Although coming from a household with a high income is not necessarily a predictor of early return to work after the birth of a child (other studies suggest that women whose husbands have low salaries are just as likely to return to their jobs soon after the birth of a child), the other factors seem to be associated with strong labour force attachment among women, including women with young children.

The size of employing organisations was also related to women's awareness of maternity leave entitlements and to the likelihood of any employee in the organisation ever having taken such leave. In the private sector 69 per cent of women who qualified for maternity leave did not take it. Of these, 45 per cent had no knowledge of their entitlement (Glezer 1988: 33). Women working in small private sector establishments were the least likely to take maternity leave. Only 16 per cent of employers with fewer than 100 staff had ever had a worker take maternity leave; this figure rose to 66 per cent in establishments with 100–499 employees; while 93 per cent of employers with over 500 staff had experienced someone taking maternity leave (Glezer 1988: 8). Large organisations presumably operate in a more bureaucratic manner, provide information about employee entitlements in a routine manner and are more easily able to adjust to staff taking various kinds of leave.

The widespread use of maternity leave in the public sector is undoubtedly one of the main factors contributing to the interest in work-based child care. It is likely to contribute to a culture where women expect to continue in their jobs after the birth of their children. The fact that women in public employment tend to have higher educational levels and more senior jobs should boost the demand for such services: traditional values about motherhood and workforce participation are associated with lower occupational status and lower education (Glezer 1984). The existence of career paths in public employment, hence opportunities for advancement, is also likely to play a part in the decision to return to work. That this is so is suggested by a study of maternity leave conducted in Victoria by Castleman, Mulvany and Wulff. These researchers found that women were more likely to return to their jobs after maternity leave if there were opportunities for them to advance in their careers. The clerical workers in their study had frequently reached the end of their career path at the time of giving birth to their first child. The longer these women had worked for their current employer, the more likely they were to resign when they had a baby. This led the authors of the study (Castleman et al. 1989: 16) to observe: 'it is not always traditional values that "keep mothers at home" but the structure and nature of work that operates to discourage their return.'

In 1985 the Commonwealth Public Service Board granted unpaid *parental* leave to commonwealth public servants. Under this scheme women could take up to 52 weeks leave following the birth or adoption of a child: twelve weeks on full pay and up to 40 weeks without pay. Men could take up to 40 weeks unpaid leave (Wolcott 1987). In July 1990 the Australian Industrial Relations Commission extended parental leave to men and women throughout the workforce. The availability of parental leave provisions in the public service increased men's awareness of their child-rearing responsibilities and contributed to greater employee pressure for work-based child care. Although the majority of public sector activists around the child care issue are women, a number of men have also been involved – something which is very unusual in child care lobbying.

The three groups whose campaigns for work-based child care are discussed briefly below (commonwealth government employees, nurses, and staff and students in higher education) illustrate the trend in the child care struggle to organise around the needs of particular groups and to put pressure on their immediate employers (such as individual commonwealth government departments, state Departments of Health and university administrations) to provide funds. The unions representing each of these groups have contributed actively to campaigns organised by NACBCS and other community child care groups against general reductions in commonwealth child care funding.

Commonwealth government employees

Attempts by public sector unions to have child care facilities provided in commonwealth government workplaces date back to the Whitlam period. Discussions between the Labor government, the ACTU and the relevant public sector unions took place as early as 1973 when detailed consideration was given to the inclusion of child care facilities in proposed new government offices. These proposals were never implemented, however, most obviously because Labor's construction program was abandoned by the Liberal-Country Party government which gained office two years later. In December 1983, with a Labor government once again in office, the ACTU re-commenced discussions with the commonwealth over the issue of work-based child care for government employees. In mid-1984 John Dawkins (Minister for the Public Service as well as Finance Minister) consented to an agreement with the relevant unions that new commonwealth government buildings would include provision for child care. When Senator Peter Walsh took over as Finance Minister the following year he reversed this decision (*Bulletin*, 2 April 1985).

In the meantime the Administrative and Clerical Officers Association (ACOA) was mounting a strong campaign amongst its members in support of work-based child care. In 1982 the women's caucus of ACOA decided to give the issue of child care priority. As a result, the Victorian branch of the union was delegated to conduct a preliminary survey. This resulted in a report documenting the widespread need for child care amongst commonwealth employees and strong support for work-based services. More than one-third of respondents, including two-thirds of respondents who were married women, said they would use a child care centre near work if one were provided. Two other measures received strong support from those surveyed. The first was the provision of paid leave to enable workers to care for children or other dependants in times of illness (ACOA Victoria 1985). The second was the re-introduction of paternity leave. One week's paid paternity leave for commonwealth public servants had been introduced by the Whitlam government in 1973, only to be removed by the Fraser government in 1978 on the grounds that it was 'unnecessary' and 'ahead of community standards' (Owen and Shaw 1979: 3).

The National Council of ACOA adopted a detailed child care policy in 1985. This linked the provision of child care to the implementation of affirmative action policies and called on the commonwealth to set an example to employers in the private sector.

> In view of the Government's clear recognition of the impact of family responsibilities on women's labour force participation, it is important that the Government, as an employer, is involved in the establishment of workplace child care amenities which will contribute significantly in alleviating one of the major barriers to women's full and equitable involvement with the workforce.
> *(ACOA 1985: Appendix 3)*

The Minister for Finance, Senator Peter Walsh, and his department continued to oppose the ACOA campaign. They argued that the provision of work-based child care for commonwealth employees would be too costly and would also be inequitable since workers in the private sector did not have this benefit. In addition, they argued that commonwealth employees were regarded by the community in general as a privileged group because of their security of employment and the fact that they enjoyed more generous conditions than private sector employees, such as paid maternity leave and parental leave. ACOA strongly rejected these arguments. Equity between male and female employees in commonwealth employment, it argued, should be of major concern to the government. Moreover, a considerable body of evidence pointed to the lack of child care provisions as a major factor contributing to the inequalities between men and women at work. For the government 'to raise the issue of equity *against* the provision of work-related child care would lead to a totally incoherent position' given the government's own efforts to encourage work-based child care in the private sector (ACOA 1985: 11).

ACOA continued to campaign vigorously on the issue of work-based child care and to persuade its members that 'child care is a union issue'. Commonwealth employees have not, however, achieved an overall victory on the issue of work-based child care. Moreover, the devolution of financial authority to individual departments and authorities has made the achievement of this global objective far less likely. The devolution of financial power has, however, opened up new possibilities. Campaigns for work-based child care have become focused on individual workplaces and in a number of instances these campaigns have been successful. Several commonwealth departments have established work-based child care and more services are being planned.

Predictably, the government's obvious unwillingness to provide child care for its own employees has been cited by some private employers as a reason for their reluctance to take part in the 'industry initiative' (*AFR* 31 January 1986). The impact of the government's attempt to inform the community of the economic benefits of providing child care has been considerably weakened, some employers say, by the fact that the government has not seen fit to avail itself of these benefits by providing work-based care for its own employees.

The New South Wales Nurses Association

In 1984 the New South Wales Nurses Association initiated a campaign for 24-hour, work-based child care for its members and other hospital employees. This campaign was initiated in the context of an acute shortage of nurses and widespread public concern about the impact this was having on the delivery of health services. A state government task force appointed to examine the factors influencing nurse recruitment and retention earlier that year had stated that the 'availability of child care facilities was universally identified as a significant factor in attracting nurses back to the workforce' (Stoll and Ridgway 1984: 5). The New South Wales Labor government, which called the inquiry, was favourably disposed to child care in general and work-based services in particular. It was under pressure from some of its own parliamentary members as well as some senior bureaucrats to take action in the area of child care for state government employees.

In August 1984 the New South Wales Nurses Association presented a detailed submission on work-based child care to the New South Wales Minister for Health, the New South Wales Minister for Youth and

Community Services, and the commonwealth Minister for Social Security. The association had consulted widely and gained endorsement for its policy proposals from the Working Women's Charter Committee of the Labor Council and the state branch of the National Association for Community Based Children's Services. The Nurses Association ran a very public campaign. Members of the association used every opportunity to argue their case. They gave radio and television interviews, wrote articles and spoke at public meetings.

Additional impetus was given to the nurses' campaign early in 1985 when the association surveyed its entire 33,000 membership on the issue of child care. Over 8,500 replies were received, making this the largest (though not necessarily the most representative) survey ever conducted in Australia on child care needs. Nurses showed a particularly strong preference for child care located at the workplace, thus 'shattering the myth that nurses' child care needs are best met by community child care in the suburbs where they live' (Stoll and Ridgway 1985: 2). On the basis of these survey results a second submission was presented to the relevant commonwealth and state ministers.

This submission included a detailed critique of the planning model introduced by the Hawke government, emphasising its failure to address needs for work-based care. To illustrate its point, the submission cited Royal Prince Alfred Hospital (a major teaching hospital in an inner Sydney suburb), where 4,500 staff were employed. Notwithstanding that nurses there expressed a very strong demand for work-related care, services in the area were filled to capacity and most had waiting lists of several hundred names. Under the planning model, however, this area was classified as one of low priority.

Within a few years of the commencement of this campaign, work-based child care centres had become a routine feature of most large hospitals in New South Wales. They usually operate for extended hours (approximately 6 a.m. to 11 p.m.) and a few are open 24 hours a day. Funding comes from several sources. In most cases the land and building have been provided by the state government, the commonwealth contributes operational assistance and fee relief, while the hospital provides administrative support and services such as meal preparation, cleaning, laundry, repairs and maintenance. Generally, hospital-based child care services provide long day care for the children of nurses and other hospital employees (including resident medical officers, administrative and clerical staff) and occasional care for the children of patients and visitors. They are not obliged to take children who do not fit into these categories as the commonwealth has accepted the argument that the hospital, with its staff, patients and visitors constitutes a 'community' in its own right.

It would be unrealistic to conclude that the establishment of these facilities simply resulted from the campaign mounted by the Nurses Association. A number of other factors were at work, particularly the severe labour shortages experienced by the industry and the state government's interest in introducing measures which would enhance its claim to being a promoter of equal employment opportunities. Providing work-based child care for nurses and other hospital employees was a good way of doing this. Because of the special circumstances of the industry it could be presented to the public as a limited measure which would not necessarily extend to other public servants.

Despite these special features, the achievement of work-based child care for hospital employees has been regarded by many workers in public employment as an important precedent. It is frequently referred to in submissions made by other groups of state employees and has boosted their morale and enthusiasm in seeking work-based care.

Staff and students in higher education

The first child care centre specifically intended for use by students and staff of an Australian university was opened in 1947 at Melbourne University. The provision of campus-based child care was confined to Melbourne for another 20 years until the newly-established Macquarie University (Sydney) opened a campus-based centre. A survey conducted by the Australian Vice-Chancellors' Committee a few years later showed that only nine of Australia's fifteen universities provided child care (Australian Vice-Chancellors' Committee 1972). The introduction of commonwealth funding for community-based services led to a brief flurry of activity in the mid-1970s when a number of groups applied successfully to the Office of Child Care for funds. By 1981 the Federation of Australian University Staff Associations (FAUSA) was able to report that all but one of the nineteen universities provided some form of child care. The laggard – Deakin University – caught up in 1983. Colleges of advanced education were far less fortunate; perhaps they lacked people with the skills and time to prepare effective submissions. Only 14 out of 57 CAE campuses surveyed by the Australian Union of Students in 1981 had any kind of child care service (Nicholls 1978).

One of the most contentious issues regarding child care in educational institutions has been determining the most appropriate source of funds. Should campus groups compete with the rest of the community for commonwealth funds provided through the Office of Child Care? Should the relevant tertiary funding authority set aside a specific amount for campus-based child care or should the institutions themselves provide (or at least contribute to) child care from their own budgets? Debate on this issue has revolved around whether or not the cost of establishing and running child care services can be considered a legitimate educational expense. In 1975 the Universities Commission, under pressure from campus administrators, students and staff to provide funds for child care, grappled with this issue:

> The Commission is conscious that the development of child care facilities at Universities represents an important element of support for the study programmes of numbers of student parents and for the employment of female academic and general staff. Opportunities for study for a growing number of student parents will depend on the development of adequate child care facilities for their children; the Commission recognises that in a very real sense such students are denied equal opportunities unless adequate child care facilities are available to them. It is also true that women will have equal opportunities for employment as academic or general staff only if they have available adequate child care facilities.
> *(Universities Commission 1975: 220)*

Nevertheless the commission decided that it would not make any special provision for the establishment of child care centres. Both it and the Advanced Education Council did, however, recommend that minor works grants provided to individual institutions could be used for the establishment of child care facilities. As a result of this decision there was some growth in the number of campus-based facilities. Without recurrent funding to meet staff costs and other on-going expenses, however, these tended to be makeshift and to rely heavily on unpaid labour.

Meanwhile, as a result of the abolition of fees for tertiary education by the Whitlam government, the number of mature-aged and female students grew steadily, thus increasing the need for child care. Whilst information on whether or not students have responsibility for dependent children is not available on a national basis, students unions at a number of individual institutions have conducted surveys. A study conducted at Melbourne University (Vowels and Beighton 1977) showed that approximately 11 per cent of students had young children. An enrolment survey of Monash University students in 1983 revealed that approximately 15 per cent of the student population were parents (Seth and Giles 1983: 25).

During the late 1970s and early 1980s, when commonwealth funding for new child care services virtually came to a halt, campus-based groups who approached the Office of Child Care for funds were informally advised that their submissions had almost no chance of success and that they should put pressure on the Tertiary Education Commission (the body which had replaced the Universities

Commission and the Advanced Education Commission). The Tertiary Education Commission, however, was just as reluctant as its predecessors to accept that child care was the responsibility of educational authorities. Whilst acknowledging that the absence of child care facilities could restrict access to tertiary education for certain groups, the commission 'doubted whether expenditures on child care centres could be regarded as strictly educational' (Tertiary Education Commission 1981: 201). To the despair of student organisations and campus-based child care groups it recommended that they should apply to the Office of Child Care!

Meanwhile, from the early 1980s student organisations seeking child care were gaining the support of academic staff through FAUSA. The introduction of equal employment opportunity programs in some states and the prospect of commonwealth legislation which would apply to all higher education institutions throughout Australia was one reason for this. Another specific reason for FAUSA's interest was the activities of a small group of women employed in junior positions in universities. Several of these women – Carol O'Donnell, Jan Craney, Lynne Davis and Lynn Shoemark – had been founding members of Children's Services Action in New South Wales. In 1981, as a result of pressure from this group, FAUSA made a submission to the commonwealth government on the need for campus-based services to assist both students and staff. At the same time, FAUSA alerted its members (that is, staff associations on all campuses) to the importance of child care in relation to equal opportunities, in both employment and education, for those responsible for young children.

One phase in the long battle with commonwealth funding authorities ended in 1984 when the Tertiary Education Commission officially sanctioned child care as a 'legitimate educational need', thus opening the way for universities and colleges to apply to it for funds to establish child care services. In order to do this, however, the institutions had to be persuaded of the importance of child care and the reasons why they should give this service priority in their funding submissions. Effectively this development shifted the struggle away from the central funding body and on to individual campuses.

Child care services within universities and colleges of advanced education have gradually increased in number but in an unco-ordinated and unsystematic fashion. Funding has been extremely patchy. As most institutions have a number of separate campuses (particularly since the amalgamation of universities and colleges into a 'unified national system' at the beginning of 1990), it is difficult to summarise the current situation. On the whole, however, child care groups at wealthier universities (such as the Australian National University and the

University of Sydney) have had the most success. While some universities make no contribution at all, at least one (Wollongong) provides total funding, including fee relief, from its own funding sources.

Undoubtedly the expectation that child care should be available to students and staff alike has grown enormously in recent years; numerous groups have sprung up to work for campus-based services. The University of Sydney provides a prime example of the explosion of interest in child care. This institution currently has five commonwealth-funded long day care centres (one of these is for the children of university employees only, the other four take children of staff, students and community members). A group of staff and students from the university's law school is aiming to have a child care centre incorporated within its proposed new building and there are at least four other child care groups working towards the establishment of child care services on outlying campuses of the expanded university.

Employer-supported child care has become far more important to the Labor government's overall strategy for children's services.

CHAPTER 8

New Players, New Rules

> By taking up child care as an industrial issue, trade unions are becoming involved in a wide range of issues which will affect the lives and living standards of their members both as parents and as workers in child care...
>
> The issue of child care is therefore being taken out of the 'welfare basket' as a service for the poor and needy and placed firmly into the category of a universal service.
> *Cliff Dolan, ACTU President 1983*

The politics of child care under the Labor governments of the 1980s and early 1990s presented a distinct contrast with previous administrations. Under the Whitlam and Fraser governments, interest in and debate about child care was largely confined to women's organisations, child care lobby groups and a small number of government members and public servants with a direct interest in the area. In a very real sense, child care was marginal to the main policy agendas of both the Whitlam and Fraser governments (even though it featured as an electoral issue for the Whitlam government).

Following the advent of the Hawke government in 1983, the level of interest in child care policy and provision greatly intensified. Steps were taken towards integrating child care with key areas of government policy, notably labour market strategies and social security reform. Even more significantly, under the Accord negotiated between the government and the trade union movement, child care was defined as an important part of the social wage. The Children's Services' Program became of interest to far more community groups, trade unions, government ministers and departments than ever before.

The Political Context of Child Care Policy Development

The attention given to child care under the Hawke government can largely be attributed to two features of the new political environment: the emergence of corporatist political structures involving the trade union movement, employers and the government, and the new priority given to women and 'women's issues' within the Labor Party.

The trade union movement and the Accord

In the months leading up to the 1983 election an agreement, or 'Accord' as it was termed, was negotiated between the ACTU and the Labor Party. The agreement was similar to compacts made between social democratic governments and labour organisations in a number of European countries. The centrepiece of the Accord was the unions' acceptance of wage restraint in return for increases in the social wage (government-provided benefits and services), the introduction of policies designed to assist growth and employment opportunities and efforts to improve the relative position of low-paid workers. This trade-off represented an implicit acceptance of the view that the wage gains which might have been achieved by industrially strong unions would have been won only at the expense of less militant and well-organised sections of the workforce. It also represented an acknowledgment that wage gains could easily be eroded by high levels of taxation, inflation and reduced social wage outlays. Under the Accord, the ACTU acquired greater influence than ever before over the broad contours of social and economic policy. A number of tripartite organisations involving unions, employers and government were established, most notably the Economic Planning and Advisory Council. These have provided the union movement with opportunities to influence economic and industry policy. Although it has subsequently been modified and re-negotiated several times, the Accord continues to provide the framework within which the union movement and the government have operated.

The new political climate also led to changes in the way that 'women's issues' have been pursued *within* the labour movement. As already noted, during the 1970s women workers succeeded in bringing a number of issues to the attention of the union movement and even achieved some important policy changes (particularly in the areas of equal pay and child care). However, the implementation of these policy changes was not always pursued with as much vigour as they might have been. According to Anna Booth and Linda Rubinstein, two prominent feminist union activists, in the early 1980s 'women were pushing against a great wall of apathy from male unionists', with policy debates on women's issues at ACTU Congresses 'notable for the inattention of most delegates' (Booth and Rubinstein 1990: 128). However, the acceleration of changes in the membership base of the union movement (particularly the decline of blue collar male unionism and the growth of female and white collar union membership), together with the determined efforts of a number of activists to promote women's issues, gradually resulted in a climate where women's interests as workers were more likely to be seriously addressed by the trade union movement. Women even made some forays into the heart of union power – the ACTU executive. In 1983, Jennie George (a representative of the Australian Teachers' Federation) became the first woman to be elected to the ACTU executive. By 1990, the 39-member executive included seven women.

Following a lengthy campaign by trade union women, the ACTU in 1984 adopted an Action Program for Women Workers based on the Working Women's Charter and the ACTU Women's Policy. The Action Program set out the priorities of the ACTU in relation to women workers and strategies that might be adopted to achieve them. The objectives include parental leave and flexible working arrangements for workers with family responsibilities, improved provision of child care, equal pay, equal employment opportunity and affirmative action, and increased involvement of women in the trade union movement. The Action Program aimed to locate issues of prime concern to women within the broader concerns of the Australian labour movement: 'it sets women's issues firmly within the general strategy of the trade union movement and integrates them into the work of most of the ACTU's officers' (Booth and Rubinstein 1990: 129–30).

Child care was one of the policy areas singled out for mention in the original agreement between the Labor government and the unions and it consistently featured in the social wage claims put forward by the union movement subsequently. The ACTU took up the child care issue in a variety of ways. It pressed for increases in the level of provision of community-based and, especially, work-related services, and urged the government to ensure that fees in subsidised services were kept at levels which could reasonably be afforded by low and middle income families. In addition, an ACTU campaign to improve the position of the low-paid identified child care workers as one of the major groups to be assisted and resulted in the mounting of a major test case concerning child care workers' salaries and conditions. Generally, the goals of the trade union movement and child care lobby groups have been consistent with one another. However, as will be discussed in the next chapter, the decision of the ACTU Working Women's Centre to support the government's extension of fee relief subsidies to the users of commercial child care services, caused some tensions between the two groups.

The ALP: 'Not just "a working man's party"?'

In the late 1970s the Labor Party began to pay serious attention to women both as voters and as electoral candidates. The Whitlam government had initiated reforms in a number of areas of concern to women but there was a feeling amongst many feminists that ALP policies were inadequate and that, regardless of written policies, there was insufficient commitment within the party to the issues which women were placing on the political agenda. Furthermore, there were accusations of discrimination against women within the ALP. In particular, women claimed that it was far more difficult for them than for men to gain preselection for winnable seats (Sawer and Simms 1984: 123–4).

Following the Labor Party's electoral defeat in 1977, a committee of inquiry was established to investigate and report on: 'the changing social, economic and demographic structure of the community'; ways of 'maximising the involvement and satisfaction of Party members'; and ways of 'communicating the policies and ideals of the Party into [sic] the Australian community' (ALP National Committee of Inquiry 1979: 5). In short, the Labor Party wanted to know why it had lost the election and what it should do to enhance its prospects of winning the next one. In its report, the committee of inquiry pointed amongst other things to the under-representation of women in all party structures and in parliaments throughout Australia. (At that time, there was not a single female Labor Party member in the House of Representatives.) The report also noted that Labor's vote was lower amongst women than men and suggested that it was time to present the ALP as 'not just "a working man's party"' (ALP National Committee of Inquiry 1979: 38). The committee suggested a broad program of affirmative action designed to increase the representation of women at all levels of the party. Guidelines for the implementation of these recommendations were endorsed at a special national executive meeting held in 1981. The following year the National Conference of the ALP included a special section on 'Women' in the party's platform. This stated, in part, that:

> The ALP recognises that Australian women do not yet experience total equality with men nor full participation in all aspects of our society. The special disadvantages of Aboriginal women, migrant women, disabled women and isolated women are also recognised ... In office, Labor will take all legislative and administrative steps including the introduction of affirmative action programmes to ensure that these problems and disadvantages are overcome; such reforms will recognise the rights of women to participate fully in all aspects of political and economic life, the crucial contribution of women to family life and the special needs of women who are childbearers.
> *(quoted in Sawer 1990: 63)*

Later that year the ALP launched a women's policy, described by one political scientist with a special interest in women as 'the most comprehensive and systematic ever put forward by an Australian political party' (Sawer 1990: 63). It included extensive discussion about women's employment, education, income security, health, housing, and access to legal services. Specific commitments were made in each of these areas. In the 1983 federal election, which brought the Hawke government to power, Labor was widely believed to have received the same level of support from female as from male voters.

Partly as a result of the affirmative action campaign within the ALP, there has been a gradual increase in the number of women pre-selected for winnable seats and elected to parliament. Before the 1970s the majority of women entering Australian parliaments came from the non-Labor parties. This pattern has now been reversed. Furthermore, most of the new women Labor members of parliament identified themselves as feminists and were keen to pursue the implementation of the party's policies on women, particularly those dealing with affirmative action and child care. (For example, Jeanette McHugh, elected to parliament in 1983, was the first New South Wales woman to represent the Labor Party in the House of Representatives. She was one of those who, in 1973, had travelled to Surfers Paradise in order to persuade the Labor Party Conference to change its policy on child care.) Although most women Labor MPs, like their male colleagues, are aligned with one or other of the party's factions, they have made strong efforts to minimise their factional differences and to work together in support of women's policy issues. According to Marian Sawer:

> Women members of federal Caucus meet together weekly during sitting weeks as the Co-ordinating Committee on the Status of Women. During the first couple of years of the Hawke Government, each woman on the committee was responsible for monitoring two or three federal Ministers to ensure that their statements were consistent with Government objectives in relation to women. Women MPs also participate in the National Status of Women Platform Committee (chaired by a woman member of the National Executive) which monitors the work of all other platform committees for the impact of their policies on women. *(1990: 66)*

Labour Market and Social Security Policies

Under the Hawke government child care policy began to be considered in relation to the broader policies and concerns, particularly labour market and social security policies. This represented an important change. No longer was child care an isolated policy issue of interest mainly to feminists on the one hand and traditional early childhood organisations on the other. Instead it was becoming integral to a number of the government's social and economic policies and of interest to a far broader range of community groups, trade unions, policy makers and government ministers than ever before.

Women's employment

The expansion of job opportunities for both men and women between 1983 and 1989 was one of the major achievements of the Hawke government. More than 1.5 million new jobs were created in these years and 56 per cent of them were filled by women. Slightly more than half of the new jobs occupied by women were full-time: women accounted for 46 per cent of full-time employment growth and 77 per cent of part-time employment growth over the period. Other indicators also suggest a strengthening of women's employment situation. During the period under consideration the total number of women employed rose by over 600,000 or 27 per cent, and women's rate of workforce participation rose from 42 to 51 per cent. (Men's participation rate actually declined over this period from 78 to 75 per cent, largely because of the reduction in participation by men aged 55–64.) Women were also recorded as having declining levels of unemployment (from 10 per cent to 7 per cent) and the number of women classified as hidden unemployed or discouraged job seekers was also substantially reduced (Department of Education, Employment and Training 1989).

During these years women were undoubtedly the star performers in the Australian labour market – in terms of participation, if not in terms of pay rates. Within the broad category of 'women', moreover, the highest rates of growth, both in labour force participation and numbers employed, were experienced by married women with children under school age. Between 1984 and 1988 the participation rate for this group grew by 32 per cent, compared with 19 per cent for all married women with dependent children and 10 per cent for those with no dependents. By 1988, 45 per cent of women with children aged four years or under were in the labour force. Twenty per cent of all married women in the labour force had children under four years (Maas 1989).

These figures, however, tell only part of the story about women's employment. Despite the significant growth in women's participation rates, the structural characteristics of the female labour force have not changed significantly. Women are still overwhelmingly concentrated in low-paid work in a limited number of occupations and industries. Indeed, some studies have suggested that gender segregation in the Australian labour market has actually increased slightly over the last two decades (Karmel and MacLachlan 1986). Women still earn considerably less than men although the female/male wages ratio is much more favourable in Australia than in countries with histories of non-centralised, or enterprise level, wage bargaining. The present ratio can partly be explained by women's location in the labour force, particularly their heavy dependence on part-time work. However, even when full-time workers are considered and overtime payments excluded, adult women still receive only 83 per cent of male earnings. There are differences, too, in the impact of age and experience on male and female earnings. As men get older and gain more experience in the labour force their earnings tend to increase; a 40-year-old, full-time male employee earns, on average, 20 per cent more than a 25-year-old male. In contrast, as women get older their earnings tend to decrease; a 40-year-old female employee earns, on average, 10 per cent less than her 25-year-old female counterpart (Anstie et al. 1988).

The fact that women continue to carry the major responsibility for child care is one of the primary reasons for their disadvantaged position in the labour market and lower earnings. Women with children are far more likely than other women (or men) to work part-time, particularly if their youngest child is below school age. Statistics on hidden unemployment also show that the absence of affordable child care is one of the major reasons for women not actively seeking work.

The Labor government introduced a number of legislative measures designed to improve the position of women in the labour market. In 1986 it passed the *Affirmative Action (Equal Opportunity for Women) Act* requiring private sector employers with more than 100 employees and all higher education institutions to introduce equal employment and affirmative action polices for women. This complemented the *Public Service Reform Act 1984*, which introduced equal employment policies into the commonwealth public service and the various state acts concerning equal employment in the public sector.

Regrettably, however, the commonwealth government's affirmative action programs do not directly address the issue of child care provision. Although it has exhorted private employers to provide child care services for their staff, and has introduced tax concessions and other measures to encourage them to do so, the commonwealth has not set an example by providing such services in the public sector – despite considerable union pressure to do so. The government has, however, introduced new guidelines governing access to long day care and family day care services provided through the Children's Services Program. Priority of access to these services has, since 1986, been given to working parents and those studying or training in order to enter the labour market. Low income families have priority within this category.

An interesting sidelight on the relationship between employment issues and child care provision is that in recent years there has been explicit recognition of the direct job creation potential of child care services. New services create short-term jobs in the building and construction industries and long-term jobs for teachers, child care certificate workers, cooks, cleaners and clerical assistants. The Labor government in Victoria, under John Cain, placed particular emphasis on the employment creation aspect of child care. The announcement of the first round of new services under the planning model in Victoria stressed that, in addition to increasing the stock of subsidised child care places by 25 per cent, the new services would create 250 permanent full-time jobs in child care centres, 100 part-time jobs in after-school care centres and hundreds of construction jobs in the building and renovation of centres (*Labor Star* September 1984).

The social security review: facilitating workforce participation by sole parents

The intensive review of social security initiated by the Minister for Social Security, Brian Howe, in 1986 and carried out under the leadership of feminist sociologist and policy analyst Bettina Cass, also contributed to the focus on child care provision. The review stimulated debate and policy change in a number of areas including the crucial one of facilitating the entry of welfare recipients – especially sole parents – into the labour force.

From the mid-1970s to the mid-1980s Australia's sole parent population increased by 73 per cent, from 183,000 to 316,400, while the number of two-parent families with dependent children rose by only 4 per cent to 1,884,400 (Raymond 1987: 31). Over the same period there was a sharp increase in the proportion of sole parents reliant on commonwealth income support. Not surprisingly, this growth in dependence on government support was paralleled by a decline in the labour force participation rates of both male and female sole parents. From 1975 to 1983 the proportion of female sole parents in the labour force declined from 48 per cent to 39 per cent; for male sole parents the decline was from 93 per cent to 80 per cent. Between 1983 (the year in which the Hawke Labor government was elected) and the end of the decade there was a steady increase in the workforce participation of sole parents.

Research studies have shown that a high proportion of sole parents wish to have a job. The barriers to their workforce participation range from low self-esteem and lack of self-confidence to the costs of working, including the poverty traps which reduce the overall benefit of undertaking paid work. Research has also shown that the lack of appropriate, affordable child care is one of the most important workforce barriers confronting sole parents. According to Australian Bureau of Statistics data, 56 per cent of sole mothers who wanted work and could start within four weeks were not actively seeking jobs because their children were too young or they could not find suitable child care (Raymond 1987: 86). A study commissioned by the Department of Social Security from Australian Market Research also showed that more than half of those not currently working saw child care as the main factor inhibiting them from seeking employment (Australian Market Research 1986). A smaller study carried out for the Social Security Review showed that 60 per cent of sole parents saw child care as the major barrier to workforce participation. According to the author of this report child care was unequivocally 'the most commonly cited workforce barrier' (Frey 1986).

Under Labor, major changes have occurred in policies towards sole parents. The government has made clear its view that it is undesirable for sole parents to remain outside the labour force for lengthy periods of time. One indication of this was the announcement in 1987 that eligibility for the supporting parent's benefit would be restricted to those whose youngest child is below sixteen years of age. (Previously, the benefit was available until the youngest child reached twenty-four years of age.) Another indication was the decision to phase out the special pension which was previously payable to widows whose dependent children had grown up. The existence of this pension reflected the assumption that middle-aged women who had raised children, and who no longer had a spouse to support them, had an inherent right to financial support from the community. Although both of these decisions met with some community protest, it was generally accepted that the benefits to women of being in paid employment outweigh the benefits of reliance on government assistance.

A number of research reports had demonstrated the strong desire of women, including those with young children, to undertake paid work in preference to long-term dependence on welfare (Montague and Stephens 1985). The policies initiated under the Hawke government do not attempt to compel sole parent pensioners with young children to join the workforce (as has been done in some parts of the United States of America); rather, they encourage and facilitate workforce participation where this is desired by sole parents themselves. In general, the policies have been designed to smooth the transition between dependence on benefits and workforce participation and to remove the 'poverty traps' and other factors which previously discouraged this move. In 1988 the government introduced Jobs,

Education and Training (JET), a scheme aimed at providing education, training and other forms of assistance to enable single parents to enter the workforce. Child care provision is an important component of JET.

Policies for workers with family responsibilities

Another change in the context of child care policy under Labor was the ratification in 1990 of International Labor Organisation Convention 156 'Equal Opportunities and Equal Treatment for Men and Women Workers: Workers with Family Responsibilities'. Ratification of this convention commits a country to promoting and encouraging the sharing of domestic responsibilities between men and women. It also implies a commitment to developing services which enable workers (and prospective workers) with family responsibilities to undertake training and educational programs as well as to take part in employment. Countries which ratify the convention commit themselves to working towards the provision of parental leave, to introducing laws which prohibit direct or indirect discrimination on the basis of marital status or family responsibilities and to providing a range of community services such as home help and child care. The ACTU has actively promoted the ratification of the convention, most notably by its support for work-based child care and its successful test case on parental leave for all workers.

All the contextual issues mentioned so far – economic policies, moves to encourage and facilitate the labour force participation of women (including single mothers), the review of social security, trade union pressures for work-based child care and other measures to secure the equal treatment of workers with family responsibilities – have contributed to an intensive focus on child care in relation to employment. The government's overall goal was an expansion of services, combined with ensuring that services funded by the commonwealth are primarily used by workforce participants. The provision of child care for reasons other than parents' workforce participation – to enhance the social development of children or to provide respite for home-based mothers, for example – received much lower priority. Also, the language of the debate about child care changed. Child care is now about 'facilitating workforce participation', 'enhancing productivity' and 'assisting the welfare to work transition'. The rhetoric of the 1970s feminist movement, which promoted child care as enhancing women's autonomy, providing alternatives to traditional nuclear family care arrangements, and encouraging independence and sociability amongst young children has all but disappeared from public debates about child care.

Early Initiatives

When it came to office in 1983 Labor had a far more detailed child care policy than it had had in 1972. The policy reflected the key concerns of trade unionists, women's organisations and child care groups. These concerns were, firstly, that a publicly-funded child care program should be maintained as the central feature of government policy; secondly, that any expansion of child care services should not rely on submissions but be planned on the basis of demographic data and other relatively objective sources of information; and thirdly, that the funding formula for child care services should remain linked to the payment of award wages for child care workers.

The ALP policy had been drafted by Eva Cox who had worked in Canberra for the shadow Minister for Community Services, Don Grimes, throughout 1981 and 1982. Cox, together with Jan Burnswoods of the ALP Left and Tricia Kavanagh of the ALP Right, had managed to get this policy written into the party platform in what has been described as 'a startling display of sisterhood at a conference characterised by extreme Left/Right confrontation' (Sawer 1990: 80).

Once in office, the new government acted swiftly to commence implementation of its promise to expand the number of child care services. In its first budget $10 million was allocated for the establishment of new services and the following year a further $30 million was made available.

The planning approach

The introduction of a planning approach was another early initiative of the Labor government. The push towards planning had come most strongly from New South Wales child care groups and Labor party women; as already noted, it was representatives from New South Wales who were responsible for drafting the ALP's federal policy on child care and having it adopted at the party's 1982 Conference. Not all child care groups were in favour of ending submissions. Some members of Community Child Care (Victoria), for example, perceived the planning approach as antithetical to the community development principles they believed should underlie child care policy. However, from the government's point of view there were obvious advantages to the new system. At one stroke, it put an end to the enormous amount of time and energy that went into unsuccessful submission writing and thereby relieved politicians of the unpleasant duty of attempting to explain to disappointed (and often irate) community groups why their proposals had been unsuccessful.

The planning approach also provided a basis for co-ordination between the commonwealth, state and local levels of government. Furthermore, it meant that there could be some streamlining of the tasks and processes involved in establishing services. Under the previous system where community groups were given complete responsibility for overseeing the construction of centres, the process could take up to five years and the costs of individual services were sometimes extraordinarily high. Above all, it was only through a planning approach that there could be any guarantee that services would be located in areas of greatest need and would be developed in line with other government objectives, such as the need for work-related care. Feminist bureaucrats working within the child care field pointed out that the development of more sophisticated planning data and a fairer way of allocating funds for child care would also assist them in arguing for increased allocations. As Gae Raby, director of the Family and Children's Services Agency of New South Wales, informed participants at a conference on planning for child care: 'The better our information base, the more chance we have of making our demands irresistible' (Raby 1984).

At the heart of its attempt to co-ordinate the activities of the various levels of government was the commonwealth's effort to attract contributions from other levels of government. In the 1984–85 financial year, some fourteen million dollars, 140 blocks of land and a number of buildings were provided by state, territory and local governments (Grimes 1985). The commonwealth also entered into agreements with particular states; in New South Wales, for example, the state government undertook to provide the capital funds required to build and equip centres, while the commonwealth provided recurrent funds and fee relief.

Planning committees were established in each state and territory to give advice on funding priorities and to represent the interests of each level of government as well as a range of community groups. The brief given to the planning committees was to provide advice on the localities which had the highest need for child care services, to comment on the most appropriate types of services to meet those needs and to establish priority rankings within the state (Department of Community Services and Health 1984). The composition of these committees varied but in addition to representatives from commonwealth, state and local governments, they generally included members of community organisations, ethnic groups and women's advisory units. The government made no direct attempt to use the state planning committees to link child care planning with labour market needs. Hence, only in New South Wales (where a number of individual members of the planning committee were strong advocates of work-related child care) was an attempt made to develop new services with a specific work-related focus. For some years the New South Wales planning committee presented two lists of priority areas to the commonwealth minister – one for general community-based services and the other for work-related care.

Funding for children with special needs

Another issue that received attention in the early years of the Labor government was the most appropriate way to assist children with special needs for child care. A review of the Children's Services Program carried out in 1979 had pointed to the need to distinguish between two quite separate types of need: assistance for *children* deemed especially in need of care (such as disabled children, children of migrants and children at risk of abuse) and economic assistance for poor *families* who could not afford to pay for care (1981: 5). This review had suggested that, in addition to assistance to parents to help with fees, a special subsidy should be provided to *services* to help them meet the costs of caring for children with special needs. In July 1983 the Labor government introduced Supplementary Services Grants (known as SUPS) for this purpose. These were intended to help to fund specialist workers, such as English language teachers and special carers to assist disabled children. They were also to provide funds for capital grants for services which might need to make structural alterations or purchase special equipment in order to accommodate particular children. A separate form of assistance, Special Economic Needs Subsidies (SENS) was introduced to assist low income families with their fees.

The expansion of services

The Labor government sought its second term in late 1984. During the election campaign Prime Minister Hawke described child care as 'a matter of high priority' and promised to create 20,000 new child care places over the following three years at a cost of around $100 million (*AFR* 14 November 1984). In expenditure terms, this was the biggest promise made by the government during the campaign. The Liberal and National parties gave much lower priority to child care and did not attempt to match the government's commitment to additional publicly-funded services. Instead they promised a 'family tax package' which included limited tax rebates for child care expenses and the introduction of income splitting. The conservative parties also promised a pilot study into the extension of fee relief to users of commercial centres.

After the election, the government announced details of the types of services to be funded under its 20,000-place strategy. Slightly more than half of the places (11,500) were to be in child care centres, about a quarter in family day care schemes (4,450) and a smaller number (3,000) in occasional care programs. The cost equivalent of 1,000 child care places was directed to support services, groups with special needs and outside school hours care. This distribution among service types was a further indication that the government's policy was geared towards improving the access of employed women to child care.

The government also announced a major reorganisation of commonwealth departments. The Office of Child Care was moved to the newly established Department of Community Services which also housed the Office of the Aged, the Office of the Disabled and the Community Support Division of the former Department of Social Security. Child care groups generally welcomed this as a positive development for children's services. Under the previous arrangement child care had been (in financial terms at least) a very small part of the overall work of the Department of Social Security. Within the new Department of Community Services it appeared not to be overshadowed to the same extent. Further, the location of the Office of Child Care within a department providing a range of community services was seen as helping to consolidate the image of child care as a normal social service, not something reserved for those who could prove their 'neediness' or inability to cope.

Tax deductibility for child care expenses?

The question of tax deductibility for child care expenses flared briefly during the election campaign of 1984. This issue had divided women's organisations and child care lobby groups for several years. The main supporters of tax deductibility were organisations representing well-paid professional women, such as the Women Lawyers' Association, the Women Members Group of the Australian Society of Accountants and the Business and Professional Women's Association. The Lone Fathers' Association also campaigned in support of tax deductibility. All major child care lobby groups, including the National Association of Community Based Children's Services, Children's Services Action, Community Child Care (in both Victoria and New South Wales) and Children's Services Resource and Development opposed the idea, as did the ALP.

Advocates of tax deductibility sought recognition of the fact that child care expenses are an essential item of expenditure incurred in the course of earning their income by taxpayers with responsibility for young children. On this view, the rejection of child care expenses was an anomaly within the system.

> If you have to pay child care expenses in order to earn an income, then, even without any other commitments, your disposable income is noticeably reduced. If the amount of tax an Australian pays is proportional to her/his ability to pay tax, then why does the parent who must pay child care pay the same tax as an individual on a similar salary without young children?
> (Johnston 1982: 111)

Recognition of these costs, it was argued, would remove one of the disincentives to workforce participation faced by those with child care responsibilities and would thus be a step towards a more neutral tax system. Proponents argued that women who cared for their own children at home did not get taxed for providing this service, and that women who could organise to exchange their own labour in return for child care were not taxed either. Only those who pay for child care from their (already taxed) earnings are required to pay tax for this service.

Detailed arguments in favour of tax deductibility were put forward in a submission to the Treasurer in 1980 by the Women Members' Group of the Australian Society of Accountants. They urged that tax deductions for child care expenses should be made available to working mothers and single fathers, claiming that such a system, by decreasing the net cost of going out to work, would encourage more women to earn taxable income (thereby increasing tax revenue). They also claimed that welfare payments would be reduced, that employment would be created as a result of increased demand for child care places and that facilitating women's return to the workforce after the birth of their children would result in a better return from public investment in the education and training of women. The submission claimed that the introduction of tax deductibility (and the consequent necessity for documentation of financial transactions involving child care) would increase tax revenue by bringing the underground child care economy into the open (Australian Society of Accountants 1980).

Many women felt a deep sense of injustice at the treatment of child care costs in the tax system compared with the treatment of other expenses incurred in earning an income.

> At one of the first child care cases to go to a Tax Tribunal, one of the Tribunal members pointed out that to earn income, it was more essential for a car salesman to be able to buy a prospective customer a pint of beer and so possibly sell a car, than it was for a mother to buy child care and so earn a wage. He knew at this time that he was talking to a sole parent. I couldn't disagree more strongly. Whereas car salesmen still sell cars without using this inducement, a sole mother cannot earn a wage without child care.
> (Johnston 1982:112)

Tax *rebates* rather than *deductions* were favoured by a few. Those who favoured rebates argued that this form of tax concession was fairer because it provided a flat-rate reduction of tax liability, thereby providing the same dollar value for everyone. Deductions, on the other hand, reduced the taxpayer's taxable income, thereby benefitting the individual at the level of his or her marginal tax rate. In fact, however, tax rebates only provide the same dollar value for those who have a high enough tax liability to benefit from it. Low income earners may not incur sufficient tax liability to benefit fully from rebates. In any case, advocacy for rebates remained a minority position. Most of those advocating recognition of child care expenses within the tax system saw the campaign for deductibility as 'a simple campaign with a distinct goal that fits into the current tax system', particularly as child care expenses 'can be compared with those deductions already allowed'. Kay Johnston, convenor of the Children's Services sub-committee of WEL (ACT), argued that the 'slow death' suffered by family allowances as a result of lack of indexation was one reason for opposing any flat-rate payment. She argued that 'funds allocated to families through Cabinet are seen as "hand-outs". They are given little or no priority and are not seen in their real context within the tax transfer system' (1982: 113-4).

The child care lobby groups and others who opposed tax deductibility did not necessarily dispute the facts or the logic of those who advocated deductibility. Their position was based on an analysis of the vertical – as against horizontal – equity issues involved in tax deductions and also on their strategic assessment of the best way to encourage public expenditure on children's services. Opponents of tax deductibility for child care pointed out that tax deductions for any purpose are regressive, in that the higher an individual's income, the greater the benefit. Tax deductions would therefore lead to a situation where a high income-earner would actually pay less for child care than a middle or low income earner. Low income-earning women with high income-earning partners could be particularly disadvantaged because, for the purpose of assessing their child care fees, both incomes would be taken into account (thus rendering them liable for a higher fee than if each personal income only was considered) while the tax deduction would most likely be claimed by their (male) partner in order to maximise the benefit. Opponents of tax deductibility also argued that the amount of revenue which would be foregone by the commonwealth in any such scheme might jeopardise the future of the Children's Services Program (Morrow 1981; Children's Services Action 1982). In 1984 the Department of Social Security estimated that tax deductions for child care expenses would cost about $400 million per year compared with expenditure on the Children's Services Program of $110 million (*AFR*

31 July 1984). The Minister for Community Services and Health, Senator Grimes, stated at this time that should tax deductions be introduced the government would regard the tax foregone as equivalent to an item of expenditure and would be unlikely to continue direct outlays on the Children's Services Program in addition to tax deductibility.

In 1984 a Full Bench of the Federal Court dismissed the appeal of a Canberra sole parent, Lorraine Martin, against a New South Wales Supreme Court decision to reject her claim for tax deductibility of child care expenses. Martin's case had been supported by the Women Lawyers' Association, the Women Accountants' Group and several state branches of the Women's Electoral Lobby. It was generally regarded as a test case on the issue. After the Federal Court's decision, the women decided to seek a High Court hearing. In the middle of the election campaign, the High Court ruled that it would not hear a test case on the issue and the Chief Justice, Sir Harry Gibbs, commented: 'If the [present taxation] rule is thought to work an injustice, then the remedy lies with the Parliament' (*SMH* 27 October 1987). This decision brought to an end the possibility of change through the courts.

Labor's Finance Minister Opens Fire

Following the government's re-election there were signs that some members of the government had serious misgivings—both economic and ideological—about the emphasis being given to the expansion of child care. The most sustained opposition to the general thrust of Labor's child care policy came from the Finance Minister, Senator Peter Walsh, and his department. Senator Walsh first publicly signalled his disquiet about child care funding in an interview with the *National Times* in May 1985. There he argued that to provide child care for all children below school age whose parents were in the workforce would require $500 million in capital construction costs and a further $500 million in annual recurrent subsidies. Walsh commented that 'child care should not have the priority entailed in that sort of expenditure', adding that to expand the program in the way outlined would be 'a misallocation of funds' (*NT* 17–23 May 1985).

The costing done, at Walsh's request, by the Department of Finance may have been intended to discredit the idea of expanding child care provision by alarming the electorate (and, perhaps, others members of the government) with projected levels of expenditure far above those which the government had contemplated. Walsh's *National Times* interview followed the announcement in the May 1985 mini-budget that commonwealth expenditure on children's services was to be substantially reduced. The proposed cuts were two-fold: complete withdrawal of the $33 million block grant for pre-school services and a reduction of $30 million in the 1985–86 child care subsidies. Given the size of the children's services budget ($158 million at that time), these cuts represented a very significant reduction; in proportional terms they were the biggest of all those announced in the mini-budget. The campaign mounted by children's services lobby groups in opposition to the proposed cuts and the response to the campaign by some senior government ministers, resulted in extremely bitter relations between the two for a period.

According to senior officers within the Office of Child Care, the cuts in child care had been insisted upon by the Department of Finance and the figure of $30 million as the target for savings had been hit upon by the crude calculation that each of the 60,000 families using child care could be called upon to pay an extra $10 per week (Coleman interview 1985). Child care activists maintained that this was unrealistic. They pointed out that 65 per cent of the families using child care were receiving fee relief and therefore could not be expected to pay much more for child care; the anticipated savings could therefore only be achieved by fee increases far higher than $10 per week for the remainder of users. The treatment of middle and high income earners was one of the major points at issue in this debate, but a resolution of the debate was not made any easier by the fact that statistics on the distribution of incomes amongst users of commonwealth-funded services who did *not* receive fee relief were not collected. Child care lobbyists (many of them directors of child care centres in daily contact with the users of services) maintained that the majority of families whose incomes put them above the cut-off point for fee relief were not particularly well-off and indeed were often struggling to pay fees which were similar to those charged by elite private schools. They also claimed that the issue of the distribution of income within families had not been taken into account and that quite often women from families with relatively high joint incomes had very little independent income of their own, and found it difficult to meet child care expenses.

The Minister for Finance and the Minister for Community Services were distinctly uninterested in the difficulties faced by families in this bracket. Senator Grimes, the Minister for Community Services, was quoted as saying that he had not opposed the cuts in Cabinet because he believed that parents on combined incomes of $30,000 should be paying more for child care than they currently were. In his words, if such a family was not able to pay more for child care it would have to be 'because they wanted to buy a Volvo or something' (*SMH, Good Weekend* 15 June 1985). As child care groups were quick to point out, $30,000 represented less than the combined incomes of a bus driver and a process worker, a clerk and a typist or two cleaners or factory hands (*NT* 14–20 February 1986). The issue seemed to arouse some particularly hostile views about the recipients of 'middle class welfare'. Women's organisations and child care groups regarded this as particularly unjust and contrasted the attitudes of Labor politicians to expenditure on the dependent spouse rebate with their attitudes to child care expenditure. The certain knowledge that many high income males benefitted from the spouse rebate did not seem to provoke any concern amongst Labor politicians, but the mere suspicion that there were wealthy beneficiaries amongst the users of child care led to changes in the system. Yet there was clearly far greater potential for savings to be made by overhauling the dependent spouse rebate. The rebate cost government more than one billion dollars per year in revenue forgone, compared with $158 million expended on the Children's Services Program. The fact that approximately 96 per cent of the recipients of the spouse rebate were male, whereas the main beneficiaries of child care were women, was seen to underlie this inconsistency. Feminists and child care lobby groups maintained that high quality, affordable child care services were fundamental to gender equity and were essential in order for women to have genuine choices about entering the paid workforce. They argued that there could be no justification for the government's spending over one billion dollars on the spouse rebate but not being prepared to spend even one fifth of that amount on child care.

From the point of view of the government the single biggest equity issue involved in child care was that of access. Even with the projected increase in the number of places, 90 per cent of children under the age of five would still not have access to commonwealth-funded child care. Further, according to a speech made by Senator Grimes (at a conference called by the National Association of Community Based Children's Services to debate the proposed changes), a new approach to funding had been necessary in order to secure Cabinet support for the continued expansion of services:

> The Cabinet felt that we were at a watershed. There were major inequities in the program, and yet we were poised to launch into another major expansion. It would have been irresponsible not to take stock of the situation, and to see whether we could design better funding arrangements. In essence, what we are doing is finding a way to use the available funds more effectively so that our goals of expanding the program can be more equitably and more rationally achieved. (*Grimes 1985c: 3*)

The government also maintained that it was inequitable to provide a very high standard of care for the few, while most children missed out altogether. Senator Grimes argued that he could not 'allow a situation to develop where some children have perhaps the highest quality of care in the western world while most have no chance of access' (Grimes 1985c: 9). Finally, the government asserted that standards of care were unnecessarily high in some services and that the level of expenditure required to maintain such standards could not be justified. For those receiving full fee relief and benefitting from the general operational subsidies which assisted all users, the total benefit was said to be equal to 12 times the value of family allowance and almost twice the value of junior unemployment benefit (Grimes 1985c).

The views of the community-based lobby groups did not prevail. However, the government did not succeed entirely in achieving its objectives. Senator Grimes appointed a committee to advise on how the government could save $30 million from the Children's Services Program, but this committee, which included representatives from the Department of the Prime Minister and Cabinet, the Treasury, the Department of Finance, the Office of the Status of Women and the Office of Child Care, recommended savings of only $10 million in a full year, not the anticipated $30 million. When the government announced its new funding arrangements for child care, in November 1985, it adopted the committee's report. According to Senator Grimes (1985d), the new arrangements were designed to create 'a fairer and simpler funding system'. They would mean fee rises of no more than $2 per week for most families and would not lead to any reduction in the quality of child care services.

This assessment of the new arrangements was not shared by users of child care or by workers in child care centres. Protest rallies and demonstrations against the government took place around Australia. The ACTU, the NSW Labor Council and the National Women's Consultative Committee issued statements condemning the new system, as did many individual trade unions and women's groups. At the height of the campaign the Prime Minister was reported to be receiving 600 letters per week on the issue – more than on any topic other than the killing of kangaroos (*Age* 13 September 1985). Child care workers in different parts of Australia held rolling strikes and, in an extraordinary development for such an industrially-weak area, centres throughout the country closed down for a full day as part of the protest.

Labor's new funding system

The central feature of the government's new funding system for child care – and the issue which raised the most opposition – was that, in contravention of ALP policy, it ended the link between subsidies and award wages, effectively implementing one of the major recommendations of the Liberal government's Spender Report. Previously, under section 11 of the *Child Care Act*, centres had received 75 per cent of the award wages of the nurses and teachers they employed. The number of staff in each of these categories for whom subsidy was received depended upon the number and ages of children attending the centre. This system meant that staff could be paid award wages and that centres would not suffer a financial penalty if they employed well-qualified, experienced staff. Centres received 75 per cent of the wages of the actual staff they employed and so, as staff gained additional qualifications and years of experience, the subsidy they attracted rose accordingly – so long as the awards which covered them included provision for such increments. This put staff employed in child care centres on a similar footing to those employed in pre-schools.

The new formula introduced a per capita subsidy for each child place within the centre. Most centres faced a cut of around 50 per cent in their operational assistance grants as a result of this new system. The government accompanied the announcement of the new funding arrangements with suggestions as to how centres should re-arrange their affairs in order to break even financially. The first suggestion was that centres could reduce their costs by employing fewer or less qualified staff. (In order to facilitate this the government repealed section 11 of the *Child Care Act* which required all commonwealth-funded centres to employ some trained staff.) The other course of action suggested by the government was that fees be raised substantially. More detailed advice was provided to individual centres by staff of the Office of Child Care. This advice included suggesting to the (entirely voluntary) management committee of one centre that they undertake fund-raising activities in order to supply the money for on-costs such as annual leave loading and long service leave (Hamilton 1986: 8).

The other significant aspect of the new funding system was a revision of the 'fee relief' system. Under the new arrangements, eligibility for fee relief was extended considerably. Families with a joint income of up to around $34,000 became eligible for some reduction in fees if they had one child in care, and a higher income limit applied to those with two or more children in care. The benefit of this, however, was substantially reduced by the necessity for most centres to raise their fees sharply.

The Labor government's decision to restructure the child care funding system in this way was regarded by the National Association of Community Based Child Care and other lobby groups as one of the most serious setbacks ever suffered by the Children's Services Program.

The budgetary reductions which had occurred during the years of the Fraser government, although vehemently opposed by child care groups, had not had such serious consequences for the structure of the program. The cutbacks during the Fraser years had stopped growth within the Children's Services Program, but the Fraser government did not attack the fundamental principle of the *Child Care Act* – that qualified staff were essential in child care centres and that commonwealth subsidies must encourage and support the employment of such staff. Labor's new funding system undermined the child care program in both respects. This approach was taken by women's organisations and child care lobby groups as an indication that the government's primary goal was expansion of the program and that the quality of care offered to children and the industrial conditions of the staff were secondary considerations.

The announcement by Senator Grimes, the Minister for Community Services, that he had not opposed the government's cuts to child care funding generated considerable hostility and brought relations between the Labor government and the major child care groups to a very low point. Senator Grimes seemed equally incensed that the child care lobby had attacked the actions of a Labor government. He spoke constantly of the increase in the number of child care places which had occurred under Labor and dismissed critical statements on the restructuring of child care funding as 'ill-informed and alarmist' (Grimes 1985a). Not until 1987, when Dr Neal Blewett was appointed the Minister for Community Services and Health (a portfolio which included child care), were better relations restored.

CHAPTER 9

Equity and Economics

> Child care is a critical part of the Government policy of economic recovery and increased productivity. In straight economic terms, child care is an investment by Government that has contributed to Australia's recovery ...
> Child care provisions are not welfare, they are a crucial part of the overall social justice and economic strategies of the Government.
> *ALP* Report of the Working Party on Child Care, *1988*

Child care policy since the late 1980s has been shaped by the persistent tension between the government's economic and social justice objectives. Labor's economic goals in this period included reducing the public sector's share of gross domestic product and lowering the budget deficit – an inauspicious environment for advocates of an expanded child care program. In the late 1980s a bitter struggle erupted within the government over the continued existence of publicly-funded child care. For a time it appeared that the program might be scrapped and child care handed over to the private sector. Neal Blewett, Minister for Community Services and Health from 1986 to 1990, emerged as a key defender of the program whose enemies included the commercial sector, key members of the Coalition opposition, Treasury and Department of Finance officials and Labor's high profile Finance Minister, Senator Peter Walsh. Blewett supported publicly-funded child care as 'an integral component of the Government's economic and social justice policies' and praised the expansion of the Children's Services Program as 'one of the greatest social and economic reforms undertaken by the Hawke Government' (Blewett 1988). In Cabinet he defeated Walsh's attempts to wind back the government's commitment to public child care and, together with allies, achieved an expansion of the program.

Nevertheless, by the early 1990s a fundamental shift had occurred in the direction of child care policy. Although the non-profit sector remained at the heart of Labor's policy, commercial and employer-provided child care had been drawn into the overall program as the government attempted to encourage other bodies (especially employers and commercial providers) to extend their involvement. Fee relief was extended to users of commerical child care centres and Labor's goals for expansion relied more and more on the private sector. The government increasingly defined its role as being one of supporting other players, rather than being the major provider of services. Efforts were made to tighten the focus of the program and to link use of child care to the labour force status of parents, rather than to children's needs.

By 1993, child care was entrenched as part of the mainstream political agenda. Both Labor and the Coalition parties made major commitments in the area during the 1993 election campaign and portrayed child care as central to their overall social and economic goals. The 'mainstreaming' of child care, however, had been achieved at a high price. Labor has moved towards ever-increasing reliance on the private sector for the expansion of child care. Further, the extension of fee relief to commercial and employer providers has effectively resulted in the establishment of a voucher system through the back door. The aspirations of feminists and community child care advocates for a national system of non-profit services based around the needs of children and their families has receded. Child care has expanded rapidly but has become a narrowly focussed instrument of economic and labour force policies.

Publicly-funded Child Care –
'An Affront to the Canons of Decency'?

As the program of establishing 20,000 places (initiated in 1985) neared completion, debate about the future direction of child care policy was rekindled. Several key groups sought further expansion of the program. The 1987 ALP Conference called on the government to set a new target for the expansion of child care places over the ensuing three years. It re-affirmed the party's commitment to the principle that government funding should only be provided for non-profit organisations. The ACTU congress, held the same year, also urged the government to set up another 20,000 child care places. Later in 1987, the ACTU executive met with Brian Howe (Minister for Social Security and Chair of the Caucus Social Justice Committee) and stressed the need for child care to be expanded as part of the government's social justice strategy. The ACTU delegation also suggested that more emphasis should be placed on work-related child care so that parents could have a choice between services located in their neighbourhood and those near their place of work. The ACTU maintained its pressure in the lead up to the 1988 budget, linking child care with the maintenance of family living standards, social justice and equal opportunities at work. In May 1988 the ACTU made a detailed submission to the commonwealth which argued for the introduction of a program which would encourage employer support for work-based child care.

The Australian Council of Social Service (ACOSS), the peak organisation representing welfare agencies in Australia, also put pressure on the government to maintain the momentum of expansion. In 1988 it issued a detailed discussion paper on child care policy, highlighting the economic benefits of public provision and stressing that these benefits accrued to the whole society, not just the individual. The paper (written by Eva Cox) stated that 'child care services make a considerable contribution to the capacity of families to remain economically independent. As well, they add to labour market efficiencies by providing employers earlier access to the skills of those women (and a few men) who take the responsibility for their children's care. It is evident that these are desirable outcomes for the community at large'. ACOSS recommended that the government embark on a ten-year expansion plan which would enable it to meet 80 per cent of work-related needs for child care by 1998 – a target described as 'warranted and perfectly achievable' (ACOSS 1988: ii). The Women's Electoral Lobby, the National Association of Community Based Child Care and the Australian Early Childhood Association supported the ACOSS position.

There were, however, strong pressures operating against the calls for expansion of public child care services. In April 1987 the Minister for Finance, Senator Walsh, presented a submission to Cabinet which argued that the government's projected target of 20,000 new child care places (due to be completed by December 1988) should be reconsidered. Walsh contended that the government should either adopt a lower target or reduce costs by substituting family day care for some of the proposed centre-based long day care services (*Age* 14 April 1987). The following month the government brought down a mini-budget which included the announcement that 1,200 centre-based places were to be replaced with family day care – a change which would save $9 million. Together with the exchange of 450 projected centre-based places for family day care announced in the previous budget, this meant that the equivalent of some 40 child care centres (assuming 40 places per centre) had been replaced by family day care within a period of a few months. The government explained this adjustment by claiming that demand for family day care was increasing relative to the demand for centre-based services. No evidence to support this claim was provided, however, and most child care groups and women's organisations were sceptical; for them, the exchange was purely a cost-cutting exercise.

Representatives of family day care organisations reacted angrily to the mini-budget announcement. In the context of attempts by caregivers to improve their industrial conditions and gain recognition for the quality of the service they offered, the government's move was seen as insulting. The Victorian Home Based Caregivers Association (which was later to play a crucial role in campaigns seeking award coverage for family day care workers) was formed at this time. Its aim was to promote family day care within the community and to lobby for increased government funding and support. This organisation publicly opposed the government's new emphasis on family day care provision – no doubt causing some confusion within the government: opposition to the expansion of family day care might have been anticipated from feminists who had ideological objections to this form of home-based provision, but here were caregivers themselves opposing the extension of family day care. The caregivers' attitudes reflected a growing confidence and assertiveness within the ranks of family day care. The newly elected president of the Victorian Home Based Caregivers Association declared that the government was promoting family day care not because it valued the service but because it regarded family day care as 'child care on the cheap'. In her words, 'the announcement that funding cuts to child care services will be achieved by transferring funds from "expensive" child care centres to "cheap" family day care is an outrage' (CCC 1987: 1).

The Finance Minister continued to voice his opposition to publicly funded child care. In a supposedly off-the-record post-budget speech to the Australian Society of Labor Lawyers, Walsh angrily claimed, 'I can give you 200, a list of 200 bloody programs off the top of my head that can't be justified by social justice, equity, or economic efficiency grounds, and the reason we haven't abandoned them is because we don't have the political courage to do so' (*SMH* 22 September 1987). Publicly-subsidised child care was high on Walsh's list. Such services, he claimed, had resulted from a 'middle class push' in the 1970s and had become far too costly for the country to afford. He argued that money was not available for further increases in public child care provision and that, in any case, on equity grounds the continuation of the program could not be justified. Instead, Walsh suggested, the establishment of new child care services should be left to the private sector with government providing assistance to low-income users: 'The money could be found for a means-tested voucher system which would then remove child care from the public sector and send it back to the private sector from whence, I believe, it should never have been enticed away' (*SMH* 22 September 1987).

Walsh appeared unaware that child care had not been 'enticed away' from the private sector but that the commonwealth government had entered the field precisely because of the failure of the market to provide a reasonable service at a price parents could afford. He also seemed not to know that one of the reasons that an across-the-board subsidy for all users had been introduced was a concern for the well-being of children: 'Child care which is beneficial to the child's overall development is prohibitively costly for the large body of parents and ... the child minding arrangements that most parents could afford fall far short of the quality required in the interests of child welfare ... ' (*CPD*, HR, vol. 81: 2289). Although only a remnant of this operational subsidy remained, after the funding changes introduced in 1985, it was regarded as important for both symbolic and financial reasons. Also, as women's groups were quick to point out, the value of the operational subsidy was only about $15 per week – several dollars less than the benefit spouses would receive (regardless of income) through the dependent spouse rebate were they to withdraw from the workforce.

Walsh's views on child care were consistent with his opinions on other areas of public policy (for example, tertiary education) where he believed that working-class taxpayers were subsiding services which primarily benefitted middle-class users. His objections to the public funding of child care were expressed in terms of three principles: equity, efficiency and expense (Jones 1988: 5). Walsh maintained that publicly-funded child care was inequitable because 'middle class' families (never defined) had gained disproportionate access to it. A further inequity arose, he argued, from the fact that low-income parents who could not find places in public sector child care (or who chose to use private centres) did not receive government assistance with their fees. Further, since less than 10 per cent of children had access to services funded under the Children's Services Program, Walsh argued that the system conferred significant benefits on a small group (not all of whom, in his view, were deserving of assistance), while doing nothing to assist the majority. On the issue of efficiency, Walsh contended that since average fees in private centres were lower than those in public centres the former must be more efficient (*Australian* 31 March 1989). This view was forcefully argued by the Australian Federation of Child Care Associations, the main lobby group representing commercial child care centres. According to Walsh and the commercial centre proprietors, the employment of unionised labour and the 'unnecessarily high' qualifications of many child care workers were the major causes of the higher costs of subsidised child care services. As to the long-term expense of the system, Walsh argued that the level of funding which would be required to make child care universally available was prohibitive. To provide care for all children below school age, he claimed, would require a capital outlay of $2 billion and recurrent expenditure of approximately $1.3 billion per year.

The community child care lobby (including a number of trade unions, welfare organisations and feminist groups) contested each of these claims. Concerning the equity of the Children's Services Program, they pointed to data from a survey conducted by the Office of Child Care (1987), which showed that the use of publicly-funded child care services was widely spread across income groups, with those on low and middle incomes being slightly over-represented. The survey showed, for example, 70 per cent of families with children in publicly-subsidised care had incomes below the $32,000 cut-off point for fee relief, compared with 55 per cent of all Australian families with children. Approximately half these families (that is, one-third of all users) had incomes below $14,000 – suggesting that they were in receipt of a government pension or benefit. Another indication of the successful targetting of the program was the fact that, although only 7 per cent of families with parents in the workforce were headed by a sole parent, approximately 28 per cent of the families using subsidised child care for work-related reasons were sole-parent families. The most serious equity issue in the child care area, community child care groups claimed, was the insufficient number of publicly-subsidised services. All community-based child care centres had long waiting lists, some with several hundred names; commercial centres frequently had vacancies. (An ABS survey published in 1989 revealed that across Australia the average vacancy rate in private child care centres was 16 per cent, with the actual rate varying from less than 7 per cent in New South Wales and Victoria to almost 20 per cent in Queensland.)

As to efficiency, community child care advocates acknowledged that average fees in commercial centres were lower than those in the public sector. However, they disputed the view that this meant the commercial sector was more efficient. A simple comparison of the costs of public and commercial child care centres failed to take into account the fact that the two sectors provided quite different services and catered to different groups. Private centres employ fewer trained staff, open for shorter hours and usually do not cater for babies and toddlers – the group requiring the most intensive and therefore most expensive care.

Furthermore, unlike public child care centres, most commercial operators do not cater for children with special needs (such as those with physical disabilities or developmental delays or both) or provide programs for children from a range of ethnic and cultural backgrounds, or accept large numbers of children deemed by state welfare officers to be at risk of abuse from their parents. All these services are expensive to provide. However their provision, according to community child care groups, contributes to the wellbeing of society and leads to savings in other areas – for example, by reducing the need for remedial education when children are older. On this view, the 'cost' of child care cannot be equated with fee levels. A far greater range of issues needs to be considered, and social benefits weighed against monetary outlays.

The Finance Minister's estimates of the costs of expansion were also challenged, notably by ACOSS. Walsh's figures were based on two assumptions: that all parents of pre-school age children wished to enter the labour force and that all would require full-time formal care for their children. Both these assumptions were unrealistic. Not even Sweden, renowned for its active encouragement of women's workforce participation, has achieved this level of participation by mothers of pre-school age children. In any case, the majority of mothers who enter the labour market work part-time and do not require full-time child care. Further, some parents will chose not to use any formal services, but will share child care between themselves, hire nannies or make their own private arrangements with family and friends. ACOSS produced its own estimates of the demand for child care and the cost of meeting this demand through public provision. It argued that continued expansion of the Children's Services Program at a rate similar to that which had occurred during 1983–1988 would result in a doubling of the existing level of provision and enable 80 per cent of work-related needs to be met within a decade. A substantial proportion of non work-related child care needs could also be met through this rate of expansion. ACOSS estimated that the initial capital outlay would cost approximately $500 million over a ten-year period, with a similar amount required for recurrent costs: an average additional cost of $100 million a year. This was a far cry from Senator Walsh's estimates.

Despite these important challenges to the validity of Walsh's arguments, his attack on child care was enthusiastically promoted by media commentators, who made no reference to any of the contervailing arguments or evidence. According to John Hyde, a columnist for the *Australian* and a former Liberal member of parliament, the availability of any form of child care subsidy for middle and upper income families was 'an affront to the canons of decency' (*Australian* 10 October 1987). David Clark, an academic economist and columnist for the *Australian*

Financial Review, described child care subsidies as 'a scandalous waste of taxpayers' money', and referred contemptuously to the advocates of publicly-funded child care as 'the potty lobby'. Clark echoed Walsh's erroneous criticisms of state regulations which required the employment of trained staff in child care centres. He argued that requirements such as these were simply devices 'to make even softer the nests of bachelors of early childhood education and their middle class well-feathered friends'; and he accused child care workers of 'slowly crippling the current system with "creeping credentialism" ':

> Do child carers really need three or four-year degrees from tertiary institutions? Do they need to be trained in political science and sociology? Are under-fives interested in 'class analysis', structuralism, or even physics and chemistry? Has the human race suffered that much from the fact that its under-fives have not been cared for by such graduates since Eve accepted the apple? *(AFR 5 July 1988)*

In fact there were (and are) no child care regulations in Australia which require the employment of staff with 'three or four-year degrees from tertiary institutions', although the employment of staff with such qualifications is the norm in pre-schools. Most child care centre directors and teachers have a two-year Certificate of Child Care Studies from a TAFE college. At the time Clark was writing, Victoria and Queensland did not require *any* staff working in child care centres to hold formal qualifications. For historical reasons, the strongest support for the employment of university or CAE graduates in child care centres has come from New South Wales; however this is not a requirement of the regulations. As already noted, commonwealth operational subsidies have, since 1986, been paid on the basis of the number of children enrolled – not on the basis of staff qualifications or award wages. Accordingly, where the management committee of a particular centre *chooses* to employ a graduate with a Bachelor of Early Childhood Education degree, the extra expense is borne by the parents, not by the government.

Vouchers or publicly-funded services?

While Senator Walsh did not elaborate in detail on what he meant by a voucher scheme, the broad outlines of his proposal were clear from his numerous public statements. The central purpose of such a scheme was to end direct government involvement in the provision of child care: there would be no more expenditure on capital items such as building and equipping centres and establishing new family day care schemes. Walsh also wished to bring to an end the operational subsidies provided to all commonwealth-funded services, thus 'levelling the playing field' and ensuring that middle-class families did not receive assistance from the public purse. A voucher to assist with the cost of child care expenses could then be made available to all families whose income was below a certain level. Families would be permitted to use the voucher at any approved child care centre, whether public or commercial.

The introduction of vouchers had been advocated by the Australian Federation of Child Care Associations (the organisation representing the interests of commercial centres) for several years. Although the association seemed to accept that publicly-funded child care centres would continue to exist for some time after the introduction of a voucher system, its eventual goal was an entirely private system of service provision with government stepping in only to help those on low incomes. The association argued that a voucher system would save the government money because it would not have to establish new services (with all the capital and recurrent costs involved); concentrating its resources on direct assistance to needy families would be cheaper (Australian Federation of Child Care Associations 1988).

The introduction of vouchers was strongly opposed by the community child care lobby. The scheme symbolised an approach to child care provision which was at odds with virtually every principle which had been fought for by feminists and community child care groups. In particular it was seen as likely to entail bringing to an end one of the most important achievements of the Hawke government – the development of planning mechanisms for the expansion of child care. Under the planning approach thousands of child care places had been established in low-income suburbs and rural areas where commercial proprietors had never shown any interest in setting up a business. The community child care lobby was sceptical of the claim that the availability of vouchers would somehow activate market forces and lead to the establishment of private child care centres in areas which had previously been neglected. They pointed out that the market had so far failed to provide services even in high income areas where there was strong demand for child care and where parents could afford to pay high fees. In the absence of a public program to ensure that services were established in areas of high need, they argued, the vagaries of private enterprise could leave low-income families without access to any service. To such families, the existence of a voucher would be of little comfort.

A voucher scheme was also seen as bringing to an end the growth of services which were accountable to users and staff rather than to owners or shareholders. The principle of parent management of child care services – the ability of autonomous, parent-controlled management committees to hire and fire staff, develop policies on matters such as discipline, health and nutrition, and determine the stance of the service on issues such as sexism and racism – is very highly valued within the community child care movement.

Another concern of the community child care movement was the fact that commercial child care centres are much less likely than non-profit services to cater for children below two years of age – the group for which there is the greatest demand for care. Rarely, if ever, do commercial centres provide multilingual or multicultural programs, as many community-based services do. Further, the community-based organisations doubted that services guided by the profit motive would be likely to establish services for Aboriginal children, disabled children or those living in remote rural communities.

Finally, there were many unanswered questions about the costs involved in a voucher system and what the implications of these might be. If the scheme simply involved extending existing levels of fee relief to the thousands of families using commercial centres then it would be extremely expensive. Indeed, it would lead to growth in the child care budget rather than achieve savings. If a decision were made to provide a lower level of fee relief to users of all services (public and private), then this would lead to higher fees for some low-income families or put further pressure on services to cut costs or both. Given that salaries represent about 80 per cent of the costs in most child care centres, this in turn was likely to mean reductions in salaries and working conditions for child care staff. The move to introduce vouchers was thus seen as an all-out assault on the fundamental principles of the community child care movement (Roughley and Philippou 1989).

Although publicly-organised child care groups such as the National Association of Community Based Children's Services and feminist organisations such as WEL were the most visible opponents of the introduction of vouchers, considerable lobbying was also undertaken behind the scenes. Feminists employed in state and commonwealth bureaucracies were involved in various ways in combatting the Finance Minister's views on child care. The NSW Women's Co-ordination Unit, for example, prepared a document entitled 'Rebutting the opposition to the Commonwealth Children's Services Program'. This was widely circulated to journalists, bureaucrats and politicians. In Canberra, several senior women bureaucrats engaged in intense lobbying of MPs and Ministers as well as providing useful information to child care groups.

The Caucus working party on child care

The repeated attacks on publicly-funded child care and the continued advocacy by Senator Walsh and others of a voucher system to replace the existing system of operational assistance, caused considerable dissension within the government. Women in the parliamentary Labor Party were infuriated by Walsh's comments. Several – particularly Susan Ryan, Wendy Fatin, Margaret Reynolds and Rosemary Crowley – who were in touch with women's organisations and child care groups became convinced that Walsh's statements were harming the image of the government.

Amidst growing concern amongst women MPs and other party members that the government might embrace the idea of vouchers, a Caucus working party (jointly chaired by Wendy Fatin and Rosemary Crowley) was set up to examine the government's role in child care and to recommend a course of action for the government to pursue once it had fulfilled its promise of 20,000 places. The working party strongly endorsed continuation of publicly-subsidised services through the Children's Services Program. It argued that child care had been a 'critical part of the Government policy of economic recovery and increased productivity' and had 'dramatically contributed to Australia's recovery' (ALP 1988: 7). It pointed out that child care services were vital in enabling women to enter (or re-enter) the workforce, which in turn provided their families with a significant buffer against the impact of reduced real wages; the presence of two income earners in the household had allowed many families to meet their mortgage payments despite very high interest rates and escalating household costs. It placed a great deal of emphasis on success of the government in integrating child care policies with other areas of government concern, such as job creation, social security, training and employment policies. Integration of this kind, it argued, was unlikely to be achieved if crucial decisions about the development of new services (such as location, hours of operation, ages of children cared for) were left to private entrepreneurs principally concerned with the pursuit of profit. The working party recommended that the government commit itself to an increase in the level of publicly-subsidised child care, setting specific targets for long day care, family day care, occasional care, out-of-school hours and vacation care. Two types of care – out-of-school-hours care and vacation programs – were singled out as needing 'serious and immediate attention' in order to maintain the impetus of women's increased participation in the workforce.

The Caucus working party report also canvassed the political importance of child care provision. In particular it noted a poll conducted for the Labor Party by Australian Nationwide Opinion Polls (ANOP) in marginal electorates in New South Wales, in which women in working-class suburbs had rated child care as their most pressing need.

In an apparent effort to repair the government's image with supporters of public child care, a number of government members made public statements at this time. Senator Susan Ryan (Minister Assisting the Prime Minister on the Status of Women, 1984-87) and Gerry Hand (the junior minister responsible for child care) were among those who publicly recorded their opposition to any system which would benefit commercial child care centres and undermine the principles of publicly-funded services (*CPD*, HR, vol.157: 1894). Deputy Prime Minister Lionel Bowen also intervened in the debate, in November 1987, warning Senator Walsh in a widely-leaked letter that he should cease making derogatory statements about publicly funded child care. Bowen's letter stressed that 'the issue of child care is a particularly sensitive one, and its provision a central objective of the ALP Platform' (*SMH* 7 November 1987).

The economics of publicly-funded child care

One of the most significant developments in the debate about publicly-funded child care occurred towards the end of 1987 when the Minister for Community Services and Health, Neal Blewett, commissioned a study from the Centre for Economic Policy Research at the Australian National University on the economic issues surrounding publicly-funded child care. The terms of reference for this study were: (1) to review and comment on the data used to evaluate the economic benefits of the Children's Services Program; (2) to identify additional data sources and to provide additional arguments on the fiscal impact of the program; (3) to provide qualitative arguments on the labour market effects of the program; and (4) to construct models which could be applied to measure the economic benefit of the program.

The Centre's report (Anstie et al. 1988) was published by the Department of Community Services and Health. It argued that publicly-funded child care resulted in major economic and social benefits and that society as a whole (not just individual parents) had an interest in the upbringing of children. According to the authors of the report, the non-taxation of child care (and other domestic services) provided in the home, plus the high costs of purchasing child care outside the home, combined to create strong disincentives to women's participation in the workforce and thus distorted their choice. This had consequences for the economic wellbeing of families since women's participation in the labour force was one of the chief ways for low-income families to avoid poverty. It also had implications for the economy as a whole, since high employment rates for able-bodied adults contributed to economic and industrial development and aided governments in providing for those people outside the labour force because of age, poor health or disability.

Another argument addressed by the report concerned the return from public investment in women's education. Government subsidisation of child care, the report argued, would help avoid the depreciation of 'human capital' associated with women's lengthy withdrawals from the labour force for child rearing purposes:

> The greater the fraction of education and training paid for by the government the greater the community interest in the decision to leave and return to the workforce. The child care subsidies should be seen as part of the contribution that government makes to the development and maintenance of the stock of human capital embodied in the labour force
> *(Anstie et al. 1988:12)*

It was also argued that society as a whole had an interest in how children were raised since 'well brought-up children make good citizens – less crime, better voters [sic], larger tax base' (Anstie et al. 1988: 15). High quality services which help children to develop their full potential were therefore socially desirable. Further, such programs were important elements in the campaign against poverty, especially child poverty:

> The child of competent, happy and well-off parents has a flying start in life, whereas the child of parents with the opposite characteristics begins with a handicap. In a variety of ways, Australian governments do much to improve the prospects of the less advantaged child, by providing free or subsidised schooling, medical attention, and so on. Increasingly, because of community expectations, there is a need to do more to assist the child in the pre-school ages. Funded childcare is an integral part of that increased effort on behalf of children. *(Anstie et al. 1988: 28)*

According to this study, publicly-funded child care (particularly schemes such as the Children's Services Program where the major beneficiaries were low and middle income families) also contributed to social equity and income redistribution. In the absence of public subsidies, the cost of child care created a significant workforce disincentive for women with low-income earning potential. The existence of such a program, therefore, by helping to facilitate entry to the labour market by single parents and second earners in low-income families contributed to a fairer distribution of jobs and income.

Probably the most influential and widely quoted aspect of the report was its assessment of the net fiscal impact of publicly-funded child care. Against direct expenditure on the Children's Services Program it set the gains to the commonwealth which accrued from increased taxation

Table 3 *Possible fiscal gain to the commonwealth from working mothers with 0–4 year-old children in commonwealth-funded services*

	Married Women $m	Sole Parents $m	Total $m
Tax Revenue	121.9	21.0	142.9
Dependent Spouse Rebate	63.3	–	63.3
Marginal Tax Rate on Unearned Income	6.3	–	6.3
Family Allowance Supplement	28.1	–	28.1
Supporting Parents Benefit and Rent Assistance	–	55.8	55.8
TOTAL	219.6	76.8	296.4

Source: Anstie et al. (1988).

revenue, savings on the dependent spouse rebate and savings on social security pensions and benefits. The report estimated that net gains from the program could have been as high as $296 million in 1987–88, compared with expenditure of $190 million. Hence, publicly-funded child care may have resulted in a net addition to the budget as high as $106 million (Table 3).

The report received extensive publicity. It proved to be a crucial weapon in countering the arguments of Senator Walsh and the Department of Finance. Dr Blewett used it to argue both publicly and in Cabinet that there were 'sound arguments for the program's expansion' (*SMH* 1 June 1988). At a time when economic considerations were paramount, it was extremely important politically that the case in favour of publicly-funded child care had been produced by a group of mainstream economists.

In the end Senator Walsh failed in his bid to end operational subsidies to non-profit child care services and introduce a voucher system, despite the fact that this approach was given strong support by the Treasury and the Department of Finance. The majority in Cabinet preferred the alternative proposal put forward by Dr Blewett, the Minister for Community Services and Health. Blewett argued that the existing system, which combined a needs-based planning approach to the development of new services with fee relief subsidies targeted to low-income workforce participants, was more consistent with ALP principles and more amenable to integration with other government policies. According to newspaper reports, Blewett presented this proposal in a vigorous and forceful manner. He was supported by submissions presented to Cabinet by the Departments of Employment,

Education and Training, Prime Minister and Cabinet and Social Security (*AFR* 20 July 1988; *Australian* 23–24 July 1988). Brian Howe was also said to have spoken strongly in support of Blewett's approach.

In conjunction with the budget, the government announced the adoption of a 'National Child Care Strategy' which would involve the establishment of 30,000 additional child care places over a four-year period. In recognition of the fact that many parents who had benefitted from services for their pre-school children had encountered difficulties finding care for these children once they reached school age, the majority of the new places (20,000) were to be in out-of-school-hours care. Family day care and centre-based day care would each be boosted by 4,000 new places and there would be 2,000 occasional care places for the benefit of parents caring for young children at home. The announcement of the strategy appeared to be a significant victory for the advocates of community-based non-profit services. However, economic rationalist principles were soon to be re-asserted with renewed vigour as the government looked towards private interests (individual commercial operators and employers) to sustain the momentum of growth.

Pressures from the commercial centres to have fee relief subsidies extended to users of their services proved an extremely difficult issue for Labor. On the one hand the government had decided, after a great deal of internal debate and dissension, to give a firm commitment to the expansion of non-profit, community-controlled services and the continued existence of operational subsidies to support them. On the other hand, its members (particularly those backbenchers whose seats were vulnerable) were sensitive to representations from constituents whose incomes would qualify them for fee relief in a community-based centre but who could not get assistance because of the type of centre their children attended.

During the 1990 election campaign Labor announced an expansion of its 1988 child care strategy. Simultaneously it announced an extension of fee relief to users of commercial child care – a measure which it justified as necessary in order to achieve equity between families using public and private services. While some sections of the community child care lobby regarded this step as a bitter blow to their aspirations for a nationwide system of publicly-subsidised, parent-controlled services, (Community Child Care Victoria described it as 'disastrous' in their July *News Sheet*), many others had softened their views on the issue by the time the announcement was made. The ACTU, once a staunch opponent of subsidies to users of commercial centres, changed its position in the run-up to the 1990 election and became a strong advocate of the move.

Peak organisations such as the National Association of Community Based Children's Services, ACOSS and the Australian Early Childhood

Association began exploring the potential of an accreditation system in the late 1980s. They were influenced by the American model of accreditation put forward by the National Association for the Education of Young Children. The rationale for accreditation was that, with increasing numbers of children spending large parts of their lives in child care, there ought to be some mechanism for 'quality assurance'. State and territory regulations (which vary considerably around the country) were not seen as sufficient for this purpose. Regulations deal with quantifiable 'inputs'; staff/child ratios, the qualifications of staff, building specifications and open space and other physical requirements. Accreditation, in contrast, requires a focus on the way in which a centre actually functions. In the words of June Wangmann (a Sydney-based academic who is a key player in the accreditation debate):

> Regulations only deal with issues which affect children before they come in the door – the number of toilets, ratio of staff, the qualifications they hold. Accreditation looks at how staff interact with children. (*SMH 4 March 1993*)

Wangmann was commissioned by the commonwealth government to prepare a report on the possible content and structure of an accreditation system. Her report (Wangmann 1991) was supported by the community sector and sections of the commercial child care industry. It suggested a process in which services undergo a process of self-assessment, using criteria determined by an industry council with wide representation. Participants in the assessment would include parents, children, staff and sponsors of the service. The centre's self-assessment would subsequently be checked by an external validator. The process of accreditation, according to its advocates, does not compel all services to operate as 'five star', luxury services. Rather, it encourages standards of good practice which, with adequate inservice training and resourcing, can be achieved by all services (Wangmann 1991: 23).

Accreditation is regarded by its opponents in the commercial sector as adding an unnecessary layer of bureaucracy and paper work to an already over-burdened sector. They argue that it will increase costs and drive out services which are needed by struggling families. The market is the best, and only appropriate arbiter of the quality of services in this view. (Some of those who are most vociferous in their opposition to accreditation have also campaigned against the existence of basic state regulations.) They also argue that the personal qualities of caregivers are far more important in guaranteeing good care than are formal qualifications.

The government's announcement of its intention to introduce an accreditation scheme for child care centres was made in conjunction with the announcement concerning the extension of fee relief to the commercial sector. It was clearly intended to allay the fears of the community child care movement concerning the standard of care in private centres. Many concerns had been expressed regarding the standard of care in commercial centres. Research conducted by the Australian Bureau of Statistics (1989) had shown that commercial centres had fewer qualified staff, four times as many staff under 18 years and fewer ancillary staff. Many in the industry (especially teachers in early childhood courses who visit many centres in the course of their duties) claimed that the quality of care in commercial centres was of a lower standard. The concept of accreditation is not new to Australia. Accreditation schemes already operate in respect of private hospitals, nursing homes and schools.

Prime Minister Hawke, announcing the scheme, focused on the role that it could play in re-assuring parents of the quality of care they were using: 'Parents are entitled to be confident they are getting quality attention for their kids whether they are using government funded or commercial centres'. Subsequently, the Minister for Aged, Family and Health Services, Peter Staples, expanded on the Prime Minister's rationale, arguing that in addition to its role in quality assurance, accreditation was 'sheer economics'. In 1992 some $223 million, or 60 per cent of the entire child care budget was spent on fee relief. By linking fee relief to accreditation the federal government saw a way of ensuring 'value for money' for itself and therefore for the taxpayer.

Following Labor's 1990 election win, a commitee of industry representatives (including commerical and community-based providers, union and parent representatives) was set up to explore the establishment of an accreditation system for centre-based day care. The committee, chaired by Labor backbencher Mary Crawford, received submissions from all sections of the industry, national child care groups, the ACTU and the Australian Council of Social Service. It presented its report in September 1990, recommending the establishment of an independent national council which would be representative of all the interest groups and which would oversee the implementation of the accreditation system.

In 1991 an Interim National Accreditation Council (INAC), chaired by Jane Singleton (a media consultant and former journalist), was formed. The INAC adopted the position that full accreditation should be voluntary but that some level of quality assurance be required as a condition of fee relief. It suggested that in order to be eligible for fee relief, centres should have to register with the accreditation council and complete the first step (or 'module') of the accreditation process. Labor endorsed this proposal in the 1993 election campaign and

Table 4 *Growth in expenditure and number of places, 1974–1993*

Financial year (end)	Total outlays ($m)	Adjusted outlays ($ 1989–1990)	Centre based long day care	Family day care	Out of school hours care	Total places
1974	2.5	10.9	–	–	–	–
1975	8.2	30.5	–	–	–	–
1976	16.9	55.6	–	–	–	–
1977	18.1	52.3	–	–	–	–
1978	25.2	66.5	–	–	–	–
1979	31.1	75.9	–	–	–	–
1980	36.1	79.9	–	–	–	–
1981	42.6	86.2	–	–	–	–
1982	47.4	86.9	18 600	15 100	7 900	41 600
1983	65.0	106.8	20 000	20 100	9 900	50 000
1984	80.1	123.3	23 000	24 300	11 600	58 900
1985	122.7	181.0	31 400	32 200	14 800	78 400
1986	150.1	204.2	34 600	34 000	15 900	84 500
1987	181.2	225.5	40 800	38 400	29 600	108 800
1988	224.9	260.8	44 200	39 500	30 200	113 900
1989	213.1	230.2	44 100	39 600	30 600	114 300
1990	215.0	215.0	44 400	41 000	37 200	122 600
1991*	243.6	231.4	82 900	43 000	45 000	170 900
1992	434.8	405.3	96 100	45 700	48 800	195 700
1993	538.2	496.6	111 000	48 200	52 100	190 600

*Introduction of subsidies for users of commercial child care
Information provided by Department of Health, Housing, Local Government and Community Services.

promised to commence building the link between accreditation and eligibility for fee relief from the beginning of 1994.

Following the return of the Labor government at the 1993 election, the National Accreditation Council, chaired by Quentin Bryce (a former federal Sex Discrimination Commissioner), was established. Some commercial child care organisations have continued to lobby strenuously against accreditation. Although they have made the issue of cost the focal point of their campaign against accreditation, this is unlikely to be their real objection. The Interim National Accreditation Council – on which the commercial sector had more representatives than the community sector – estimated that the cost of accreditation would be in the order of one dollar per child per week. Compliance with accreditation, it argued, would not involve large outlays on buildings, equipment or highly qualified staff – all these matters are governed by state and territory regulations with which centres must already comply in order to receive a license. What then is the issue? The process of accreditation is likely to alert parents and staff to ways in which the functioning of their services might be altered to improve outcomes for children. Effectively, it will enable them to challenge the power of private operators over the management of their services. The real 'threat' of accreditation is not to do with monetary costs, it is to do with questions of power and control. Labor's willingness to stand up to the commercial lobby on this issue will be seen by the community child care lobby as a major test of the extent to which social justice objectives form part of its commitment to child care.

By 1993, child care was entrenched as part of the mainstream political agenda. The level of funding and service provision had increased significantly over the previous two decades (Table 4). Both Labor and the Coalition made major commitments in the area during the 1993 election and portrayed child care as central to their overall social and economic goals. The 'mainstreaming' of child care, however, had been achieved at a high price. Labor has moved towards ever increasing reliance on the private sector for the expansion of child care. Further, the extension of fee relief to commercial and employer providers has effectively resulted in the establishment of a voucher system through the back door. The aspirations of feminists and community child care advocates for a national system of non-profit services based around the needs of children and their families has receded. Child care has expanded rapidly but has become an instrument of economic and labour force policies.

Conclusion

Women in Australia have been 'policy shapers', not 'policy takers' in relation to the development of child care. In this they differ from their counterparts in the Nordic countries, Britain and the USA – the countries with which Australia is most often compared. In Sweden, Finland and Denmark child care policies have developed as an aspect of welfare state expansion. Services in those countries are aimed at meeting a variety of policy goals including the encouragement of women's workforce participation, gender equality and the provision of high quality educational and developmental opportunities for children. Such goals are, of course, shared by many women, especially feminists. However, it is notable that in none of these countries has an organised women's movement been important in policy debate or formulation. The same is true in Britain and the USA, where child care services are far more limited. Both those countries have been undergoing an expansion of services in the last five years but the major impetus in each case has been private employers seeking to improve their retention of staff, reduce absenteeism and encourage workplace flexibility.

The politics of child care in Australia have grown increasingly complex over the century, especially in the last two decades. The elaboration and intensification of the demands and claims which have been articulated by various groups are key indicators of this. From the 1890s, when small groups of upper-class women provided voluntary services backed by private donations and with minimal government support, the scene has changed to the current situation where dozens of groups and organisations are articulating specific, sometimes contradictory, demands upon the state and upon other sections of society (such as employers). This complexity has built up particularly over the last twenty years. The simple, somewhat glib, call for 'free 24-hour child care', characteristic of feminist demands of the late 1960s and early 1970s, has been replaced with detailed claims relating to particular types of services, preferred styles of management, the groups which should receive priority of access, fee levels and industrial conditions of workers.

In the late 1960s, when the demand for women's labour became more pressing and women's liberation emerged, the commonwealth government became the focus of sustained claims and women's efforts lost their exclusively philanthropic character. Throughout the 1970s and 1980s a variety of individuals and organisations endeavoured to move child care onto the political agenda. Feminist activism within government, bureaucracy and community organisations was crucial throughout this phase. The rhetoric of the period portrayed child care as liberating both for women and children. The provision of community-controlled, non-profit services was seen as a way of extending responsibility for children beyond the family and enabling *women* (rarely men) to challenge their traditional roles. Moreover, child care was explicitly seen to have benefits for children. These included opportunities to form relationships with adults outside the immediate family, companionship with other children, early detection of developmental problems and, for children from poor families, access to books, toys, games, outings and activities which could not be provided by their families. In the last ten years, as child care provision has been linked increasingly to economic and labour force goals, and as non-profit, community-based services have made way for commercial and employer-supported care, such goals have disappeared from public debate. The emancipatory ideals once central to feminist and community child care advocates have been replaced by a highly instrumental approach which values children's services not for the benefits they bring to *children* but for their ability to free adults for participation in employment and other activities. There is little expressed concern about children's needs and interests, except in the context of the accreditation debate.

Into the mainstream – at a price

Australia's child care program is now twenty years old. It has grown rapidly over the last two decades, especially under the Labor government which has held power since 1983. There are more than 200,000 commonwealth-subsidised child care places around Australia (Table 5) and some 300,000 children attend these services each week (Department of HHLGCS 1993b: 3). It is notable that the major growth in children's services has occurred in a political and economic context characterised by strong pressures to reduce overall commonwealth expenditure. The explanation for this is that the Labor government has become increasingly receptive to the argument that expenditure on child care is not simply a drain on the economy but, if linked to workforce participation, can lead to increased taxation revenue and reductions in certain kinds of welfare expenditure such as sole parent pensions and family payments. The fact that women's workforce participation has been crucial in cushioning the impact of recession for many families has also contributed to government support for expanded child care provision.

Undoubtedly child care is now a mainstream issue in Australia, but how adequate are the policies and the level of provision? The answer to this question, of course, depends upon the criteria employed to make the judgment. According to the department which administers the Services for Families with Children Program, its philosophy is based on 'the simple principle that Australian families have a right to affordable, quality child care'. This 'simple principle' is immediately qualified by the statement that 'resources are finite' and must be directed to where they are needed most, namely, 'to working parents on low to middle incomes' (Department of Health, Housing and Community Services 1992: 43). If we accept the commonwealth's goal of focusing on work-related child care needs, then the existing program, although incomplete, is functioning well. Australian provision is not exceptionally high in comparison with the best served nations (Finland, Sweden, Denmark and France) but in comparison with the United States and Britain, Australia is doing very well. Approximately two-thirds of the demand for formal work-related child care services for 0–4-year olds has been met as has 40 per cent of the demand for work-related care for school age children (Department of Community Services and Health, 1992). The government is committed to meeting the remaining needs by the turn of the century. Further, Australia has a national scheme of assistance with child care fees, regulations which govern most service types (the major exception being out-of-school hours care) and the beginnings of an accreditation system.

If, however, the criteria used to assess national performance are broader than the work-related goals expressed by the government, then there are major gaps and problem areas. One area of concern is the marginalisation of the child care needs of families where both parents are not in the workforce. The 1990 survey of child care arrangements conducted by the Australian Bureau of Statistics indicated that there is a very high level of unmet demand for formal child care services for non-work-related reasons. Of those expressing a demand for formal

Table 5 *Number of operational child care places, states and territories, 30 June 1993*

Service type	NSW	Vic	Qld	SA	WA	Tas	NT	ACT	Australia
Long day centres									
Community-based	15 420	10 541	6 689	3 585	3 594	1 260	816	872	42 777
Commercial	16 825	9 671	20 497	1 759	3 904	139	107	1 018	53 920
Employer and other non-profit	1 853	2 672	491	758	667	153	195	666	7 455
Family day care	14 478	13 198	8 872	3 924	3 019	1 462	747	2 155	47 855
Occasional care	1 003	718	320	347	355	92	62	132	3 029
Neighbourhood centres	0	500	158	105	157	51	0	0	971
Multifunctional services	45	80	95	51	108	0	116	0	495
Multifunctional Aboriginal children's services	467	170	120	125	117	27	105	0	1 131
Outside school hours care	18 518	12 256	8 355	4 125	3 611	1 335	571	1 569	50 340
TOTAL	68 609	49 806	45 597	14 779	15 532	4 519	2 719	6 412	207 973

Information provided by Department of Health, Housing, Local Government and Community Services, 1994.

child care, only around 40 per cent gave work-related reasons. The other 60 per cent cited either their children's needs or their own personal needs (other than workforce participation) as the reason for seeking care. The parents of 54,300 children expressed a demand for pre-school and more than 166,000 children require occasional care (ABS 1992: 21). These children and their families are increasingly marginalised in Australian child care policy.

A second area of concern to many participants in the child care debate is that, in the rush to expand the sheer number of child care places, the policies of the Labor government have brought to an end the goal of a national system of non-profit, community-based child care. The government's shift towards reliance upon the private sector to provide services for pre-school aged children has become more pronounced with each successive announcement of growth. By the 1993 round of promises, only slightly more than half the new places were to be community-based. Of the forshadowed new places for children below school age, almost 80 per cent were in commercial and/or employer-sponsored services. Commercial and employer-supported services now account for the majority of centre-based places available to 0–4-year olds across Australia. This predominance is mainly due to the large numbers of such services in New South Wales and Queensland. In Victoria, South Australia Western Australia and Tasmania as well as the Northern Territory and the Australian Capital Territory most care for 0–4s is provided by the community sector. New South Wales and Victoria are the leaders in employer-supported care (Table 5). When *all* services including family day care, out-of-school hours care and the smaller service types are taken into account, the community sector is still the main provider of places and most children who use formal child care use community-based services.

A similar trend towards commercial and employer-provided care has been noted in other countries. Clare Ungerson warns of the trend in Britain to emphasise the responsibility of employers rather than government as providers of child care. The focus of employer-supported child care, she argues, is to maintain the profits of companies, not to build greater equality between men and women. Further, such an approach is extremely vulnerable to the vicissitudes of the labour market. Moreover, the policy is aimed not at women as carers, but specifically at the sub-group of women who are workers in the paid labour force (1990: 187). A similar trend has been reported in Denmark. In that country there have been substantial cutbacks in public expenditure on child care and corresponding attempts to privatise responsibility for children. Admission to child care centres is now 'closely linked to the employment situation of the parents'

(Borchorst and Siim 1987: 140). Peter Moss, co-ordinator of the European Childcare Network (an organisation of representatives from the countries of the European Union), raised the following questions in his annual report for 1992: 'Are [child care] services an occupational benefit for certain workers or a right of citizenship for children and parents? Can a recognition of the economic importance of services be combined with a recognition of their social and educational importance? Should services for children with employed parents be conceived and developed in isolation from other children?' (Moss 1993: 26). Such questions are also being raised in Australia. They have particular relevance for unemployed parents and Aboriginal families.

A third problematic feature of Australian child care policy is the partial abandonment of the principle that new services receiving government assistance should be located in areas of highest need. Although needs-based planning is still used to determine the location of new services established by the non-profit sector, such services represent an ever-diminishing proportion of the total. Commercial operators can start up where they wish and still attract commonwealth government child care assistance. Moreover, they are not required to provide care for babies and toddlers, even though there is clear evidence that this is the type of care in greatest demand. The extra costs involved in caring for very young children (due to the higher staff ratios required) make this an unattractive option for many commercial providers. Hence, community-based providers are likely to be left literally 'holding the babies', resulting in higher charges in these centres and further accusations that they are inefficient compared to commercial services.

The 1993 election campaign

During the 1993 election campaign Prime Minister Paul Keating announced Labor's child care policies not as part of its women's program but as part of his economic statement 'Investing in the Nation'. According to the Prime Minister, 'the time has come to move child care out of the welfare area and into the economic mainstream where it belongs' (*SMH*, 23 February, 1993). As an extension of this view, Labor promised a non-means-tested child care rebate to supplement the existing child care assistance (or fee relief) program. The new rebate, planned to come into effect in mid–1994, will apply to a family's work-related child care expenses for children up to and including 12 years old. 'Work-related child care expenses' will include those incurred in relation to parents' studying, training or looking for work as well as expenses incurred while parents are actually employed. Further, the rebate will be available regardless of the type of care used (formal or informal) as long as it meets state and territory standards, the carer is over 18 years and has an 'approved carer' provider number. The new rebate will enable families to claim 30 per cent of their child care costs above a minimum fee. The maximum level of assistance will be $28.20 per week for families with one child in care and $61.20 per week for families with two or more children in care. The rebate has been constructed as a clear alternative to a tax rebate and appears to be intended to bring to an end the debate about tax concessions for users of child care. Parents will be able to claim the rebate through local Medicare offices on a weekly, fortnightly, monthly or annual basis. This contrasts with a tax rebate or deduction which would most likely be claimed in a taxpayer's annual tax return. Importantly, the cash rebate will be available to low income individuals and families who would not have paid sufficient tax to benefit from a tax concession.

In order to head off claims that its child care policies benefit women in the workforce but neglect those caring for children at home, Labor also announced the introduction of a Home Child Care Allowance to come into operation in mid–1994. The Home Child Care Allowance will replace an existing tax measure – the dependent spouse rebate – for families with young children. In the past, the dependent spouse rebate has been heavily criticised for providing a benefit to the waged partner, while ignoring the needs of the person providing services in the home. The new allowance will mean that regular cash assistance will go to the primary carer (almost always the mother) rather than a tax rebate going annually to the main breadwinner (almost always the male partner). The Home Child Care Allowance is in line with moves in several European countries to provide economic assistance to parents providing full-time care for their young children at home. One criticism of the Home Child Care Allowance is that while it is a gesture towards recognition of the economic needs of parents caring for children in the home, it does nothing to address their needs for child care services.

Labor also promised during the 1993 election campaign that it would meet all demands for work-related child care by 2001. How realistic is this goal? To date, there has been considerable difficulty in proceeding with the long day care places promised in Labor's earlier child care strategies. To some extent, Labor has promised, but not yet delivered. The government went into the 1993 election with only a little more than half the promised places from the 1988 strategy actually operating. *None* of the centre-based long day care places promised in the 1990 strategy were operational at that time. The reluctance of state governments to enter into cost sharing arrangements, difficulties in finding sponsors able to raise capital and problems in finding suitable land have been the major difficulties. Labor has now made available new partnership arrangements to both non-profit organisations and employers. Under these arrangements, non-profit groups can receive a grant equal to half the capital cost of establishing a service (up to $6,000 per place), plus an interest free loan to be repaid over twenty years to cover the balance. Employers will also be eligible for interest free loans to cover 50 per cent of the establishment costs of new services. Despite these generous new provisions, Labor's biggest problem is likely to be finding sponsors for its promised services. Since the commonwealth no longer puts up the total capital, the fulfilment of the government's pledge is largely beyond its control.

Child care also featured prominently in the Coalition's election campaign. According to the Coalition parties, 'affordable quality child care is a basic right of all parents' (Liberal and National Parties 1993: 2). The Liberal and National parties castigated Labor for 'ignoring children who are being cared for in the home' and for what they termed its 'obvious bias in favour of those in the full-time paid workforce' (Liberal and National Parties 1993: 4). Like Labor, the Coalition promised a significant expansion of services, setting a target of 360,000 places by 2001 compared with Labor's estimate of 354,000 new places. The Coalition, however, did not present any strategy for providing these places. It did not follow Labor's lead of offering capital subsidies to non-profit organisations and interest free loans to employers and its suggested level of government expenditure on new services was well below Labor's. Presumably the Coalition's assumption was that commercial operators and employers would be responsible for establishing most of the new services.

As a measure to address the high costs of child care, the Coalition, like Labor, offered a cash rebate to parents. However, the Coalition proposal was for a *means-tested* rebate – Labor's non-means-tested policy was described as 'child care for millionaires' (Liberal and National Parties 1993: 21.) Interestingly, the Coalition offered to introduce a common level of child care assistance for all forms of care, thus ending the less favourable treatment of occasional care, before- and after-school care and vacation care. This policy initiative has been strongly supported by community organisations. In regard to the contentious issue of accreditation, however, the Coalition strongly opposed the stance of the major community child care organisations. In line with its general policies of reducing government regulation in business affairs, the Coalition expressed support for a voluntary system of accreditation only, arguing that 'parents are undoubtedly the best judges of the quality of available services' (Liberal and National Parties 1993: 6).

Clearly, as the prominence of child care issues in recent election campaigns suggests, there is little consensus between the major parties about the nature and direction of commonwealth child care policy. The current Children's Services Program is regarded by community child care groups as extremely vulnerable to a change of government. Although the policy statement of the Coalition parties at the last election suggested a high level of support for the continuation of a strong commonwealth government presence in child care, the broader policies and philosophies of the opposition parties have consistently emphasised market solutions rather than government provision in most areas of community service provision (Hewson and Fischer 1993). In the past, the Coalition has been equivocal about its commitment to operational subsidies for non-profit services. In the event of a change of government, the structure of child care provision and funding that has developed under Labor is such that it would not be difficult for a conservative government to further privatise the system. This could be achieved by eliminating the operational subsidies which currently support non-profit child care (a possibility which was explored very seriously even by the Labor government) and changing the present fee relief sytem into a voucher system. Given Labor's extension of fee relief to users of commercial centres, the introduction of vouchers would only be a minor, largely superficial, change from the present system. Alternatively, or in addition, tax concessions could be introduced. Existing non-profit services could be sold to the private sector.

Undoubtedly the biggest challenge for Australian child care policy is to achieve a balance between the need for work-related child care and the broader goal of providing services which are focused upon all children and their needs. Those who wish to see the current system retained and extended will need to develop a policy framework which links child care in a more integrated way with other policies for children and parents. Child care provision needs to be linked to other policies such as economic support for parents, support and assistance for those caring for children at home, flexible employment practices and paid parental leave. Some moves towards a broader conception of family needs have been made as a result of Australia's ratification of ILO convention 156 concerning workers with family responsibilities. The work done in the context of the International Year of the Family (IYF) has also contributed to a more inclusive understanding of the needs of families.

The great strength of the Australian child care system and the feature which makes it of particular interest in terms of international comparison, is the extent to which it has been shaped by the energies of women working in, or closely allied with, community-based organisations – from the philanthropists of the late nineteenth century to the feminists, trade unionists and bureaucrats of the last two decades. The harnessing of relatively high levels of public resources into a nationally organised, high quality system which retains a strong community focus and provides opportunities for parental involvement (at least in the non-profit sector) is unusual in international terms. Preserving this system in the face of growing pressures towards privatisation and a narrowly focused, workforce-oriented program is the challenge of the coming decades, no matter which party is in office.

References

a'Beckett, A. M. (1939) 'Presidential Address', in *First Biennial Conference of the Australian Association for Pre-School Child Development*, AAPSCD, Melbourne, 12–20.

Adam, J. (1991) *Employer Sponsored Child Care – An Issues Paper*, prepared by Community Child Care, Victoria, for the National Women's Consultative Council, Melbourne.

Adams, C. Teich and Winston, K. Teich (1980) *Mothers at Work: Public Policies in the United States, Sweden and Britain*, Princeton University Press, Princeton, N.J.

Administrative and Clerical Officers Association (1985) *The Case for Work-Related Child Care in Australian Government Employment*, Sydney.

Administrative and Clerical Officers Association (Victoria) (1985) *Child Care Survey Report*, Melbourne.

Alexander, J. et al. (1980) *One Step Forward, Two Steps Back: The Hidden Problems in Community Management of Children's Services*, Social Research and Evaluation Ltd., Sydney.

Allen, J. (1979) 'Breaking into the Public Sphere', in J. Mackinolty and H. Radi eds., *In Pursuit of Justice: Australian Women and the Law 1788–1979*, Hale & Iremonger, Sydney, 107–117.

——(1982) 'Octavius Beale Reconsidered: Infanticide, Babyfarming and Abortion in New South Wales, 1880–1939', in Sydney Labour History Group, *What Rough Beast?: The State and Social Order in Australian History*, Allen & Unwin, Sydney, 111–29.

Allport, C. (1984) 'The Princess in the Castle: Women and the New Order Housing', in *All Her Labours*, (selected papers from the Third Women and Labour Conference, Adelaide, 1982), Vol. 2, Hale & Iremonger, Sydney.

Anderson, M. (n.d.) *The Story of the Free Kindergartens and Playgrounds*, Kindergarten Union of NSW, Sydney.

Anstie, R., Gregory, R.G., Dowrick, S. and Pincus, J. J. (1988) *Government Spending on Work-Related Child Care: Some Economic Issues*, Centre for Economic Policy Research, Australian National University, Canberra.

Apps, P. (1975) *Child Care in the Production-Consumption Economy*, Victorian Council of Social Service, Collingwood, Victoria.

Association of Child Care Centres of NSW (1981) 'Discrimination and Mismanagement of Existing Child Care Funding', *National Journal of Child Care*, 3 (3), 7–9.
—— (1988) Response to Caucus Committee on Welfare and Community Services Report on Child Care, Sydney.
Australian and New Zealand College of Psychiatrists (1971) 'Memorandum on Some Aspects of the Welfare of Infants and Children Aged Under Three Years Whose Mothers are in Full-Time Employment', *Medical Journal of Australia*, February.
Australian Bureau of Statistics (1970) *Child Care*, May 1969 (Cat. No. 17.2, Canberra.
—— (1974) *Child Care*, May 1973 (Cat. No. 17.2), Canberra.
—— (1978) *Child Care*, May 1977 (Cat. No. 4402.0), Canberra.
—— (1981) *Child Care Survey, Australia* June 1980 (Cat. No. 4402.0), Canberra.
—— (1985) *Child Care Arrangements, Australia* November 1984 (Cat. No. 4402.0), Canberra.
—— (1987) *Child Care Arrangements, Australia*, (Cat. No. 4402.0), Canberra.
—— (1989) *Commercial Long Day Child Care Australia* (Cat. No. 4414.0), Canberra.
—— (1990) *Labour Force Status and Other Characteristics of Families, Australia, 1980–1989*, (Cat. No. 6224.0) Canberra.
—— (1992) *Child Care*, Australia, (Cat. No. 4402.0), Canberra.
Australian Council of Social Service (1971) *Day Care for Children*, ACOSS, Sydney.
—— (1988) *Child Care: A Background Paper*, Sydney.
Australian Council of Trade Unions (1981) *Child Care Kit*, Melbourne.
—— (1984) *Child Care Facilities in Australian Government Employment*, Melbourne.
Australian Family Association (1980) *National Seminar on the Family*, University of Melbourne, AFA, Melbourne.
—— (1981) *National Seminar on the Family*, University of Melbourne, AFA, Melbourne.
Australian Federation of Child Care Associations (1981) Submission to Senator F. M. Chaney, February, *National Journal of Child Care*, 3 (2), 25–27.
—— (1988) *The Politics of Child Care – You Should Know the Truth*, Australian Federation of Child Care Associations, Hawthorn, Victoria.
Australian Institute of Family Studies (1990) *The Coalition Parties' Family Tax Package*, Australian Family Income Transfer Bulletin No. 7, Melbourne.
Australian Labor Party (1972) *Policy Speech 1972*, ALP, Canberra.
—— (1973) *Platform, Constitution and Rules*, Canberra.
—— (1979) *National Committee of Inquiry: Discussion Papers*, (APSA Monograph No. 23), ALP and Australian Public Service Association, Bedford Park, South Australia.
—— (1983) *Platform, Constitution and Rules*, Canberra.
—— (1988) *Report of the Working Party on Child Care to the Caucus Committee on Welfare and Community Services*, Canberra.
Australian Market Research (1986) *A Study to Identify the Information Needs and Networks of Low Income Families*, Canberra.
Australian Pre-School Association (1970) *Day Care Centres in Australia: Standards and General Principles*, Canberra.
Australian Pre-Schools Committee (1974) *Care and Education of Young Children*, (The Fry Report), AGPS, Canberra.

Australian Society of Accountants, Women Members' Group (1980) *Submission to the Federal Treasurer on Tax Deductibility for Child Care Expenses*, Sydney.

Australian Vice-Chancellors' Committee (1972) Child Minding Facilities, Memorandum 42/72, Canberra.

——(1977) Child Care Facilities, Memorandum 50/77, Canberra.

Bailey, E. (1952) Transcript of Evidence to Western Australian Royal Commission on Kindergartens (no page numbers). (Held at Battye Library, Perth.)

Balbo, L. (1987) 'Crazy Quilts: Rethinking the Welfare State Debate from a Woman's Point of View', in A. Showstack Sassoon ed., *Women and the State: the Shifting Boundaries of Public and Private*, Hutchinson, London, 45–71.

Baldock, C.V. and Cass, B. eds. (1988) *Women, Social Welfare and the State*, (2nd ed.), Allen & Unwin, Sydney.

Beazley, K. (1973). Transcript of Interview on *A.M.* (ABC Radio), 15 October 1973 (personal papers, Elizabeth Reid).

——(1977) 'The Labor Party in Opposition and Government', in I.K.F. Birch and D. Smart eds., *The Commonwealth Government and Education 1964–1976: Political Initiatives and Developments*, Drummond, Melbourne, 94–119.

——(1980) 'The Commonwealth Ministry of Education: An Experience in the Whitlam Government 1972–75', in Stephen Murray-Smith ed., *Melbourne Studies in Education*, Melbourne University Press, Melbourne, 1–60.

Bethune, D. (1971) Early History of Kindergartens as Community Centres, Typescript (held at Institute of Early Childhood, Kew, Victoria.)

Blewett, N. (1988) Unpublished speech notes for official opening of Hyde Park Child Care Centre, Sydney, May 30.

Bonython, J. (1966) 'The Lady Gowrie', *Australian Pre-School Quarterly*, 6 (3), February, 5–6.

Booth, A. and Rubinstein, L. (1990) 'Women and Trade Unions in Australia', in S. Watson ed., *Playing the State: Australian Feminist Interventions*, Allen & Unwin, Sydney, 121–35.

Borchorst, A. (1990) 'Political motherhood and child care policies: A comparative approach to Britain and Scandinavia' in C.Ungerson ed., *Gender and Caring: Work and Welfare in Britain and Scandinavia*, Wheatsheaf, Hemel Hempstead.

Borchorst, A. and Siim, B. (1987) 'Women and the Advanced Welfare State – A New Kind of Patriarchal Power?', in A. Showstack Sassoon ed., *Women and the State: The Shifting Boundaries of Public and Private*, Hutchinson, London, 128–57.

Bowen, L. (Special Minister of State) (1974a) Press statement, 'Establishment of a Children's Commission', 19 September.

——(1974b) Press statement, 'Interim Committee for the Children's Commission', 29 October.

Bowlby, J. (1951) *Maternal Care and Mental Health*, World Health Organisation, Geneva. Abridged version *Child Care and the Growth of Love*, (2nd ed. 1965), Penguin, Harmondsworth.

Brennan, D. (1982) *Children's Services in Australia: The State of Play: A Review of Commonwealth and State Policies, 1972–1982*, Family and Children's Services Agency, Sydney.

——(1983a) 'Government Changes in the Direction of Children's Services', Keynote address, *Child Care is a Political Issue*, (Papers of the National

Association of Community Based Child Care Conference) Sydney, July, 10–13.
——(1983b) *Towards A National Child Care Policy*, Institute of Family Studies, Melbourne.
Brennan, D. and O'Donnell, C. (1986) *Caring for Australia's Children: Political and Industrial Issues in Child Care*, Allen & Unwin, Sydney.
Brotherhood of St Laurence (1972a) *Report Covering the First Six Months Operation of the Family Day Care Service*, May, BSL, Melbourne.
——(1972b) *Report Covering the Second Six Months Operation*, April -September 1972, November, BSL, Melbourne.
——(1973) *Third Progress Report*, December 1972 to September 1973, October, BSL, Melbourne.
——(1977) 'Family Day Care', *Australian Child and Family Welfare*, 2 (3).
Burgess, A., Keeves, E. and Prest, E.J. (1975) *Jubilee History of the Kindergarten Union of South Australia, 1905–1955*, KUSA, Adelaide.
Burns, A. (1980) *The Child Care Conflict*, Paper presented at WEL Conference Sydney, June.
Burns, A., Fegan, M., Sparkes A. and Thompson, P. (1974) *Working Mothers and Their Children*, The Electrical Trades Union Study, School of Behavioural Sciences, Macquarie University, Sydney.
Burns, A., Fegan, M., Sparkes, A. and White, D. (1975) *An Alternative in Quality Child Care: A Feasibility Study of Family Day Care in an Inner City and an Outer Suburban Area of Sydney*, School of Behavioural Sciences, Macquarie University, Sydney.
Burton, B. (1986) 'Bad Mothers? Infant Killing in Victoria', BA hons. thesis (History), University of Melbourne.
Burud, S. (1989) 'Employer Supported Child Care in the USA', in *Corporate Child Care: The Bottom Line* (Papers from a National Conference on Employer Supported Child Care, Sydney, November 1989) CCAW, Sydney, 7–15.
Butler, B. (1992) 'Aboriginal and Torres Strait Islander Children: Present and Future Services and Policy' (Paper presented at Northern Territory Annual Children's Services Conference) August.
Callinan, (Sir) B. (1980) 'The Australian Family Association', in AFA, *National Seminar on the Family*, University of Melbourne, 4–5.
Campbell, Dame Janet (1930) *Report on Maternal and Child Welfare in Australia*, Department of Health, Canberra.
Cass, B. (1982) *Family Policies in Australia: Contest over the Social Wage*, Social Welfare Research Centre (University of New South Wales) Reports and Proceedings No. 21, Kensington, NSW, May.
——(1988a) 'Population Policies and Family Policies: State Construction of Domestic Life', in Baldock and Cass 168–89.
——(1988b) 'Redistribution to Children and to Mothers: a History of Child Endowment and Family Allowances', in Baldock and Cass 54–88.
——(1990) 'Private Life, Work and Citizenship: Social Policy Challenges for the 1990s', Paper presented at Public Lecture Series, Department of Social Work and Social Policy, University of Sydney, July.
Cass, B., Keens, C. and Moller, J. (1981) 'Family Policy Halloween: Family Allowances: Trick or Treat?', *Australian Quarterly*, 53(1), 56–73.
Castleman, T., Mulvany, J. and Wulff, M. (1989) *After Maternity: How Australian Women Make Decisions about Work and Family*, Swinburne Institute of Technology, Centre for Women's Studies, Hawthorn, Victoria.

REFERENCES

Castles, F. (1985) *The Working Class and Welfare: Reflections on the Political Development of the Welfare State in Australia and New Zealand, 1890–1980,* Allen & Unwin, Sydney.
Central Advisory Council for Education (UK) (1967) *Children and Their Primary Schools,* (The Plowden Report), Her Majesty's Stationery Office, London.
Centre for Urban Studies (n.d.) *Evaluation of the Child Care Catalyst Program in Victoria,* Swinburne Institute of Technology, Hawthorn, Victoria.
Chaney, F.M. (Minister for Social Security) (1981a) 'Children's Services Program', Press release, 19 August (81/51).
——(1981b) Speech at Opening of Curzon Street Child Care Centre, 28 August.
——(1981c) 'The Role of Voluntary Organisations', Address to Sydney Day Nursery and Nursery Schools Association, 23 October.
Child Welfare Department of New South Wales (1955–66). *Annual Reports.*
Childcare at Work Ltd. (1990) *Corporate Child Care: Management's View,* AGPS, Canberra.
Childhood Services Council of South Australia (1980) *Children's Services in Metropolitan Adelaide,* Adelaide.
Children's Commission – A Progress Report (1975) AGPS, Canberra.
Children's Services Action, (1978–81). Minutes of meetings.
——(1982) *The Case Against Tax Deductions for Child Care Expenses,* pamphlet, Sydney.
Chipman, L. (1981) 'National Family Policy – A Concept', in AFA, *Second National Seminar: The Family Education and Community Support,* University of Melbourne, 7–20.
Choo, C. (1990) *Aboriginal Child Poverty,* Brotherhood of St. Laurence, Melbourne.
Clements, F.W. (1964) 'Programmes and Problems for Children Needing Day Care', in *Report of 10th Biennial Conference of APA,* Brisbane.
——(1966) 'Maternal Deprivation – A Review', *Australian Pre-School Quarterly* 6 (4), 9–12.
——(1967) 'The Need for and the Trends of Day Nurseries', in Australian Pre-School Association, *Children and their Families* (Proceedings of 11th National Conference of APA, Canberra, 1967), Canberra 63–72.
Cochran, M. ed. (1993) *International Handbook of Child Care Policies and Programs,* Greenwood Press, Westport, Connecticut.
Cohen, B. (1988) *Caring for Children: Services and Policies for Childcare and Equal Opportunities in the United Kingdom,* European Commission, London.
——(1993) 'United Kingdom', in Cochran 515–34.
Coleman, M. (1978a) The Children's Services Program in Australia, Paper presented at OECD Conference on Early Childhood Care and Education, New Zealand, February.
——(1978b) 'An Idea Before its Time', in A. Graycar ed., *Perspectives in Australian Social Policy: A Book of Readings,* Macmillan, Melbourne, 144–56.
Committee on Pre-School and Kindergarten Education in Tasmania (1968) *Education from Three to Eight,* Education Department, Hobart.
Community Child Care (NSW) (1977–90) *Annual Reports.*
——(1978–86) *Newsletter,* Nos. 1–29.
——(1981) *Children's Services in New South Wales: A Community Perspective,* Sydney.
——(1987a) *Public versus Private: How are the Interests of Australian Families Served in Child Care Provision?,* Sydney.

——(1987–1990) *Rattler*, Nos. 1–14.
Community Child Care Victoria (1975–76) *Newsletter*, Nos. 1–9.
——(1977–82) *Ripple*, Nos. 10–26.
——(1978a) 'Planning for Children: "People" Resources and Children's Services', *Royal Australian Planning Institute Journal*, 16, May, 44–45.
——(1978b) *Child Care – Workable Policies for Working Women*, Melbourne.
——(1983–90) News Sheet.
Coughlan, W. G. (1957) 'Marriage Breakdown', in A.P. Elkin ed., *Marriage and the Family in Australia*, Angus & Robertson, Sydney, 115–63.
Council of Commonwealth Public Service Organisations (1974) Supplementary Submission to the Australian Pre-Schools Committee and the Social Welfare Commission Concerning Child Care Facilities.
Cox, E. (1988) ' "Pater-patria": Child-rearing and the State', in Baldock and Cass 190–204.
Cox, E. and Baker, C. (1975) 'Possibility and Portents: Child Care in New South Wales', *Papers from the Sydney Women's Commission*, Sydney.
Cox, E. and Martin, J. (1976) *There is No 'Come in for a Cuppa, Love' for Us: Stress and Conflict amongst Migrant Women*, NCOSS, Sydney.
Cox, E., Jobson, S. and Martin, J. (1976) *'We Cannot Talk Our Rights': Migrant Women*, NCOSS and School of Sociology, University of New South Wales.
Cox, L. (1971) *Review of Current Research on Children of 'Working Mothers'*, Department of Labour and National Service, Melbourne.
Crawford, P. (1988) 'Early Childhood in Perth, 1940-1945: From the Records of the Lady Gowrie Child Centre', in P. Hetherington ed., *Childhood and Society in Western Australia*, University of Western Australia Press, Nedlands, 187–207.
Creche and Kindergarten Association of Queensland (1907–84) *Annual Reports*
——(1937) Typescript. (Held at Lady Gowrie Centre, Brisbane.)
Creswick, A. (1939) 'Finance', in Australian Association for Pre-School Child Development, *First Biennial Conference*, Melbourne, AAPSCD.
Cropley, J. and Chadwick, J. (1981) *The ACTU Moorabbin Child Care Project*, ACTU, Melbourne.
Crow, R. (1976) 'Child Care: An Expediency or a Right?', *Join Hands*, No. 3, March, 22–25.
——(1983) 'Child Care and the People's Front against Fascism', *Join Hands*, Winter/Spring, 3–10.
——(various dates) Papers, records and photographs relating to involvement in campaigns for child care in Melbourne since the 1930s, especially the Brunswick Children's Centre and other wartime children's centres. (The Crow Collection. Held at Urban Studies Unit, Victoria University of Technology, Footscray.)
Cullen J. et al. (1975) *Mothers' Child Care Preferences: A Report to the Australian Government Advisory Committee on Child Care*, Health Commission of New South Wales, Sydney.
Cumpston, J.H.L. and Heinig, C. (1944) *Pre-School Centres in Australia: Building, Equipment and Programme: The Lady Gowrie Child Centres*, Commonwealth Department of Health, Canberra.
Curthoys, A. (1976) 'Men and Childcare in the Feminist Utopia', *Refractory Girl*, 10, March, 3–5.
Davis, L. (1983) 'Now You See It, Now You Don't: The Restructuring of Commonwealth Government Child Care Policy', *Australia and New Zealand Journal of Sociology*, 19 (1), March, 79–95.

REFERENCES

——(1987a) 'The Brunswick Children's Centre: A Forgotten Model Children's Service?', *Australian Journal of Early Childhood*, 12 (1), February 42–8.
——(1987b) 'Minding Children or Minding Machines', *Labour History*, 53, November, 86–97.
——(1988) 'Minding Children or Minding Machines. Women's Labour and Child Care in Australia During World War II and the Post-war Reconstruction', PhD thesis, Macquarie University, Sydney.
Davison, G. (1983) 'The City-Bred Child and Urban Reform in Melbourne, 1900-1940', P. Williams ed., *Social Process and the City*, Allen & Unwin, Sydney, 143–74.
de Coney, J. (1945) 'Motherhood on Strike', *Australian Women's Digest*, 1 (6).
de Garis, B.K. (1974) '1890-1900', in F.K. Crowley ed., *A New History of Australia*, Heinemann, Melbourne, 216–259.
de Lacey, P. R. and Fisher C. H. (1972) 'Educational Need and Provision for Urban Pre-School Children', *Australian Journal of Education*, 16 (2).
de Lemos, M. (1968) 'Some Recent Developments: Theory and Practice', *Quarterly Review of Education*, 1 (4).
de Lissa, L. (1955) *Talks Given at the Golden Jubilee of the Kindergarten Union of South Australia*, unpublished typescript, Adelaide.
Deagan, C. (1978) 'The Trivialisation of Women's Work – The Case of Child Care', *Refractory Girl*, 16, May, 3–7.
——(1979) 'The "Flying Dutchman" Principle in Children's Services', *Interim Report to the Family and Children's Services Agency from the New South Wales Council of Social Service Evaluation Unit*, Sydney, December.
——(1980a) '"Volunteers and Conscripts": Women Working in Child Care', *Refractory Girl*, 18/19, [joint issue], 6–8.
——(1980b) 'Research and Planning in Children's Services: The Politics', *National Child Care Conference 1980*, Women's Advisory Unit, South Australian Premier's Department, Adelaide.
Denison, D. (1978) *Education Under Six*, Croom Helm, London.
Department of Community Services and Health (1984–92) *Annual Reports*.
——(1986) *Children's Services Program – Guidelines for the Establishment and Funding of Work-Related Child Care in Conjunction with Private Sector Employers*, Canberra.
——(1988) *Industry Initiative: Information and Guidelines*, Canberra.
——(1989) *1988 Census of Day Care Services*, Canberra, 1989.
Department of Education, (1981) *Major Trends and Developments in Australian Education 1977–78*, AGPS, Canberra.
Department of Education and Science (1972) *Pre-School Teachers' Colleges Annual Report*, AGPS, Canberra.
Department of Education, Employment and Training (1989) *Recent Trends in the Australian Labour Market*, Economic Analysis Branch, DEET, Canberra.
Department of Health, Housing and Community Services (1992) *Annual Report 1991–92*, AGPS, Canberra.
Department of Health, Housing, Local Government and Community Services (1993a) *Annual Report 1992–93*, AGPS, Canberra.
Department of Health, Housing, Local Government and Community Services (1993b) *Census of Child Care Services*, AGPS, Canberra.
Department of Labour and National Service (1968) Women's Bureau, *Married Women in Industry: Three Surveys*, (Women in the Work Force Series Booklet No. 4), Melbourne.

——Women's Bureau (1970) *Child Care Centres,* (Women in the Work Force Series Booklet No.7), Melbourne.
Department of Social Security (1976–92) *Annual Reports,* AGPS, Canberra.
Derody, B. and Sheehan, P. J. (1978) *The Demand for and Supply of Kindergarten Teachers in Victoria 1977–1984,* Australian Council for Educational Research, Hawthorn, Victoria.
Development of Pre-School Education in South Hobart, (1971) 1910–1971, An Historical Sketch, Hobart. (Held at Lady Gowrie Centre, Hobart.)
Dolan, C. (1983) 'Child Care – the Industrial Issues', in *Child Care is a Political Issue,* (Papers of the National Association of Community Based Child Care Conference), Allen & Unwin, Sydney, July, 4–10.
Dowse, S. (1988) 'The Women's Movement's Fandango with the State: The Movement's Role in Public Policy Since 1972', in Baldock and Cass 205–26.
d'Souza, N. (1993) 'Aboriginal Child Welfare: Framework for a National Policy', *Family Matters,* 35, 40–45.
Ebbeck, F.N. (1980) *The Kindergarten Union of South Australia through Seventy-Five Years: 1905–1980,* KUSA, Adelaide.
Edgar, D.E. (1967) 'The Educational Ideas and Influence on Victorian Education of Dr. John Smyth', MEd thesis, University of Melbourne.
Edney, J. (1983) 'Grassroots Organisation of Child Care Workers', in *Child Care is a Political Issue,* (Papers of the National Association of Community Based Child Care Conference) Sydney, 29–31.
Eisenstein, H. (1983). 'The Gender of Bureaucracy: Reflections on Feminism and the State', in J. Goodnow and C. Pateman eds., *Women, Social Science and Public Policy,* Allen & Unwin, Sydney, 104–115.
——(1990). 'Femocrats, Official Feminism and the Uses of Power', in S. Watson ed., *Playing the State: Australian Feminist Interventions,* Allen & Unwin, Sydney, 87–103.
——(1991) *Gender Shock,* Allen & Unwin, Sydney.
Elefsiniotis, J. (1981) 'Parent Control versus Parent Involvement: The Effects on Migrant Communities', Australian Pre-School Association (Victorian Branch) *Newsletter,* 3 (1), December, 13–32.
Elliott, G. (1982) 'The Social Policy of the New Right', in M. Sawer ed., *Australia and the New Right,.* Allen & Unwin, Sydney, 120–134.
Elliott, G. and Graycar, A. (1979) 'Social Welfare', in A. Patience and B. Head eds., *From Whitlam to Fraser: Reform and Reaction in Australian Politics,* Oxford University Press, Melbourne, 89–102.
English, B. et al. (1978) *Families in Australia – a Profile,* Family Research Unit, University of New South Wales, Kensington.
Esso Australia Ltd. and Lend Lease Corporation (1989) Messenger's Cottage Evaluation Report, 1987–1988, Sydney.
Ethnic Child Care Development Unit (1980) *Latch Key Kids,* Marrickville.
——(1982) *Report of the 1982 Survey of Child Care Needs in Newtown and Surry Hills,* Marrickville, NSW.
——(1983) *Report on the Child Care Needs of Ethnic Families in the Rockdale Municipality,* Marrickville, NSW.
Ethnic Communities Council of New South Wales (1984) *Ethnic Child Care and Australian Society,* Sydney.
Faro, C. (1983) 'Social Constructions of Women and Work: Australia, 1939 to 1954', BA hons. thesis (Economic History), University of Sydney.

Family and Children's Services Agency (1979) *Child Care Services in Western Sydney*, FACSA, Sydney.
——(1981) New South Wales Children's Services Study, FACSA, Sydney.
Ferguson, S. and Fitzgerald, H. (1954) *Studies in the Social Services*, Her Majesty's Stationery Office, London.
Fitzgerald, R.T. (1968) 'Facilities for Pre-Schooling in Australia', *Quarterly Review of Education* 1 (4).
Fitzgerald, R.T. and Crosher, J. A. (1971) *Pre-School Education in Australia: A Review of Recent Developments*, Australian Council for Educational Research, Melbourne.
Forbath, B. (1983) 'National Perspectives', in *Child Care is a Political Issue*, (Papers of the National Association of Community Based Child Care Conference) Sydney, 36–40.
——(1985) 'Unionising Workers in Children's Services', Working Women's Information Service, *Bulletin* No.85/1.
Forbath, B. and Dolan, C. (1983) 'Child Care – the Industrial Issues', in *Child Care is a Political Issue*, (Papers of the National Association of Community Based Child Care Conference), Sydney, 4–10.
Franzway, S., Court, D. and Connell, R.W. (1989) *Staking a Claim: Feminism, Bureaucracy and the State*, Allen & Unwin, Sydney.
Free Kindergarten Union of Tasmania (Kindergarten Union of Tasmania from 1958) (1939–78) *Annual Reports* (held at Tasmanian College of Advanced Education, Hobart).
Free Kindergarten Union of Victoria (1910–90) *Annual Reports* (held at State Library of Victoria).
——(1987) *Bringing Their Tales: Recollections of Pioneers in Early Kindergartens of Victoria*, Melbourne.
Freudenberg, G. (1986) 'The Program', in *The Whitlam Phenomenon*, (Fabian Papers), McPhee Gribble, Melbourne, 130–44.
Frey, D. (1986) *Survey of Sole Parent Pensioners' Workforce Barriers*, Social Security Review, Canberra.
Fry, J. (1961) 'The Working Mother', *Tasmanian Pre-School News*, 8 (1).
——(1969). Day Care – the Australian Scene, Address to the Day Care Committee of the Australian Pre-School Association (Victoria), (mimeo).
——(1972) 'Caring for Other People's Children', *Social Service*, 23 (5), March/April , 2–5.
Galbally, F. (1978) *Migrant Services and Programs: Report of the Review of Post-Arrival Programs and Services for Migrants* (The Galbally Report), AGPS, Canberra.
Gardiner, L. (1982) *The Free Kindergarten Union of Victoria, 1908–80*, Australian Council for Educational Research, Melbourne.
Gayler, B. (1976) 'The Multi-Cultural Society: What About Child Care?', *Ekstasis*, 15, August.
George, J. (1985) 'Women and Unions', Paper presented at the Women and Post-Secondary Education Conference, Sydney, February.
Gelb, J. (1990) *Feminism and Politics: A Comparative Perspective*, University of California Press, Berkeley.
Gifford, J. (1988) *Family Day Care in the ACT: A Look at the Issues*, ACT Family Day Care Association, Canberra.
——(1992) *Child Care Funding Re-assessed: Operational Subsidies, Fee Relief and Taxation Measures*, Australian Early Childhood Association and National Association of Community Based Children's Services, Canberra.

Glezer, H. (1984) 'Changes in Marriage and Sex-Role Attitudes Among Young Married Women: 1971–1981', in *Family Formation, Structure and Values*, Proceedings of the Australian Family Research Conference, November 1983, vol. 1, Institute of Family Studies, Melbourne.

——(1988). *Maternity Leave in Australia: Employee and Employer Experiences*, Australian Institute of Family Studies, Melbourne.

Goodnow, J. and Burns, A. (1984) 'Factors Affecting Policies in Early Childhood Education: An Australian Case', in L. Katz, P. J. Wagemaller and K. Steiner eds., *Current Topics in Early Childhood Education*, Ablex, New York, 189–207.

Grimes, D. (Minister for Community Services) (1985a) Children's Services – Progress Report, Council of Social Welfare Ministers Conference, May.

——(1985b) 'Child Care', Press Release, 7 August.

——(1985c) Speech to 'Save Children's Services' Conference, Canberra, 14 September.

——(1985d) 'Child Care', Press Release, 6 November.

Groenewegen, P. D. (1979) 'Federalism', in Allan Patience and Brian Head eds., *From Whitlam to Fraser*, Oxford University Press, Melbourne, 63–69.

Hamilton, L. (1986) 'The Cuts – Already Upon Us', Community Child Care (NSW) *Newsletter* no. 26, February–March.

Hargreaves, K. (1982) *Women at Work*, Penguin, Ringwood, Victoria.

Harrison, R. (1985). *The Sydney Kindergarten Teachers' College, 1897–1981*, Sydney Kindergarten Teachers College Graduates Association, Sydney.

Hayden, B. (1978). 'Planning and Integration of Welfare Services: An Australian Government Viewpoint', in A. Graycar ed., *Perspectives in Australian Social Policy: A Book of Readings*, Macmillan, Melbourne, 120–26.

Heinig, C.M. and Duncan, A. Co. (1943) Report on an Experimental Period in Three Wartime Children's Centres, Melbourne, (no page numbers). (Held at Institute of Early Childhood, Kew, Victoria.)

Henderson, G. (1983) 'Fraserism: Myths and Realities', *Quadrant*, June.

Hernes, H.M. (1985) 'The Welfare State Citizenship of Scandinavian Women', in Kathleen B. Jones and Anna G. Jónasdóttir eds., *The Political Interests of Gender: Developing Theory and Research with a Feminist Face*, Sage, London, 87–213.

——(1987). 'Women and the Welfare State: The Transition from Private to Public Dependence', in A. Showstack Sassoon ed., *Women and the State: The Shifting Boundaries of Public and Private*, Hutchinson, London, 72–92.

Hewson, J. and Fischer, T. (1993) *Fightback!*, Liberal and National Parties, Sydney.

History of the Victorian Association of Day Nurseries, (typescript, n.d. held at VADN, Melbourne.)

Huntsman, L. (1989) *A Guide to Regulations Governing Children's Services in Australia*, Community Child Care Co-operative, Sydney.

Hurwitz, H. (1977) 'Factory Women' in A. Bordow ed. *The Worker in Australia*, University of Queensland Press, St. Lucia, 222–67.

Isbister, C. (1973) 'The Rights of the Child', *Social Service*, 24 (6), May, 4–7.

——(1982) 'The Child Care Issue', *Australian Family*, 3 (4), 22–25.

Jackson-Nackano, A. (forthcoming) *Children's Business: A History of the Australian Early Childhood Association*.

Johnston, K. (1982) 'An Argument Towards the Recognition of Child Care Expenses as Tax Deductions', in *Women and Taxation*, (Proceedings of

Women and Taxation Conference, Melbourne, June 1981), Status of Women Committee, United Nations Association of Australia, Melbourne, 111–16.

Joint Parliamentary Committee on Social Security (1945–46) *Eighth Interim Report*, Commonwealth Parliamentary Papers, Vol. III.

Jones, A. (1983) *Selectivity in Children's Services Policy*, Social Welfare Research Centre (University of New South Wales) Reports and Proceedings No.32, Kensington, NSW.

Jones, A. (1988) 'Child Care Policy: Where to Now?', *Current Affairs Bulletin*, 65 (6), 4–9.

Jones, H. (1975) 'The Acceptable Crusader: Lillian de Lissa and Pre-School Education in South Australia', in S. Murray-Smith ed., *Melbourne Studies in Education*, Melbourne University Press, Melbourne, 126–53.

Judge, C. (1978) 'Day Care Workers', in K. Gallagher Ross ed., *Good Day Care: Fighting For It, Getting It, Keeping It*, Women's Press, Ontario, 133–36.

Kamerman, S. B. and Kahn, A. J. (1981) *Child Care, Family Benefits, and Working Parents: A Study in Comparative Policy*, Columbia University Press, New York.

——(1991) *Child Care, Parental Leave, and the Under 3s: Policy Innovation in Europe*, Auburn House, New York.

Kaplan, G. (1992) *Contemporary Western European Feminism*, Allen & Unwin, London.

Kapp Howe, L. (1977) *Pink Collar Worker*, Avon, New York.

Karmel, T. and MacLachlan, M. (1986) *Sex Segregation – Increasing or Decreasing?*, Bureau of Labour Market Research, Canberra.

Kelly, Jan (1988) 'Not Merely Minded: The Sydney Day Nursery and Nursery Schools Association, 1905–1945', PhD thesis, University of Sydney.

Kindergarten Union of New South Wales (1895–1989) *Annual Reports*.

Kindergarten Union of South Australia (1905–1986) *Annual Reports*.

——(1980) *The Kindergarten Union of South Australia through 75 Years, 1905–1980*, Adelaide.

Kindergarten Union of Western Australia (1911–1987) *Annual Reports*, (Held at Battye Library, Perth.)

King, E. (1957) Report of Contacts with Various Child Welfare Agencies and Children's Homes During Recent Visit to Canada and the USA as a Delegate to the Conference of the International Council of Women, (mimeo).

——(1986) *Dreams Become Deeds*, [published by the author], Melbourne.

——Papers and records relating to involvement in the Free Kindergarten Union of Victoria, National Council of Women (Victorian branch), Australian Early Childhood Association (National and Victorian levels), Melbourne Kindergarten Teachers College. (Held by Ethleen King, Melbourne).

Kingston, B. (1975) *My Wife, My Daughter and Poor Mary Ann*, Nelson, Melbourne.

Kramar, R. (1982) 'Female Employment During the Second World War', *Women and Labour Conference Papers* vol. 2, 448–60

Lady Gowrie Child Centres – Sydney, Melbourne, Adelaide, Brisbane, Perth, Hobart. General records, photographs, newspaper cuttings, minutes of meetings.

Larmour, C. (1975) 'Women's Wages and the WEB', in A. Curthoys, S. Eade and P. Spearritt eds., *Women at Work*, Australian Society for the Study of Labour History, Canberra, 47–58.

Laster, K. (1985) 'Frances Knorr: "She Killed Babies Didn't She?"', in M. Lake and F. Kelly eds., *Double Time: Women in Victoria – 150 Years*, Penguin, Ringwood, Victoria, 148–56.

Lazerson, M. (1971). 'Social Reform and Early Childhood Education: Some Historical Perspectives', in R. H. Anderson and H. G. Shane eds., *As the Twig is Bent: Readings in Early Childhood Education*, Houghton Mifflin, New York, 22–33.

Leira, A. (1992) *Welfare States and Working Mothers*, Cambridge University Press, Cambridge.

Levy, Jennifer (1980) *Overview of Working with Migrant Children*, Early Childhood Development Unit, Sydney.

Liberal and National Parties (1993) *New Directions for Parents and their Children*, Canberra.

Lowenstein, Wendy (1978) *Weevils in the Flour: An Oral Record of the 1930s Depression in Australia*, Hyland House, Melbourne.

Lynch, L. (1984) 'Bureaucratic Feminisms: Bossism and Beige Suits', *Refractory Girl*, No. 27, May, 38–44.

Maas, F. (1989) 'Demographic Trends Affecting the Workforce', in *Corporate Child Care: The Bottom Line*, (Papers from a National Conference on Employer Supported Child Care, Sydney, CCAW, Sydney, 16–24.

Macchiarola, F.F. and Gartner, F. eds. (1989) *Caring for America's Children*, Academy of Political Science, New York.

Macintyre, S. (1985) *Winners and Losers*, Allen & Unwin, Sydney.

Manning, P. (1974) 'Big New Deal for Pre-Schoolers', *Bulletin*, October 26.

Matthews, J.J. (1984) *Good and Mad Women: The Historical Construction of Femininity in Twentieth Century Australia*, Allen & Unwin, Sydney.

Matthews, J.K. and Fitzgerald, R.T. (1975) 'Education Policy and Political Platform: The Australian Labor Government', *Australian Education Review*, 14.

McCaughey, W. (1972) 'Day Care – Liberating Who for What?', *Dissent*, 28, Winter, 3–8.

——(1978) 'History and Development of the Child Care Movement', in *Child Care – an Industrial Issue*, (Proceedings of a seminar sponsored by ACSPA), Melbourne, 5–10.

——(1983) 'Parent Control and Management', in *Child Care is a Political Issue*, (Papers of the National Association of Community Based Child Care Conference), Sydney, 21–25.

McCaughey, W. and Sebastian, P. (1977) *Community Child Care: A Resource Book for Parents and Those Planning Children's Services*, Greenhouse, Melbourne.

McGregor, C. (1989) 'Feminism's new concern', *National Times*, 2–8 March.

McHugh, J. (1990) Speech at Community Child Care (NSW) Annual General Meeting, Sydney, April.

McKenzie, R., Kearney, P. and Mason, S. (1993) *Child Care*, Discussion Paper 55, Australian Law Reform Commission, Sydney.

Media Women's Action Group (1972) *Child Care: A Community Responsibility*, Sydney.

Meehan, E. (1985). *Women's Rights at Work: Campaigns and Policy in Britain and the United States*, Macmillan, London.

Melvin, F. (1989) 'The Great Child Care Non-debate', *Refractory Girl*, Nos. 31–32, [joint issue] 40–41.

Montague, M. and Stephens, J. (1985) *Paying the Price for Sugar and Spice: A Study of Women's Pathways into Social Security Recipiency*, AGPS, Canberra.

Morrow, A. (1982) 'Arguments Against Tax Deductions for Child Care Expenses', in *Women and Taxation*, (Proceedings of Women and Taxation Conference, Melbourne, June 1981), Status of Women Committee, United Nations Associations of Australia, Melbourne, 117–26.

Moss, P. (1982) 'Community Care and Young Children', in A. Walker ed., *Community Care: The Family, The State and Social Policy*, Basil Blackwell and Martin Robertson, Oxford.

—— (1991) 'Day Care for Young Children in the United Kingdom', in E. Melhuish and P. Moss eds., *Day Care for Young Children: International Perspectives*, Routledge, London.

—— (1993) 'Around Europe with the Network' in *European Commission Network on Childcare, Employment, Equality and Caring for Children*, Commission of the European Communities, Brussels.

National Association of Community Based Children's Services (1983–88). Minutes of meetings (author's personal collection).

National Council of Women, Victoria (1972) Working Committee on Day Care, Submission on All Day Care for Children, Melbourne.

National Health and Medical Research Council (1937–38) *Reports of Sessions 1–4*, (held at Department of Public Health, University of Sydney).

National Population Inquiry (1975) *First Main Report, Population and Australia*, Vol. 1 (W. D. Borrie, Chairman), AGPS, Canberra.

New, C. and David, M. (1985) *For the Children's Sake: Making Childcare More Than Women's Business*, Penguin, Harmondsworth.

New South Wales Association for Mental Health, Subcommittee of the Industry Standing Committee (1971) *Pre-School Centres in Industry*, Sydney.

New South Wales Council of Social Service (1980) *'She's the Perfect Substitute Mother': An Evaluation of Family Day Care*, Family and Children's Services Agency, Sydney.

New South Wales Department of Youth and Community Services (1980–84). *Annual Reports*.

New South Wales Labor Council (1983) *Survey of Family Day Care*, Sydney.

New South Wales Labor Women's Committee (1974) Letter to all Members of the Parliamentary Labor Party, 5 August (Personal papers, Elizabeth Reid).

Nicholls, J. (1978) *Campus Child Care Survey*, Australian Union of Students, Canberra.

—— (1982) 'Attacks on Childcare', in *Women Under Attack*, Australian Union of Students, Women's Department, Canberra.

Norgren, J. (1982) 'In Search of a National Child Care Policy: Background and Prospects', in Ellen Boneparth ed., *Women, Power and Policy*, Pergamon, New York, 124–43.

Norris, A. (1978) *Champions of the Impossible: A History of the National Council of Women of Victoria 1902–1977*, Hawthorn Press, Melbourne.

Nott, W. E. (Chairman) (1972), *Pre-School Education in Western Australia*, Department of Education, Perth.

O'Brien, A. (1988) *Poverty's Prison: the Poor in New South Wales, 1880–1918*, Melbourne University Press, Melbourne.

O'Donnell, C. and Hall, P. (1988) *Getting Equal: Labour Market Regulation and Women's Work*, Allen & Unwin, Sydney.

Office of the Status of Women, Department of Prime Minister and Cabinet (1989) *Child Care in the Workplace*, AGPS, Canberra.

Owen, M. and Shaw, S. (comps.) (1979) *Working Women: Discussion Papers from the Working Women's Centre*, Sisters, Carlton, Victoria.

Panckhurst, F. (1984) *Workplace Childcare and Migrant Parents*, AGPS, Canberra.
Pateman, C. (1989) *The Disorder of Women*, Polity Press, Cambridge.
Paul, H. (1945) 'The Pre-School Movement and the Community', *Health Bulletin*, 82, 2211–14.
——(1946) 'More Pre-School Centres are Needed', *Health Bulletin*, 83, 2240–42.
Pendred, G.E. (1964) 'Pre-School Centres in Australia', in *Review of Education in Australia 1955–62*, Australian Council for Educational Research, Melbourne, 387–416.
Pincus, G. and Shipley, J.(1976) 'The Politics of Early Childhood Services in Australia', *Australian Journal of Early Childhood*, 1(2), 3–6.
Poole, R. (1983). 'Markets and Motherhood: The Advent of the New Right', in A. Burns, G. Bottomley and P. Jools eds., *The Family in the Modern World*, Allen & Unwin, Sydney, 103–20.
Preston, Y. (1973) 'Areas of Need: Outer Suburbs', paper presented to WEL Child Care Conference, Sydney.
Prior, T. (1982) 'My Forty-Five Years in Industry', in M. Bevege, M. James and C. Shute eds., *Worth Her Salt: Women at Work in Australia*, Hale & Iremonger, Sydney, 123–33.
Priorities Review Staff (1974) *Early Childhood Services*, AGPS, Canberra.
Raby, G. (1984) 'The Implementation of the Planning Approach in New South Wales', unpublished paper, Sydney.
Rawson, D.W. (1986) *Unions and Unionists in Australia*, (2nd ed.), Allen & Unwin, Sydney.
Raymond, J. (1987) *Bringing Up Children Alone: Policies for Sole Parents*, Social Security Review, Canberra.
Reid, E. (1973–75) Papers and records relating to her period as Women's Adviser to the Prime Minister. (Held by Elizabeth Reid, Canberra.)
——(1985) 'The Child of Our Movement: A Movement of Women', unpublished paper.
——(1986) 'Creating a Policy for Women', in *The Whitlam Phenomenon*, (Fabian Papers), McPhee Gribble, Melbourne. 145–55.
Reiger, K. (1985) *The Disenchantment of the Home: Modernizing the Australian Family 1880–1940*, Oxford University Press, Melbourne.
Reisman, B., Moore A.J. and Fitzgerald K., (1988) *Child Care: The Bottom Line. An Economic and Child Care Policy Paper*, Child Care Action Campaign, New York.
Reynolds, M. (Minister for Local Government and Minister Assisting the Prime Minister on the Status of Women), (1988) 'Child Care – From Margin to Mainstream', Address to Australian National University Public Affairs Conference, December 1988
Riches, L. (1978) 'Child Care as an Industrial Issue in Conciliation and Arbitration', in *Child Care – an Industrial Issue*, (proceedings of a seminar sponsored by ACSPA), Melbourne, 39–44.
Richmond, K. (1974). 'The Workforce Participation of Married Women in Australia', in D. Edgar ed., *Social Change in Australia: Readings in Sociology*, Cheshire, Melbourne, 267–305.
Rigg, J. (1972) 'The control of women workers', *Nation Review*, October 14–20.
Riley, D. (1983) ' "The Serious Burdens of Love?": Some Questions on Child-Care, Feminism and Socialism', in Lynne Segal ed., *What is to Be Done About The Family?*, Penguin, Harmondsworth, 129–56.

Robertson, S. and Cox, E. (1980) *Scarce for Kids*, NSW Council of Social Service, Sydney.
Roughley, S. and Philippou, L. (1989) 'Future Provision of Child Care. Will the Tax System or a Voucher System Provide Viable Funding Alternatives?', paper presented to Women's Tax Convention, Canberra, March.
Rubinstein, L. (1978) 'The Role of Unions in the Child Care Movement', in *Child Care – an Industrial Issue*, (proceedings of a seminar sponsored by ACSPA), Melbourne, 33–38.
Rudduck, L. (1966). 'The Early History and Establishment of the Lady Gowrie Child Centres', *Australian Pre-School Quarterly*, 6 (3), February, 4–7.
—— (1973) 'Pre-School in Australia – An Overview', *Independent Education*, 3 (1).
Ruggie, M. (1984) *The State and Working Women: A Comparative Study of Britain and Sweden*, Princeton University Press, Princeton, N.J.
Ruopp, R., Travers, J., et al. (1979) *Children at the Center: Final Report of the National Day Care Study*, Abt Associates, Cambridge, Mass.
Russell, G., James, D. and Watson, J.(1988) 'Work/Family Policies', *Australian Journal of Social Issues*, 23 (4).
Ryan, E. and Conlon, A. (1975) *Gentle Invaders: Australian Women at Work 1788–1914*, Nelson, Melbourne.
Ryan, L. (1990) 'Feminism and the Federal Bureaucracy 1972–1983', in S. Watson ed., *Playing the State: Australian Feminist Interventions*, Allen & Unwin, Sydney, 71–84.
Ryan, P. (1988) Speech to ACTU Child Care Conference, March 28.
Sassoon, A. Showstack (1987) 'Women's New Social Role: Contradictions of the Welfare State', in A. Showstack Sassoon ed., *Women and the State: the Shifting Boundaries of Public and Private*, Hutchinson, London, 158–90.
Sawer, M. (1989) 'Women: The Long March Through the Institutions', in B. Head and A. Patience eds., *From Fraser to Hawke: Australian Public Policy in the 1980s*, Longman Cheshire, Melbourne, 427–62.
—— (1990) *Sisters in Suits: Women and Public Policy in Australia*, Allen & Unwin, Sydney.
Sawer, M. and Simms, M. (1984) *A Woman's Place: Women and Politics in Australia*, Allen & Unwin, 1984.
Schubert, J. (1989) 'Welcome and Opening Address' in *Corporate Child Care: The Bottom Line*, (Papers from a National Conference on Employer Supported Child Care, Sydney, November 1989) CCAW, Sydney, 4–6.
Scotton, R. B. (1980) 'The Fraser Government and Social Expenditures', in R. B. Scotton and H. Ferber eds., *Public Expenditures and Social Policy in Australia*, Vol. 2, Longman Cheshire, Melbourne, 1–27.
Seth, S. and Giles, G. (1983) *Childcare: An Education Issue* (Submission to the Universities Council from Macquarie University Student Council). Sydney.
Siim, B. (1990) 'Women and the Welfare State: Between Private and Public Dependence', in C. Ungerson ed., *Gender and Caring*, Harvester Wheatsheaf, Hemel Hempstead.
Simpson, M. (1980) 'Women, the State and Family Day Care', *Refractory Girl*, Nos. 20–21 [joint issue], 42–6.
Smart, D. (1977) 'Accelerating Commonwealth Participation, 1964–1975', in I. K. F. Birch and D. Smart eds., *The Commonwealth Government and Education 1964-1976: Political Initiatives and Developments*, Drummond, Melbourne.
Social Welfare Commission (1974) *Project Care: Children, Parents, Community*, AGPS, Canberra.

——(1975) *Family and Child Care Project: Needs Data by Regions*, AGPS, Canberra.
Spalding, B. (1976) 'The Children's Commission in Retrospect', *Australian Child and Family Welfare*, 1 (2) 53–5.
Spaull, A. (1982) *Australian Education in the Second World War*, University of Queensland Press, St. Lucia.
Spearritt, J. (1980) 'Working for the Pre-School Cause: The Role of the Australian Pre-School Association', MA thesis, Macquarie University, Sydney.
Spearritt, P. (1974a) 'The Kindergarten Movement: Tradition and Change', in D. Edgar ed., *Social Change in Australia: Readings in Sociology*, Cheshire, Melbourne, 583–96.
——(1974b) 'The Politics of Pre-School Education: A Case Study', in D. A. Jecks ed., *Sources of Influence in Australian Education*, Novak, Sydney, 324–66.
——(1975) 'Women in Sydney Factories, 1920-50', in A. Curthoys et al. eds., *Women at Work*, Australian Society for the Study of Labour History, Canberra, 31–46.
——(1977) 'Playing Politics with the Under-Fives', in I. K. F. Birch and D. Smart eds., *The Commonwealth Government and Education 1964–1976: Political Initiatives and Developments*, Drummond, Melbourne, 199–215.
——(1979) 'Child Care and Kindergartens in Australia, 1890–1975', in P. Langford and P. Sebastian eds., *Early Childhood Education and Care in Australia*, Australia International, Melbourne, 10–38.
Spedding, P. (1993) 'United States of America', in Cochran (ed.) pp. 535–58.
Spender, J. (1981) *Review of the Children's Services Program*, Canberra.
Staden, F., Rezai, S. A. and Buckley, S. (1985) *Child Care and Arabic Speaking Women in Sydney*, Ethnic Affairs Commission of NSW, Sydney.
Stamp, I. (1975) *Young Children in Perspective: A Review of Thirty-Five Years of the Lady Gowrie Child Centres in Partnership with the Australian Pre-School Association*, APA, Canberra.
Steinfels, M. O'Brien (1973) *Who's Minding the Children? The History and Politics of Day Care in America*, Simon and Schuster, New York.
Stewart, A. (1978) 'Unions and Employers: Current Policies and Attitudes', *Child Care – an Industrial Issue*, (proceedings of a seminar sponsored by ACSPA), Melbourne, 25–32.
Stilwell, F. (1986) *The Accord and Beyond ... The Political Economy of the Labor Government*, Pluto Press, Sydney.
Stoll, P. and Ridgway, B. (1984) Submission Regarding Work-Related Child Care for Nurses in New South Wales, Part 1, NSW Nurses Association, Sydney.
——(1985) Submission Regarding Work-Related Child Care for Nurses in New South Wales, Part 2, NSW Nurses' Association, Sydney.
Stone, L. (1911) *Jonah*, Angus & Robertson, Sydney.
Stonehouse, A. (1988) 'Nice Ladies Who Love Children: The Status of the Early Childhood Professional in Society', Australian Early Childhood Association, *Conference Proceedings*, (18th National Conference, Canberra, 1988) AECA, Canberra.
Storer, D. et al. (1976) *'But I Wouldn't Want My Wife to Work Here': A Study of Migrant Women in Melbourne Industry*, Centre for Urban Research and Action, Fitzroy, Victoria.
Sumerling, P. (1983) 'Infanticide, Baby-farming and Abortion in South Australia, 1870–1910', MA (History) thesis, University of Adelaide.

REFERENCES

Summers, A. (1979) 'Women', in A. Patience and B. Head eds., *From Whitlam to Fraser*, Oxford University Press, Melbourne, 189–200.
——(1986) 'Mandarins or Missionaries?: Women in the Federal Bureaucracy', in N. Grieve and A. Burns, eds. *Australian Women: New Feminist Perspectives*, Oxford University Press, Melbourne, 59–67.
Sydney Day Nursery and Nursery Schools Association (1937–89) *Annual Reports*
Sydney Day Nursery Association (1905–36) *Annual Reports*.
Sydney Labour History Group (1982) *What Rough Beast? The State and Social Order in Australian History*, Allen & Unwin, Sydney.
Terrey, I. and Ponsford, J. (1966) 'The Program – Over Twenty-Five Years', *Australian Pre-School Quarterly*, 6 (3), February, 21–27.
Tertiary Education Commission (1981) *Report for the 1982–1984 Triennium*, AGPS, Canberra.
Thame, C. (1974) 'Health and the State: The Development of Collective Responsibility for Health Care in Australia in the First Half of the Twentieth Century', PhD thesis, Australian National University, Canberra.
Tiffin, S. (1982) 'In Pursuit of Reluctant Parents', in Sydney Labour History Group, *What Rough Beast?: The State and Social Order in Australian History*, Allen & Unwin, Sydney, 130–50.
Tinney, P. (1975) *Home Away from Home?*, Brotherhood of St. Laurence, Melbourne.
Ungerson, C. ed. (1990) *Gender and Caring: Work and Welfare in Britain and Scandinavia*, Harvester Wheatsheaf, Hemel Hempstead.
Universities Commission (1975) *Sixth Report*, AGPS, Canberra.
Victorian Association of Day Nurseries (1910–87) *Annual Reports*.
Victorian Council of Social Service (1970) *Caring for the Children of One-Parent Families and Working Wives*, Melbourne.
Vowels, L. and Beighton, F. (1977) *Student Parents at Melbourne University: Their Needs and Problems*, Melbourne University Press, Melbourne.
Waerness, K. (1987) 'On the Rationality of Caring', in A. Showstack Sassoon ed., *Women and the State: the Shifting Boundaries of Public and Private*, Hutchinson, London, 207–34.
Walker, M.(1964) 'The Development of Kindergartens in Australia', MEd thesis, University of Sydney.
Wangmann, J. (1991) *Accreditation of Early Childhood Services in Australia*, Report to the Department of Health, Housing and Community Services, Canberra.
Watson, S. ed. (1990) *Playing the State: Australian Feminist Interventions*, Allen & Unwin, Sydney.
Weller, P. (1989) *Malcolm Fraser PM*, Penguin, Ringwood, Victoria.
Wheatley, N. (1988) 'All in the Same Boat? Sydney's Rich and Poor in the Great Depression', in V. Burgmann and J. Lee eds., *Making a Life. A People's History Since 1788*, McPhee Gribble/Penguin, Melbourne, 205–25.
Whitbread, N. (1972) *The Evolution of the Nursery-Infant School: A History of Infant and Nursery Education in Britain, 1800–1970*, Routledge and Kegan Paul, London.
White, C. (1983) 'Industrial Issues – Funding', in *Child Care is a Political Issue*, (Papers of the National Association of Community Based Child Care Conference), Sydney, 26–29.

Whitebrook, M. et al. (1982) 'Caring for the Caregivers: Staff Burnout in Child Care', in L. Katz ed., *Current Topics in Early Childhood Education*, Vol. 4, Ablex, Norwood, N. J., 211–35.
Whitlam, E.G. (1974a) Speech notes, 'Care and Education of Young Children', Lane Cove, 6 May. (Personal papers, Elizabeth Reid).
——(1974b) Speech notes, Inaugural Meeting of the Interim Committee of the Children's Commission, 31 October. (Personal papers, Elizabeth Reid).
Wilenski, P. (1986) *Public Power and Public Administration*, Hale & Iremonger/ Royal Australian Institute of Public Administration, Sydney, 117–36.
Wolcott, I. (1987) *Workers with Family Responsibilities: Implications for Employers*, Australian Institute of Family Studies, Melbourne.
Women's Electoral Lobby (1973–78) *Newsletter*.
——(1974) Objections of WEL (National) to the November Report of the Australian Pre-Schools Committee, February, unpublished.
Women's Electoral Lobby (National) (1987) Survey of Employer Attitudes to Work-related Child Care, Sydney.
Women's Electoral Lobby (NSW) *WEL-Informed*, Nos. 1–200.
Working Women's Information Service (1980) *Child Care – an Industrial Issue*, (Bulletin No.80/3).
Wyse, T. (1983) 'Industrial Issues in Family Day Care', in *Child Care is a Political Issue* (Papers of the National Association of Community Based Child Care Conference) Sydney, 31–36.
Yeatman, A. (1990) *Bureaucrats, Technocrats, Femocrats: Essays on the Contemporary Australian State*, Allen & Unwin, Sydney.
Zigler, E. and Valentine, J. eds. (1979) *Project Head Start: A Legacy of the War on Poverty*, Free Press, New York.

Index

AAP, *see* Australian Assistance Plan
AAPSCD, *see* Australian Association for Pre-School Child Development
a'Beckett, Ada, 32, 39
Aborigines, 5, 167; *see also* multifunctional Aboriginal children's services
  Aboriginal Child Care Agencies (ACCAs), 6
  access to child care, 41, 57, 195
  past policies towards, 5–6
  Secretariat of National Aboriginal and Islander Child Care groups (SNAICC), 6
  special child care needs, 6
ACCAs, *see* Aborigines, Aboriginal Child Care Agencies
Accord, 164–7
  and child care as a social wage component, 10, 164–7
accreditation of child care services, 5, 201–4, 207, 209, 213; *see also* Interim National Accreditation Council; National Accreditation Council
  link to fee relief, 203
ACER, *see* Australian Council for Education Research
ACOA, *see* Administrative and Clerical Officers Association
ACOSS, *see* Australian Council of Social Service
ACSPA, *see* Australian Council of Salaried and Professional Associations
Action for Adequate Child Care, 67
Action Program for Women Workers, 166
ACTU, *see* Australian Council of Trade Unions
ACTU Working Women's Centre, *see* Working Women's Centre

Administrative and Clerical Officers Association (ACOA), 157–8
AECA, *see* Australian Early Childhood Association
AFA, *see* Australian Family Association
Affirmative Action (Equal Opportunity for Women) Act (1986), 170
affirmative action policies, 149, 157, 166, 167, 168, 170
ALP, *see* Australian Labor Party
Anderson, Francis, 15, 16
APA, *see* Australian Pre-School Association
APC, *see* Australian Pre-Schools Committee
Association of Child Care Centres (NSW), 111
Association of Child Care Centres (Victoria), 60
Australian Assistance Plan (AAP), 74, 92; *see also* Whitlam government, child care policies of
Australian Association for Pre-School Child Development (AAPSCD) 32–3, 37, 39, 40, 52, 53, 55;
  see also Australian Early Childhood Association (AECA); Australian Pre-School Association (APA)
Australian Council for Education Research (ACER), 57, 58
Australian Council of Salaried and Professional Associations (ACSPA), 142, 147, 148
Australian Council of Social Service (ACOSS), 188, 192, 200–1, 203
Australian Council of Trade Unions (ACTU), 10, 67, 120, 128, 141–2, 165–6, 200, 203; *see also* Accord; trade unions

233

as child care lobbyist, 142–3, 147–8, 156, 166, 173, 183, 187–8
Australian Early Childhood Association (AECA), 102–3, 188, 200–2; *see also* Australian Association for Pre-School Child Development (AAPSCD); Australian Pre-School Association (APA)
Australian Family Association (AFA), 78, 104–5
Australian Federation of Child Care Associations, 190–1, 194
Australian Labor Party (ALP), 48, 71–2, 83, 165; *see also* Hawke/Keating government; Whitlam government
and women, 167–8
child care policy of, 5, 9, 10, 46, 64, 68–9, 163, 174, 177, 183–4, 187, 197, 199
Australian Pre-School Association (APA), 53, 60, 65, 68, 82, 85, 101, 102, 121, 125–6; *see also* Australian Association for Pre-School Child Development (AAPSCD); Australian Early Childhood Association (AECA)
as child care lobbyist, 8, 9, 61, 63, 77, 78, 124–5
relationship with feminists, 81, 124–5
Australian Pre-Schools Committee (APC), 78–9, 83, 87, 133
report of, (Fry Report), 83–6, 87, 88, 92, 133
Australian Women's Charter, 50

baby farming, 24; *see also Infant Life Protection Act* (1890)
Baker, Carole, 81, 135
Beaurepaire, Dame Beryl, 109, 112
Beazley, Kim (snr), 77, 78, 81, 82, 83, 85, 88, 104, 133
Blewett, Neal, 185, 186, 197, 199
Booth, Anna, 165
Bowen, Lionel, 85, 90, 91, 197
Bowlby, John, 8, 59, 63; *see also* maternal deprivation
Brotherhood of St Laurence
pilot family day care scheme, 132–3
reports of, 132
Brunswick Children's Centre, 45–6

Campbell, Dame Janet, 33–4
Care of the Child in War-time Committee (Sydney), 44, 50; *see also* Co-ordinating Committee for Child Care in War-time
Cass, Bettina, 49, 104, 171, 214
casual care, *see* occasional care

Caucus working party on child care 195–6
CCAW, *see* Child Care at Work
Centre for Economic Policy Research, Australian National University, report of, 197–8
Chaney, Fred, 107, 109, 110, 111, 112
Chifley, J.B., 46
Child Care Act (1972), 9, 67–9, 78, 89, 110, 114, 124, 126, 184, 185
child care allowance, 64; *see also* Home Child Care Allowance
child care assistance, *see* fee relief
Child Care at Work (CCAW), 153; *see also* corporate child care
Child Care Charter, 67
Child Care Federal Funding Campaign, 108, 112, 129
child care policies; *see also* Australian Labor Party, child care policies of; Coalition parties, child care policies of; Fraser government, child care policies of; Hawke/Keating government, child care policies of; Whitlam government, child care polices of
'education' vs. 'care', 7, 8, 51, 52–4, 56, 57, 77–8, 88–9, 90, 101, 103, 124, 126
influence of the Second World War on, 7, 33, 43–7, 50–1
integration with other government policies, 10, 164, 168–9, 173, 175, 177, 186, 187, 196, 199, 204–5, 207
in Britain, 1, 2, 4, 56, 206, 210
in Denmark, 1, 3, 206, 210
in Finland, 1, 3, 206
in Sweden, 1, 3–4, 192, 206
in USA, 1, 2, 56–7, 130–1, 172, 206; *see also* Project Head Start
public vs. private responsibility for, 1–4, 8–9, 146, 186–7, 189–90, 193, 196, 210, 213–14
role of Catholic church, 48, 57, 89
role of feminists, 5, 7, 8–9, 65–7, 68, 76, 79–83, 98, 108, 112, 117, 142, 168, 174, 195, 207; *see also* feminists; femocrats; Labor Women's Committee (NSW), Media Women's Action Group, United Women's Action Group, Women's Electoral Lobby; Women's Liberation movement
role of media, 80, 84, 192–3
role of union movement, 7, 48, 57, 139–40, 142, 147–8, 165–6, 187–8
role of women, 5, 9, 108–9, 117, 141–2, 166, 168, 174, 196, 206; *see also* child care policies, role of feminists

child care rebate, 211–12
child care services: *see also* child care policies; commercial services; community-based services; day nurseries; demand for child care; distribution of commonwealth child care funds; employer-sponsored services; equity issues in child care; family day care centres; funding of child care services; funding models; kindergartens; mobile services; multifunctional Aboriginal children's services; multifunctional services; neighbourhood centres; occasional care; out-of-school hours care; playgroups; special child care needs; vacation care; work-based care
  adequacy of, 114, 182, 209–10
  as instrument of other government policies/strategies, 10, 95, 186–8, 196, 204, 205, 213
  as source of employment, 126, 134, 135, 171
  community management of, 5, 9, 126–8, 131, 145, 175, 194; *see also* funding models, submission-based
  cost of, 39–40, 47, 58, 67, 89, 90, 130t, 174, 176, 179, 180–5, 188, 189–90, 191–3, 195, 198–9, 203t, 204
  cost recovery in, 110, 114, 115, 117
  early commonwealth involvement in, 7, 32, 39, 43, 45–7, 50–1, 53, 58–9, 62
  expansion of, 10, 106, 123, 126, 135, 173–4, 176, 182, 185, 186, 187–8, 200, 203t, 204, 207, 208t, 209
  government regulation of, 5, 25, 111, 124, 131–2, 146, 149, 193, 202, 204, 209
  indirect benefits of, 10, 63, 106, 148, 188, 192, 196, 197–9, 207, 209
  national approach to, 5, 6, 39, 46, 51, 72, 91, 95, 97, 99, 112, 150, 175, 200, 209, 210
  opposition to expansion of, 180–83, 186, 188–90, 192–3
  reliance on private sector, 10, 187, 189–90, 193, 200, 205, 210, 211
  role of feminists, 5, 8–9, 65–7, 195
  role of parents, 87, 122, 145, 148, 194
  role of union movement, 67, 119, 129, 139–40, 142–3, 147–8, 154, 156–63, 166, 173, 183, 187–8
  state vs. commonwealth control over, 39, 91, 98, 101, 108, 110, 117, 123–4; *see also* distribution of commonwealth child care funds
Child Care Standards Committee, 78, 83

child care subsidies, 5, 53, 54, 61, 62, 68, 94, 102, 114–15, 124, 127–8, 153, 181, 183, 190, 193–4, 198, 200, 207, 213; *see also* commercial services, subsidies for; fee relief; Special Economic Needs Subsidies
  links to award wages, 110, 129, 183–4
  non-indexation of, 102, 108, 114, 139
  per number of children enrolled, 110, 184, 193
child care workers; *see also* family day care workers
  class base of, 120–1, 125–6, 134–5
  in day nurseries, 36, 125
  industrial conditions of, 10, 36, 120, 122, 123–4, 125, 127–31, 133–4, 136–8, 139, 166, 185
  in pre-schools (and kindergartens), 10, 30, 36, 58, 93–4, 122–3, 124–5
  politicisation of, 10, 108, 118, 119–20, 126, 128–9, 131, 183
  role of union movement, 10, 119–20, 137, 139–40, 166
  training of, 17, 27–30, 55–6, 58–9, 84, 120–3, 125–6, 193
  unionisation of, 10, 119, 126, 128
  wages of, 40, 55–6, 58, 93–4, 120–4, 128, 133–5, 166, 184
child endowment
  Royal Commission on (1927), 33
Child Welfare Advisory Council, 44
children at risk of abuse
  access to child care, 192, 201
  special child care needs of, 176
Children's Protection Society, 20
Children's Services Action, 108, 112, 129, 162, 177
Children's Services Program
  cost of, 179–80, 182, 183, 192
  equity of, 190, 191, 198
  under Fraser government, 101, 102, 106, 109–10, 113, 117, 176, 185; *see also* Fraser government child care policies of
  under Hawke/Keating government, 149, 170, 179–80, 182, 183, 184, 185, 186, 196, 197, 201, 213
Coalition parties, child care policies of, 9, 58–9, 63, 67–8, 156, 176, 186, 187, 204–5, 212–3; *see also* Child Care Act (1972)
  under Gorton, 63, 64
  under McMahon, 67
Coleman, Marie, 64, 73, 92, 96, 100, 112
commercial services, 11, 53, 61–2, 110–11, 152, 187, 191–2, 194, 197, 208t, 210
  attitudes to accreditation, 202, 204

fee relief for, 166, 176, 187, 195, 200–1, 202–3, 205, 214
restrictions on access to, 11, 191–2, 195, 211
standard of care in, 202–3
subsidies for, 103, 110–11, 112, 117, 166, 176, 187, 195, 211
Communist Party, 7, 45
community-based services, 11, 66, 92, 103, 111, 144, 146, 148, 149, 150, 160, 191, 195
Community Child Care, (NSW), 114, 129, 177
Community Child Care, (Victoria), 52, 66, 67, 78, 80, 86, 115, 117, 146, 174, 177, 200
Co-ordinating Committee for Child Care in War-time (Melbourne), 45, 48; *see also* Brunswick Children's Centre; Care of the Child in War-time Committee
corporate child care, 151–3; *see also* Child Care At Work
Council for Women in War Work, 44
Country Party, *see* Coaltion parties
Cox, Eva, 4, 81, 102, 116, 135, 174, 188
Cox, Lenore, 64, 78, 86
Crawford, Mary, 203
Creche and Kindergarten Association of Queensland (CKA), 20–1, 54
Crow, Ruth, 45, 48
Crowley, Rosemary, 196
Cumpston, Dr J.H.L., 38, 46

day nurseries, 131, 203t, 208t, 212; *see also* Sydney Day Nursery and Nursery Schools Association (SDN & NSA); Sydney Day Nursery Association (SDNA); Victorian Association of Day Nurseries (VADN)
access to, 62, 170, 201
attitudes towards, 36, 37–8, 54–5, 59–62, 64–5, 67, 79, 85, 135
class base of staff, 30
demand for, 61, 63, 212
establishment of, 7, 26–7
funding of, 30–32, 36, 61–2, 177, 196, 200
ideals of, 7, 26–27, 28
role of feminists, 65–7, 81
staff training, 28, 125–6
Deagan, Carole, 103, 116
deLissa, Lillian, 18–20, 28
demand for child care, 5, 8–9, 47, 49–50, 53, 55, 61, 62–3, 116, 143, 155–6, 157, 159, 161, 188, 191–2, 195, 196, 209, 211; *see also* day nurseries, demand for; maternity leave, and demand for child care; migrants, demand for child care services; trade unions, union demands for child care services; work-based care, demand for
demonstration centres, *see* Lady Gowrie centres
Department of Community Services (and Health), 177, 197
Department of Education (Commonwealth), 58, 61, 71, 78, 83, 85, 86
Department of Finance, 180–1, 183, 199
Department of Health, 32, 33, 46, 61
Report on Maternal and Child Welfare, 33–4
Department of Labour and National Service, 44, 46, 49, 61–4, 71, 86; *see also* Women's Bureau
Department of Social Security, 71, 83, 99, 112, 177, 179, 200
dependent spouse rebate 182, 190, 199, 212
Depression, the, 34–36
disabled children
access to child care, 41, 192, 195
special child care needs, 176
distribution of commonwealth child care funds; *see also* child care services, community management of; funding models, submission-based
via community groups, 126–7, 144–5, 175
via local governments, 87–8, 126–7
via state governments, 101–2
Duncan, Constance, 46, 49

employer-sponsored services, 11, 62–3, 64, 145–6, 148–53, 156–63, 170, 187, 208t, 210, 212; *see also* work-based care; corporate child care
access to, 148, 150
fee relief for, 149, 150, 163, 187, 201, 205
equal employment opportunity policies, 142, 151, 153, 160, 162, 166, 170, 188
equity issues in child care, 97, 116, 118, 157–8, 179, 182–3, 189–91, 198, 200
Ethnic Child Care Development Unit, 144
Ethnic Communities Council, 145

Family and Children's Services Agency, 136, 137
family day care centres, 11, 53, 84, 91, 124, 131–39, 203t, 208t, 210
access to, 170, 201

INDEX

as cheaper alternative, 84, 110, 129, 139, 188–9
feminist opinions on, 81, 134–5, 189
Fry Report on, 84, 133
funding of, 102, 138–9, 177, 196, 200
regulation of, 131–2
Spender Report on, 110, 138–9
Social Welfare Commission Report on, 88, 133–4
family day care workers, 131, 133; *see also* child care workers
class base of, 134–5
development of industrial consciousness, 119–20, 137–9
politicisation of, 138–9, 189
union coverage of, 139–40
working conditions of, 136–8, 139
wages of, 133–5, 139
Fatin, Wendy, 196
FAUSA, *see* Federation of Australian University Staff Associations
Federal Health Council, 34, 38; *see also* health; National Health and Medical Research Council
Federation of Australian University Staff Associations (FAUSA), 160, 162
fee relief, 150, 181, 183, 184, 199, 200–1, 211, 213–14
cost of, 195, 203
for commercial services, 195, 200–1, 202–3
for employer-based services, 149–50, 201
link to accreditation, 203
two-tier system, 201
feminism, *see also* feminists; 'femocrats'
first wave, 14, 21
ideals of, 2, 9, 65–7, 75, 106, 135, 173, 194, 207
second wave, 3, 8, 65–7, 74, (211); *see also* Women's Liberation movement
feminists, 2, 4–5, 8, 50, 71, 74–6, 100, 112; *see also* child care policies, role of feminists; child care services, role of feminists; feminism; 'femocrats'; Labor Women's Committee (NSW); Media Women's Action Group; United Women's Action Group; Women's Electoral Lobby; Women's Liberation movement
achievements of, 2, 5, 9, 82, 174
American, 2–4, 75
attitudes to child care, 65–7, 79–82, 124–5, 134–5, 207
British, 2–3, 4
Swedish, 3–4
'femocrats', 2, 4–5, 75, 99, 100, 109, 117, 134, 175, 195; *see also* feminism; feminists
Fraser government, 96–118; *see also* Review of Commonwealth Government Functions
attitudes to pre-schools, 100–1
child care policies of, 9–10, 99–102, 106, 109–10, 112, 113–15, 117–18, 125, 157, 164, 185
compared with Thatcher, Reagan, 106, 107
funding of child care services, 9–10, 99, 101–2, 106, 109–10, 114–15, 117–18, 124, 128, 185
lack of community consultation, 96, 117
'new federalism' of, 98, 101
philosophy of, 96–9, 100–1, 103–4, 113, 118
relationship with feminists, 96, 98, 100
Free Kindergarten Association (FKA), 21
Froebel, Friedrich, 14–15
Fry, Joan, 61, 78–9
Fry Report, *see* Australian Pre-Schools Committee
funding of child care services; *see also* child care subsidies; day nurseries, funding of; distribution of commonwealth child care funds; family day care centres, fee relief; funding of; Fraser government, funding of child care services; funding models; Hawke/Keating government, funding of child care services; kindergartens, funding of; Second World War, funding of child care during; Whitlam government, funding of child care services; work-based care, funding of
by commonwealth government, 32, 45, 46, 58, 68–9, 94, 98, 124, 127, 130t, 175, 180–5
by community groups, 127
by local government, 45, 62, 175
by parents, 58, 110, 115, 127
by state governments, 32, 45, 58, 62, 122, 126, 175, 212
cuts to, 9–10, 36, 90, 99, 102, 106, 114, 118, 128–9, 180–5
public vs. private sector, 10, 187–97, 200
funding models; *see also* funding of child care services
needs-based, 91–2, 93, 113, 116, 199, 211
planning approach, 159, 174–6, 194, 199
submission-based, 68–9, 92–3, 115–17, 118, 127, 145, 174

George, Jennie, 166
Gorton, John, *see* Coalition parties, child care policies of
Gowrie, Lady Zara, 37
Grimes, Don, 174, 180, 181, 182, 183, 185
Guilfoyle, Dame Margaret, 68, 106, 112

Hawke/Keating government, 164–85; *see also Affirmative Action (Equal Opportunity for Women) Act* (1986); affirmative action policies; equal employment opportunity; *Public Sector Reform Act* (1984)
  child care policies of, 154, 159, 164–5, 166, 170, 173–85, 186–7, 201–5, 210, 211–13
  funding of child care services, 176–85, 186, 193–4, 202–3, 207, 211–13
  integration of child care and labour market policies, 164, 168–9, 173, 175, 177, 186, 187, 196, 204–5, 207, 211
  integration of child care and social security policies, 164, 168–9, 177, 186, 196, 204–5
  policies towards sole parents, 171–3
  policies towards women, 165, 168, 170, 177
  reliance on private sector, 10, 187, 189–90, 193, 200, 205, 210, 211
  structural changes in, 177
Hawker, Reverend Bertram, 18–19
health, 38; *see also* Federal Health Council, National Health and Medical Research Council
  Aboriginal, 6
  calls for government intervention, 34
  child, 32–6, 40, 51
  government funding for, 38
  maternal, 33–4
  Royal Commission on, 34
Hewson, John, *see* Coalition parties, child care policies of
Home Child Care Allowance, 211; *see also* child care allowance
Hospital Employees Federation, 129
Howe, Brian, 171, 187, 200

ICCC, *see* Interim Committee for the Children's Commission
INAC, *see* Interim National Accreditation Council
International Labor Organisation (ILO) Convention 156, 173, 214
Infant Life Protection Act (1980), 24–5; *see also* baby farming
infant schools, 6, 25
informal care, 12, 53, 192
Interim Committee for the Children's Commission (ICCC), 90–1, 93, 94–5, 99, 132
Interim National Accreditation Council (INAC), 203, 204

Keating, Paul, *see* Hawke/Keating government
kindergartens, 11, (52–4): *see also* child care policies; child care services; kindergarten unions
  as instruments of education, 16, 26, 40, 52–4, 56, 77, 120–1
  as instruments of social reform, 16–17, 19
  class base of children attending, 14–15, 53–4, 57–8, 95, 100
  class base of staff, 16, 21, 29–30, 120–21, 122, 125–6
  commonwealth government involvement in, 39, 58–9, 77, 94, 101, 124
  funding of, 8, 11–12, 30–2, 36, 39–40, 54, 58, 61, 89, 93–6, 100, 101, 122, 124, 126, 180–1
  ideals of, 6–7, 13–21, 26, 28–9, 37, 40, 52–4, 121–2
  industrial conditions of workers, 122
  in ACT, 12, 58
  in NSW, 11–12, 16, 18, 57–8, 123
  in Queensland, 20–1, 56, 58
  in South Australia, 12, 18–20, 28, 58
  in Tasmania, 12, 21, 56, 58, 123
  in Victoria, 11, 17, 29, 57–8, 123
  in Western Australia, 12, 20, 56, 58
  origins of, Australia, 6, 13, 15–16
  origins of, Europe, 14–15
  origins of, USA, 15
  role of feminists, 14
  role of parents, 11, 54, 55, 122
  Royal Commission into, 55
  state government involvement in, 15, 28, 54, 56–8, 124
  teacher training, 17, 27–30, 55–6, 58–9, 120–3, 125–6
  wages of workers, 121–4
kindergarten unions, 7, 8, 17, 18t, 27, 29, 37–8, 39, 47, 52, 81, 92, 101, 121, 122, 124; *see also* Australian Association for Pre-School Child Development; Australian Early Childhood Association; Australian Pre-School Association; kindergartens; Lady Gowrie centres
  Free Kindergarten Union (of Victoria) (FKU), 17, 18t, 29, 35, 37, 38–9, 47, 50, 54, 60, 94
  Hobart Free Kindergarten Association (HFKA), 18t, 21

INDEX

Kindergarten Union of New South Wales (KUNSW), 16, 18t, 26, 28
Kindergarten Union of South Australia (KUSA), 18–20, 37
Kindergarten Union of Western Australia (KUWA), 18t, 20, 55
King, Ethleen, 60

Labor Council of New South Wales, 137, 153, 159, 183
Labor Women's Committee (NSW), 80, 82–3, 91, 134
labour force participation, *see* workforce participation
Lady Gowrie centres, 7, 32–3, 39–43, 46, 50–1, 61, 62; *see also* kindergartens, philanthropy
  aims/rationale, 7, 40–1
  class divisions, 42–3, 57
  restrictions on access to, 41, 57
Liberal Party, *see* Coalition parties
long day care centres, *see* day nurseries
low income families, 114, 198, 207, 211
  access to child care, 57, 170, 191, 194
  special child care needs, 176
  Special Economic Needs Subsidies (SENS), 176

Mahlab, Eve, 112
maternal deprivation, 8, 59, 61, 63; *see also* Bowlby, John
maternity leave, 62, 77, 141–2, 151–2, 154–5, 157
  and demand for child care, 155
  public sector vs. private, 154–5
McCaughey, Winsome, 52, 66, 117
McMahon, William, *see* Coalition parties, child care policies of
Media Women's Action Group, 80
migrants, 114; *see also* Ethnic Child Care Development Unit; Ethnic Community Council; VICSEG
  access to child care, 41, 57, 65, 144, 192, 195
  and work-based care, 143–4
  demand for child care services, 143, 147
  special child care needs, 65, 144, 145, 167, 176
Miscellaneous Workers Union, 128
mobile services, 12
multifunctional Aboriginal children's services, 12, 208t; *see also* Aborigines
multifunctional services, 12, 208t
Municipal Employees Union, 128, 139

NACBCS, *see* National Association of Community Based Children's Services

National Accreditation Council, 203–4; *see also* accreditation; Interim National Accreditation Council
National Association of Community Based Children's Services (NACBCS), 10, 112, 139, 152, 156, 159, 177, 182, 184, 188, 195, 200–1
National Child Care Strategy, 150, 200
National Council of Women, 44, 60, 142
National Health and Medical Research Council (NHMRC), 38, 49; *see also* health, Federal Health Council
National Party, *see* Coalition parties
National Women's Advisory Council (NWAC), 108–9, 112
NCOSS, *see* New South Wales Council of Social Service
neighbourhood centres, 12, 124, 208t
Neighbourhood Children's Centres Association of Victoria, 129
New South Wales Council of Social Service (NCOSS), 116, 136
New South Wales Nurses Association, 158–60
Newton, Frances, 18
NHMRC, *see* National Health and Medical Research Council
Nott Report, 56
NWAC, *see* National Women's Advisory Council

occasional care, 12, 91, 177, 196, 200, 208t, 209–10
Office of Child Care, 64, 99, 100, 112, 113, 138, 144, 146, 147, 160, 161–2, 177, 181, 183, 184, 191
Office of the Status of Women, 150, 183
Office of Women's Affairs, 106
out-of-school hours care, 7, 12, 64, 67, 82, 91, 110, 177, 196, 200, 201, 203t, 208t, 209, 210

parental leave, 156, 157, 166, 173, 214
philanthropy, 6–7, 13, 15, 16, 19, 21, 42, 54, 57, 120, 207; *see also* Lady Gowrie centres; voluntarism
  and educational reform, 16
  and social reform, 13, 16, 19
  tradition of, in child care, 13, 47, 51, 57, 79, 126, 206
playgroups, 12, 91
pre-schools, *see* kindergartens
Preston, Yvonne, 90, 92
Priorities Review Staff (PRS), 86
  report of, 88
Project Head Start, 56, 57, 77; *see also* child care policies, in USA
Public Service Reform Act (1984), 170

Reid, Elizabeth, 73, 76, 79, 80, 81, 82, 85, 89, 98, 134
Review of Commonwealth Government Functions, 107–8, 109; *see also* Fraser government
Reynolds, Margaret, 150, 196
Rischbieth, Bessie, 14
Royal Commissions
 into Aboriginal deaths in custody, 6
 into human relationships, 143
 into wage rates (1920), 33
 on child endowment (1927), 33
 on health, 34
 on kindergartens, 55
Rubinstein, Linda, 143, 165
Rural/isolated communities
 access to child care, 194, 195
Ryan, Lyndall, 75, 88
Ryan, Susan, 196, 197

Sawer, Marian, 4
Scantlebury Brown, Vera, 38, 54
SDN & NSA, *see* Sydney Day Nursery and Nursery Schools Association
SDNA, *see* Sydney Day Nursery Association
Second World War; *see also* Brunswick Children's Centre; Women's Employment Board
 effect on child care policy, 7, 33, 43–7, 50–1
 effect on women's employment, 7, 43–4
 funding of child care during, 7, 45–7
 compared with England, 47
 compared with USA, 47
SENS, *see* Special Economic Needs Subsidies
Smyth, John, 17, 29
SNAICC, *see* Aborigines, Secretariat of National Aboriginal and Islander Child Care groups
Social Welfare Commission (SWC), 73–4, 86, 92, 93, 100, 133
 report of (*Project Care*), 86–88, 100, 133–4
sole parents, 106–7, 114, 171–3, 180, 191
 access to child care, 62, 172, 191
 special child care needs, 171–3
Spalding, Barbara, 91, 132
special child care needs, 125, 176, 192, 195; *see also* Aborigines; children at risk of abuse; disabled children; low income families; migrants; rural/isolated communities; sole parents, Special Economic Needs Subsidies; Supplementary Services Grants
Special Economic Needs Subsidies (SENS), 176; *see also* low income families
Spence, Catherine, 14, 19
Spender, John, 109
Spender Report (1981), 109–10, 111, 112, 115, 117, 129, 139, 184
Summers, Anne, 82, 98, 108
SUPS, *see* Supplementary Services Grants
Supplementary Services Grants (SUPS), 176
SWC, *see* Social Welfare Commission
Sydney Day Nursery and Nursery Schools Association (SDN & NSA), 47, 79, 121; *see also* day nurseries
Sydney Day Nursery Association (SDNA), 26–7, 28, 30–1, 33, 35, 62; *see also* day nurseries

Tax concessions for child care, 64, 81, 103, 150, 170, 176, 177–80, 211–12, 214; *see also* dependentspouse rebate
 in Britain, 2
 in USA, 2
 Coalition policy on, 176
Torres Strait Islanders, *see* Aborigines
trade unions; *see also* Accord; Australian Council of Trade Unions; kindergarten unions; Administrative and Clerical Officers Association; Australian Council of Salaried and Professional Associations; Federation of Australian University Staff Associations, Hospital Employees Federation; Miscellaneous Workers Union; Municipal Employees Union, New South Wales Nurses Association
 attitudes to women's issues, 62, 140, 141, 165–6
 objections to women working, 22, 48
 role of women unionists, 67, 141–3, 147, 157, 165–6
 union demands for child care services, 67, 119–20, 129, 139–40, 142–3, 147–8, 154, 156–63, 166, 173, 183, 187–8
 unionisation of child care workers, 119, 126, 128
 unionisation rates, men vs. women, 121, 141, 148, 166

unemployment, 16, 97, 103, 106–7, 169, 201; *see also* Depression, the
 effect of lack of child care on, 107, 170, 172, 197
 hidden, 169, 170
 of Aborigines, 6
 of men, 169
 of women, 35, 169, 170

INDEX

Union of Australian Women, 67, 142
United Associations of Women, 50
United Women's Action Group, 81
vacation care 12, 64, 67, 110, 196
VADN, *see* Victorian Association of Day Nurseries
VCOSS, *see* Victorian Council of Social Service
VICSEG, *see* Victorian Cooperative on Children's Services for Ethnic Groups
Victorian Association of Day Nurseries (VADN), 26, 30–1, 60, 62, 79; *see also* day nurseries
Victorian Cooperative on Children's Services for Ethnic Groups (VICSEG), 144
Victorian Council of Social Service (VCOSS), 60, 67, 73, 84
  Report of (1970), 64
voluntarism, tradition of in child care, 6–7, 30, 57, 119–22, 126, 136, 138, 139, 206; *see also* philanthropy
voucher system, 10, 187, 190, 193–5, 199, 205, 214
  opposition to, 194–6, 199

wage rates
  effect of Second World War on, 44
  effect of Women's Employment Board on, (44)
  equal pay, 48, 55, 77, 82, 141, 142, 165, 166
  'family' wage, (141–42)
  'living' (minimum) wage, for men, 23
  'mother's' wage, 8
  of child care workers, 40, 55–6, 58, 93–4, 120–4, 128, 133–5, 166, 184
  of women, 23, 126, 169–70
  pre-school vs. school, 55–6, 58, 123
  Royal Commission into (1920), 33
Walsh, Peter, 156, 157, 180, 186, 188, 189, 190, 191, 192, 193, 195–6, 197, 199
Wangmann, June, 201
WEL, *see* Women's Electoral Lobby
Whitlam government, 70–95
  attitudes to pre-schools, 77–8, 88, 89, 95, 124
  child care policies of, 9–10, 71, 74, 77–9, 83, 86, 88–95, 96–7, 98, 99–100, 101, 164
  funding of child care services, 71, 97, 89–91, 92–5, 122–3, 124
  personnel changes in, 73
  philosophy of, 70–4, 77, 85, 97, 98, 100
  policies towards women, 71, 76–7, 167
  relationship with feminists, 78–83, 88, 98, 104, 167

  structural changes in, 72–3
Wilenski, Peter, 72, 76
Windeyer, Margaret, 15
Wolstenholme Anderson, Maybanke, 14, 15–16
Women Lawyers' Association, 177, 180
Women Members' Group of the Australian Society of Accountants, 177, 178, 180
Women's Action Committee, 141
Women's Bureau, 61–2, 64, 86
Women's Electoral Lobby (WEL), 74–5, 78, 80, 81, 82, 86, 90, 108, 112, 142, 149, 179, 180, 188, 195
Women's Employment Board (WEB), 44; *see also* Second World War
Women's Liberation movement, 73, 74–6, 207; *see also* feminism, second wave; Women's Electoral Lobby
Women's Services Guild, 50
Women's Trade Union Commission (WTUC), 142, 146, 147, 153
WTUC, *see* Women's Trade Union Commission
work-based care, 62, 63, 103, 143–63, 211–12; *see also* Child Care at Work; corporate child care; employer-sponsored services
  access to, 146, 148, 150
  Australian Labor Party policy on, 5, 148–50, 154, 159
  and migrants, 143–5
  demand for, 5, 143, 155–6, 157, 159, 161, 188, 209
  for commonwealth public servants, 156–8
  for educational institutions, 160–63
  for NSW hospital staff, 158–60
  funding of, 146, 148–50, 153, 159, 160–3
  objections to, 145–6
  parent involvement in, 146, 148, 150, 153
  public vs. private sector provision of, 153–5, 156, 157–8
  role of union movement, 147, 154, 156–8, 166, 173, 188
workforce participation; *see also* affirmative action policies; equal employment opportunities
  influence of Second World War on, 43
  need for women workers, 7, 9, 43, 44, 53, 63, 151–2, 158, 160, 207
  objections to women working, 22, 42–3, 45, 48, 59–60, 62, 63–4, 68, 94, 104–5, 113–14

of married women, 43–4, 53, 59, 132, 141, 169
of men, 169
of migrant women, 143
of sole parents, 24, 106, 171
of women, 8, 23, 43–4, 48, 59, 132, 135, 142, 169, 207
of women with children, 8, 23–4, 35, 62, 131, 169
type of work performed by women, 21–2, 23–4, 35, 43, 44, 151, 169, 170
Working Women's Centre, 137, 142, 143, 147, 166
Working Women's Charter, 142, 166